VICTORY '45

www.penguin.co.uk

Also by James Holland

Non-fiction

FORTRESS MALTA
TOGETHER WE STAND
HEROES
ITALY'S SORROW
THE BATTLE OF BRITAIN
DAM BUSTERS
AN ENGLISHMAN AT WAR
BURMA '44
BIG WEEK
RAF100: THE OFFICIAL STORY
NORMANDY '44
SICILY '43
BROTHERS IN ARMS
THE SAVAGE STORM
CASSINO '44
THE WAR IN THE WEST Volume I: Germany Ascendant 1939–1941
THE WAR IN THE WEST Volume II: The Allies Fight Back 1941–1943

Ladybird Experts

BLITZKRIEG
THE BATTLE OF BRITAIN
BATTLE OF THE ATLANTIC
THE DESERT WAR
THE EASTERN FRONT 1941–43
THE PACIFIC WAR 1941–43
THE BOMBER WAR
THE WAR IN ITALY
THE BATTLE FOR NORMANDY 1944
THE WAR IN BURMA 1943–44
VICTORY IN EUROPE 1944–45
VICTORY AGAINST JAPAN 1944–45

Fiction

THE BURNING BLUE
A PAIR OF SILVER WINGS
THE ODIN MISSION
DARKEST HOUR
BLOOD OF HONOUR
HELLFIRE
DEVIL'S PACT
DUTY CALLS: DUNKIRK
DUTY CALLS: BATTLE OF BRITAIN
ALVESDON

For more information on James Holland and his books, see his website at www.griffonmerlin.com

Also by Al Murray

WATCHING WAR FILMS WITH MY DAD
COMMAND
ARNHEM: BLACK TUESDAY

VICTORY '45

THE END OF THE WAR IN EIGHT SURRENDERS

James Holland
&
Al Murray

bantam

TRANSWORLD PUBLISHERS

UK | USA | Canada | Ireland | Australia
India | New Zealand | South Africa

Transworld is part of the Penguin Random House group of companies
whose addresses can be found at global.penguinrandomhouse.com.

Penguin Random House UK,
One Embassy Gardens, 8 Viaduct Gardens, London SW11 7BW

penguin.co.uk

Penguin
Random House
UK

First published in Great Britain in 2025 by Bantam
an imprint of Transworld Publishers

001

Typeset in 12/17pt Calluna by Jouve (UK), Milton Keynes
Printed and bound in Great Britain by Clays Ltd, Elcograf S.p.A.

The authorized representative in the EEA is Penguin Random House Ireland,
Morrison Chambers, 32 Nassau Street, Dublin D02 YH68.

A CIP catalogue record for this book is available from the British Library

ISBNs
9780857507952 hb
9780857508355 tpb

Penguin Random House is committed to a sustainable future for our business, our readers and our planet. This book is made from Forest Stewardship Council® certified paper.

FSC
www.fsc.org
MIX
Paper | Supporting responsible forestry
FSC® C018179

For Tony Pastor and Joey McCarthy
great friends and collaborators

CONTENTS

Principal Personalities ix

Prologue: Unconditional Surrender 1

1 A BULLET TO THE HEAD
The Surrender of Berlin, *2 May 1945* 15

2 THE DUEL PART 1
The Surrender in Italy, *2 May 1945* 39

3 THE DUEL PART 2
The Surrender in Italy, *2 May 1945* 61

4 MONTY'S MEN
Lüneburg Heath, *3–4 May 1945* 87

5 THE CAMP
The Surrender in Southern Germany, *5 May 1945* 117

6 THE SUPREME COMMANDER WILL SEE YOU NOW
Reims, *6–7 May 1945* 143

7 VE DAY
Twenty-four Hours in London, *8 May 1945* 167

8 HAPPY BIRTHDAY, MR PRESIDENT
VE Day in America, *8 May 1945* 191

9 AMID THE RUINS PART 1
The Surrender in Berlin, *9 May 1945* 217

10 AMID THE RUINS PART 2
The German Surrender to the Soviet Union in Berlin, *9 May 1945* 237

11 LOST IN TRANSLATION
The Surrender of Japan, *15 August 1945* 257

12 THE FINAL ACT
The Japanese Signing of the Surrender, *2 September 1945* 291

Postscript 317

Timeline 331
Notes 347
Selected Sources 359
Acknowledgements 365
Picture Acknowledgements 367
Index 371

PRINCIPAL PERSONALITIES

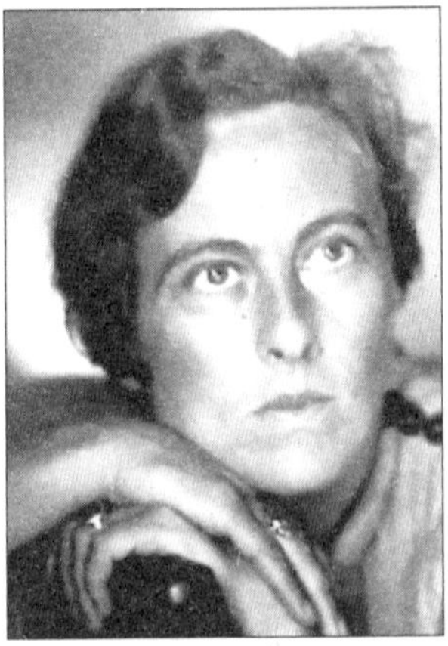

Ruth Andreas-Friedrich

Major-General Merton Beckwith-Smith

Lieutenant-General Walter Bedell Smith

Jimmy Byrnes

Winston Churchill

Grossadmiral Karl Dönitz

General Dwight D. Eisenhower

Generaladmiral Hans-Georg von Friedeburg

Bella Gryn

Géza Gryn

Hugo Gryn

General Masaharu Homma

Generaloberst Alfred Jodl

Yelena Kagan

Obergruppenführer Ernst Kaltenbrunner

Feldmarschall Wilhelm Keitel

Ed Kennedy

Andrik Krassnow

General Hans Krebs

General Douglas MacArthur

Field Marshal Sir Bernard Montgomery

Staff Sergeant Alan Moskin

Major John Poston

Lieutenant Sherman W. Pratt

Captain Kay Summersby

President Harry S. Truman

General Jonathan M. Wainwright

General Helmuth Weidling

Obergruppenführer Karl Wolff

General Tomoyuki Yamashita

PROLOGUE

Unconditional Surrender

PRESIDENT FRANKLIN D. ROOSEVELT flew into Casablanca in French Morocco on Thursday, 14 January 1943, touching down after a forty-eight-hour flight that had taken him from Washington DC to Miami, to Brazil, across the Atlantic to Gambia and then on to his final destination. It was the first time a sitting president had flown beyond the shores of the United States and had not been without risk – flying could be a dangerous business even when there were no marauding enemy planes about – but was even more arduous for Roosevelt, crippled as he was with polio-stricken legs.

None the less, he had been thrilled by the journey. The final leg, in a C-54 transport plane from Gambia, was a seven-hour stretch that took the President over desert then the snow-capped Atlas Mountains. 'Then we suddenly came on the fertile fields of N. Africa,' noted Harry Hopkins, his closest friend and advisor, 'looking like the Garden of Eden should look and probably doesn't – camels – olive groves – oranges – wheat fields – no cows – rain – miles of black earth. The President missed nothing.' They landed at a dusty airfield fifteen miles from the city, where the President's son, Elliott, was waiting for him in a limousine with windows blacked out with mud. They drove to Anfa, on the outskirts of the city, a resort hotel, now surrounded by barbed wire, soldiers and artillery, and from there to a luxury bungalow villa, Californian in style, where the President would be staying. Churchill was in a house fifty yards away. That night, the President held a dinner at which the Joint Chiefs of Staff – the most senior military men of both countries – were invited. 'Much good talk of war,' noted Harry Hopkins, 'and families and the French.' Hopkins turned in at midnight, but the President and Prime Minister Winston Churchill stayed talking until two.

The President had given considerable thought to what the post-war world might look like once the Allies had won the war. That they would win had never been in doubt, not once he had overseen the transformation of the United States from the world's largest consumer economy into what he had termed the arsenal of democracy. This transformation had begun in the summer of 1940, when the German Blitzkrieg was in full swing, France collapsed and Britain's army scuttled back across the Channel from Dunkirk. By the time the Japanese launched their attack on Pearl Harbor in Hawaii on 7 December 1941, American factories had already transformed the United States into a war-winning warfare state. Yet even as long ago as August 1941, during Roosevelt's first wartime face-to-face meeting with Churchill, he had proposed a series of eight high-minded, morally upright principles in which nations would coexist peaceably in a world free of want and fear. It had become known as the Atlantic Charter and had preceded America's entry into the war by four months.

At the Casablanca Conference the Allies thrashed out their strategic priorities, but it was clear that while Roosevelt was not present at all the discussions, he had been giving much further thought not only to what the world might look like in the future but the means by which they might end this current cataclysmic war. He had been drawing upon history and, specifically, the lessons provided by Ulysses S. Grant, Civil War general turned president. Grant, fighting for the Union eighty years previously, had won a surprise victory at Donelson, Tennessee in 1862, demanding of the Confederate fort that it surrender unconditionally. The demand had worked because rather than face the full wrath of the Union Army, Donelson had thrown in the towel. Unconditional Surrender – Grant's initials after all – became a nickname that would stick.

It was, perhaps, unsurprising that FDR had been poking into American history for examples of surrender; he'd lived through historic times himself. Had witnessed them too, and not least the post-war conference at Versailles in 1919 which had meted out punishment to Germany and the Central Powers. He had watched the seismic events that followed, from the rise of Nazi Germany to the collapse of the League of Nations, as it faced the challenges posed by the rejection of international order by the Fascist Powers. And despite being first elected President on an isolationist ticket back in 1932, by 1939, as Europe descended into war, he had recognized that the United States faced an existential threat not only from the sabre-rattling of Imperial Japan but also from Nazi Germany and the rise of fascism. And as he led the United States into a brave new world of massive war production and immense rearmament, he also understood that he needed to find a new way to express the Allies' intentions. One that offered far less wriggle room for the defeated than Woodrow Wilson's ill-fated efforts had done. This had been his consistent line from the very start of hostilities: in his address to the nation on 8 December 1941, the day after

Pearl Harbor, he resolved the country to 'win through to absolute victory'.

The Casablanca Conference came at a key moment in the war. Future prospects for the Allies looked promising, but the previous couple of months had provided a distinctly uncomfortable ride. All were keenly aware the war still had a heck of a way to go. In North Africa, the only theatre at the time where the Allies were fighting German troops on the ground, the British Eighth Army was pursuing Rommel's army across Libya from the east, while the British First Army – which included the US II Corps – had been sweeping in from the west. The grand plan was to sandwich the enemy armies in Tunisia in a giant vice and crush them there once and for all, but it was taking much longer than had been anticipated and the First Army had become horribly bogged down in northern Tunisia as Hitler had dramatically reinforced the country. There was, however, encouraging news from the Eastern Front, where, at Stalingrad, the German drive to the Caucasus had come fatally unstuck. The Red Army, reinvigorated with strong and clear leadership from the top and also benefiting from the arrival of Lend-Lease supplies, now had the German Sixth Army entirely surrounded and on the cusp of a humiliating and catastrophic surrender. Yet in the Atlantic – the Allies' vital lifeline – U-boats were still sinking vast amounts of Allied shipping, while in the skies of Europe the strategic air campaign against Germany was still currently under-delivering. Priorities of future ground operations still had to be ironed out. Certainly, many hard battles lay ahead.

There was, then, much to discuss at this conference of Britain's and America's war leaders. In truth, the British had arrived better prepared than their American counterparts, with plans already fleshed out and a global strategy – upon which British imperial minds were naturally focused – that left the Americans feeling rather as though they'd been bounced.

Argument about what to do next dominated, and disagreement about whether to maintain momentum in the Mediterranean, rather than invade north-west Europe, defined a great deal of discussion. The British attitude was that fighting the Germans in the Mediterranean, on their periphery, was the best way forward to leverage Allied advantages. All Allied warfare was expeditionary, relying on shipping and naval power, so drawing the Germans into a battle further from Germany was more of a complication for the enemy than for the Allies. And prosecuting the war in Italy might precipitate the collapse of Mussolini's fascist government in Rome too, weakening the Axis and sending a message to Berlin, and to Tokyo, that the Allies were taking control of the war.

The Italian strategy had the added benefit of drawing German forces away from north-west Europe as well as the Eastern Front. The British line of thinking, rendered more abstract by Stalin's absence from the conference, was that Germany needed to be far more worn down by fighting before they could commit to a second front. American impatience with this approach was seen by some of the British as an expression of their partner's naivety; fighting the Germans was something of which the British had that much more experience than their allies, and consequently they had no illusions about how easy it might be. Yet during the ten-day conference in Casablanca, the scale of the tasks before them, and the clearest way forward given the state of shipping, of industrial production line projections and the enormity of the build-up of forces needed to dominate the skies first in North Africa and then in north-west Europe, all began to deliver the shape of future Allied strategy – albeit one that remained flexible in execution and adjustable as necessary. The POINTBLANK memorandum, eventually signed off some months later in June 1943 but first proposed at Casablanca, was a case in point. This laid out a policy for prioritizing the destruction of the Luftwaffe and German aircraft industry, but which amounted to an open-ended accommodation of the differing British and American approaches to bombing the Reich. The United States Army Air Forces – USAAF – would focus almost entirely on this single-minded objective during daylight hours, while RAF Bomber Command would follow the same policy while maintaining their right to choose other targets. In other words, they could, for the most part, ignore POINTBLANK. Instead, they were hell-bent on continuing a strategy of 'bombing everything in order to bomb anything'; this was also termed 'area bombing' and 'dehousing' in a euphemistic blend of pragmatism and vengeance. Air Chief Marshal Sir Arthur Harris, in charge of Bomber Command, planned to begin his all-out bomber offensive, with new navigational aids and more four-engine heavy bombers, against the Ruhr industrial heartland at the beginning of March 1943. He'd once vowed that the Germans would reap what they'd sown for subjugating Britain to the Blitz. German cities and civilians were about to experience this vengeance; bombs would rain down relentlessly on Germany until the very end of the war. By contrast, the USAAF remained determined to rely on technology and ideology, and its commanders to convince themselves that they were engaged in a moral and precise bombing campaign. In reality, the effects of this approach would prove hardly more accurate than those of their Bomber Command partners.

Other matters of contention were the extent to which the Americans were committed to the strategy of prioritizing the defeat of Nazi Germany above that of Imperial Japan. The US Navy was considerably more committed to fighting in the Pacific than against the Axis forces in Europe, and Admiral Ernest King, its Commander-in-Chief, was doing what he could to draw American maritime commitment to the eastern theatre. The US Navy had its own aircraft and troops in the form of the US Marine Corps, as well as a major US Army component, and the distances involved in the campaigns were so gigantic they could not be undertaken half-heartedly. Moreover, although Roosevelt believed the Atlantic was no longer the barrier it had once been to North American security, the war in Europe and North Africa could not be framed as one of national self-defence quite so obviously as it could in the Pacific. Germany had declared war on the United States on 11 December 1941, and FDR had leaned into this as the war to win first; none the less, an American entanglement in Europe was exactly the sort of strategy isolationists had warned against between the wars.

And entanglements were all that seemed to be on offer now that the war was under way. The Americans had taken the lead in both pre-invasion clandestine conversations with the pro-Axis Vichy French in North Africa, as well as the subsequent TORCH landings on 8 November 1942. This was partly because an American, General Dwight D. Eisenhower, was commander of the Allied invasion force, as was his deputy, General Mark W. Clark. But it was primarily because the British were despised by Vichy after the fall of France in 1940 and the subsequent British attack on the French fleet at Mers-el-Kébir near Algiers in which some 1,300 French sailors were killed. The Americans, by contrast, were viewed more neutrally.

Yet Operation TORCH had proved scarring for the Americans. Competing assessments of French intentions and interests within the US State Department, the Office of Strategic Services – OSS, the wartime forerunner of the CIA – as well as the US Army were all confounded. American soldiers had gone ashore in North Africa not knowing if the Vichy French would resist; 'play ball' was the code that indicated they were to return fire at the French, and fighting took on a different shape everywhere as local commanders decided what to do according to taste. The American generals on the ground, as well as Robert Murphy, the senior US diplomat to Vichy North Africa, did what they could to co-opt a French commander and save American and French lives, unwilling as they were to back Charles de Gaulle, whom they regarded as having cultivated too many risky associations with Communists. They – and the Vichy French government – were outmanoeuvred by Amiral François Darlan, who struck a deal with Eisenhower on 22 November that outraged not only the Free French but also the British government and opinion back home in the States. The legendary broadcaster Ed Murrow likened it to liberating Norway and putting the traitor Vidkun Quisling into power. Eisenhower had found dealing with the French impossible; after one meeting he commented to General Mark Clark that what he needed was a plane crash to solve his problems. The morally compromised cat's cradle that followed pleased no one, and in the end the solution to the mess the Americans found themselves in was the assassination of Amiral Darlan by a disaffected French royalist, Fernand Bonnier de La Chapelle, on Christmas Eve 1942. British Foreign Secretary Anthony Eden confided to his diary that he had never felt so relieved at the news. No Darlan, no problem. These botched efforts, as well as the way in which French imperialism was allowed to continue in French North Africa unfettered, seemed to blatantly undermine the moral crusade on which the Americans had embarked the previous December, 1941, when they'd entered the war. Even before that decisive moment, there had been the Atlantic Charter of August 1941 in which territorial gains were to be eschewed and it was acknowledged that all people had a right to self-determination. Supporting the ongoing colonial ambitions of the French, despite the rise of Arab nationalism, seemed to be flying in the face of earlier, loftier moral concepts.

Despite this, the moral aims of the war were crystal-clear to Roosevelt. Germany would be disarmed, it would be dismantled, its military power neutered, its military classes – whom FDR held responsible for the war – dissolved and dispossessed. Given how far the Allies were from victory and how much there was still to do before Germany could be defeated, it is striking that Roosevelt insisted on this formulation. Hitler's own mentality, which was beginning to harden as Germany's high tide of victory was dramatically beginning to ebb, revealed the hidden shipwrecks of his strategy as well as his generals' eagerness to pursue it. Overreach, the tumult of over-extension fighting deep into the Soviet interior, the ideological spoil of alienating the populations the Soviets had previously abused, the huge blow to German prestige of the imminent surrender at Stalingrad – all were taking Hitler to the view that it was more than a war of conquest; rather, it was a war of annihilation. It was all or nothing. A 1,000-Year Reich or Armageddon.

Roosevelt's call for unconditional surrender accepted the challenge that Hitler now offered the world. It acknowledged that there could be no negotiating with the Nazis. Ten years of the Nazi regime had shown that with crystal clarity: the bad faith that Hitler had exhibited in the 1930s, blazing his way through the Versailles settlement while the West dithered about his intentions; his betrayal of his Soviet ally; the total disregard for human life, for institutions, the repression of so many, and the grotesque ideology that was the evil counterpoint to the ideals Roosevelt had proposed in the Atlantic Charter. Everything Hitler and the Nazis had done and stood for told Roosevelt there could be only one outcome in this war: the complete, total and unconditional surrender of Germany. The irony was that within Nazism, a core aim, a bitter principle, was to avoid any repetition of the end of the First World War. The myth of betrayal, the so-called 'stab in the back' of 1918, could never be allowed to gestate and fester in Germany again. Unconditional surrender would ensure that it did not, that this time the war would come to the centre of the Reich, to Berlin, to the Reichstag, to within mortar range of the Führerbunker; that however the Allies chose to fight following the Casablanca Conference, the end of this war would be nothing like 1918. The generals would not be allowed to blame politicians, capitalists and unseen dark forces such as religious minorities. Ulysses S. Grant's defeat of the Confederacy forces at Donelson in 1862 would come to the Brandenburg Gates.

The announcement that the Allies would be pursuing unconditional surrender was made by President Roosevelt at Casablanca without prior consultation on the morning of 24 January. The President, sat beside the Prime Minister, Winston Churchill, on the lawn of his villa, smiled benignly for the fifty pressmen assembled cross-legged like schoolchildren before them, waiting for their remarks at the conclusion of the ten-day conference. Roosevelt spoke first, reading from notes. 'The elimination of German, Japanese and Italian war power', he said in his precise, patrician and clipped East Coast accent, 'means the unconditional surrender by Germany, Italy, and Japan.' He paused for a brief moment then added a caveat. 'That does not mean the destruction of the population of Germany, Italy or Japan,' he continued, 'but it does mean the destruction of the philosophies in those countries which are based on conquest and the subjugation of other people.'

Roosevelt later claimed that the phrase had just 'popped into my mind'; Churchill was certainly wrong-footed by it, although he immediately supported the President. Yet while the announcement of this war-changing policy might have been unrehearsed, the two men had discussed it beforehand; Churchill had even written a long memo to the British War Cabinet four days earlier in which he specifically told them he and Roosevelt were anxious to announce their intention of pursuing unconditional surrender. FDR had also discussed the issue in Washington ahead of the conference. The President's son, Elliott, even recalled Churchill making a toast to 'unconditional surrender' at a dinner ahead of the press conference that Sunday. Sitting there, in the sunshine of that warm January day in Morocco, Roosevelt may have told the press that his policy was the same as General Grant's at Appomattox in 1865, but he was far from being the only person in the American establishment familiar with Civil War history, and besides he had misremembered Grant's victory at Donelson.

All of this was neither here nor there, of course. The world now knew that the Allies would only end the war against the Axis Powers when they accepted unconditional surrender. Arguments raged at the time and have done so ever since about whether such a policy was too rigid and whether, ultimately, it extended the war longer than necessary. But by demanding unconditional surrender the Allies were offering moral clarity in clear political terms; it forged the Allies in agreement, and spared them the complications that trying to treat with Vichy France had thrown up. It was definitive yet at the same time vague: a plain demand that was short on detail but heavy with intent. Unlike the Fourteen Points President Woodrow Wilson had proposed back in 1919 – which had come to little – there were no matters of argument to engage with and twist, no promises made that could be misinterpreted or regurgitated at a later date. The Germans, the Japanese and the Italians must surrender, without any conditions whatsoever.

Then the Allies would dictate terms.

CHAPTER 1

A BULLET TO THE HEAD

The Surrender of Berlin, *2 May 1945*

Decrepit, scruffy, often completely exhausted German soldiers and officers are laying their guns down everywhere in the streets and squares, and giving themselves up in droves as prisoner to our troops. The Germans are flying white flags on many houses. Right at this minute I see two Hitler officers walking with lowered banners and no guns from the Tiergarten Park towards the Brandenburg Gate, near which there lies a pile of guns, and crowds of German soldiers and officers are standing.

Piotr Zevelyov, Red Army soldier, in a letter to his parents, 30 April 1945

It was around 10 p.m. on Monday, 30 April that a lone Red Army soldier unfurled the Soviet hammer and sickle from the north-west corner of the Reichstag. The German parliament building, at the heart of Berlin, one of the most iconic landmarks in the city, was now a wreck: blackened, spattered, chipped and gouged. Around it the ground was littered with burnt-out vehicles, shell holes and dead bodies. Inside, it was a shell as fighting continued. More rubble, more wreckage, more dead. It was an apocalyptic scene.

The fighting in and around the building and government quarter of the city had continued after the flag had been raised and it was not until around 1 a.m. on Tuesday, 1 May that Red Army troops snuffed out the last pocket of SS troops that had been fighting fanatically around the Reichskanzlei – the Reich Chancellery – half a mile to the south. Then an eerie silence, followed by a single rifle shot in the night air, and then silence again. A ceasefire of sorts.

This allowed General Hans Krebs, the chief of the German Army General Staff, to carefully drive his way south through the shattered streets towards the command post of General Vasily Chuikov, commander of the Soviet Eighth Guards Army, which now held much of the southern half of Berlin. The ceasefire had taken since late on the evening of 30 April to negotiate, but eventually Chuikov issued orders for Krebs's safe conduct to his command post, a house in the Schulenburgring on the west side of Tempelhof airfield.

The forty-seven-year-old Krebs – swarthy, bald and a career soldier – was immaculately turned out in full uniform and leather greatcoat, complete with monocle; the contrast with the dishevelled Volkssturm men and young boys in ill-fitting field jackets who had been attempting to halt the swarm of Red Army troops could hardly have been greater. He reached Chuikov's command post in the early hours, accompanied by Oberst Theodor von Dufving and a Latvian SS translator. Chuikov kept them waiting until 4 a.m. He too presented a starkly contrasting picture to the sartorial Krebs: thick, dark hair, a heavy scarred and furrowed brow and silver false teeth. He looked like the peasant he was despite his general's epaulettes. Krebs had been practising his Russian and without the help of a translator announced that Hitler was dead, telling Chuikov he was the first outside person to be told this stunning news. To unsettle Krebs, however, Chuikov pretended he already knew; he then went off to call Marshal Georgy Zhukov, commander of the 1st Belorussian Front and overall Soviet commander of the Battle for Berlin. Zhukov in turn immediately sent his deputy, General Vasily Sokolovsky, to Chuikov's command post – he didn't want Chuikov taking any of the glory – and then rang Stalin. The Soviet leader was asleep but Zhukov insisted he be woken.

'Pity we couldn't take him alive,' was Stalin's comment. 'Where's Hitler's corpse?'

'According to Krebs,' Zhukov told him, 'his body was burnt.'

'Tell Sokolovsky no negotiations except for unconditional capitulation, with either Krebs or any others of Hitler's lot. And don't ring me until the morning if there is nothing urgent.'

Meanwhile, first Chuikov and then Sokolovsky, once he had reached the Eighth Guards Army command post, tried to pressure Krebs into surrendering the city. Krebs, a committed Nazi and a general who took his oath of loyalty to a ludicrous degree, refused to agree anything until the Soviets formally recognized the new German government under Grossadmiral Karl Dönitz. Krebs was instead arguing for a truce ahead of a formal surrender by Dönitz. The Russians were not fooled; Krebs was playing for time to allow more Germans to head west into the arms of the Allies. Zhukov was having none of it. 'Tell him', he told Sokolovsky, 'that if Goebbels and Bormann do not agree unconditional surrender, we'll blast Berlin into ruins.' Krebs was allowed to head back to the Führerbunker with a warning that the ceasefire would be over at 10.15 a.m. that same morning, 1 May 1945.

Having heard nothing more from the German leadership, the massed guns of the 1st Belorussian Front subjected the city and its more than 2 million civilians to another storm of fire. The Battle for Berlin was not over just yet.

Back in 1937, Hitler's favourite architect, Albert Speer, had been given a mighty project: the transformation of Berlin from the somewhat sprawling city it was into a stunning new capital at the heart of the Third Reich. 'As world capital,' Hitler said of his vision a few years later, 'Berlin will only be comparable with Ancient Egypt, Babylon and Rome!' London and Paris, he claimed, would be nothing against the magnificence and glory of this remodelled city. Nor would it be called Berlin any more. Rather, the new capital was to be renamed 'Germania'. The vision of this remodelling was grandiose to say the least: its centrepiece would be a vast Volkshalle – People's Hall – able to seat 160,000 and the world's largest suspended dome by a huge margin. This gigantic edifice would stand at the top of a three-mile-long boulevard running north to south, to be called the Prachtallee – the Avenue of Splendours. It was giddy stuff, but in pre-war Berlin anything seemed possible. After all, since taking power in January 1933 Hitler had overseen a dramatic upturn in the economy, begun massive rearmament and public works projects, reduced unemployment and started the process of reversing the reviled Versailles Treaty that had brought such despair and humiliation on Germany. The Rhineland had also been reoccupied. Further triumphs were to come: in March 1938, Austria would become joined at the hip and morphed into the Third Reich. A year on, Czechoslovakia would follow suit. All without a shot being fired. It was miraculous. The Führer had transformed Germany. Pride had been restored, historic wrongs righted; optimism reigned. Hitler had spoken eloquently of this golden age being the beginning of a 1,000-Year Reich. And Germania would be a fitting expression of German supremacy, brilliance and righteousness, and of the restoration of the Aryans, the white, northern European peoples, to their rightful place as the master race of the world.

The war had stopped such lofty plans in their tracks, but few would have doubted in late June 1940 that Hitler's transformation of Berlin would one day take place. Poland had succumbed in weeks; Denmark in a matter of hours. Norway had followed, then Holland and Belgium. The British Army had scuttled back across the Channel leaving most of its weapons and vehicles behind, and then, on 22 June, mighty France had surrendered too. Much of Europe lay at Hitler's feet. For the majority of Germans, the rapid conquest of France, especially, signalled what they assumed was the end of the war. Hitler called for bells to be rung for a week and flags to be flown. Everywhere, the vivid red, black and white of the swastika fluttered in the summer air. Widespread relief was felt throughout the Reich and was accompanied by joyous celebrations. Hitler took Speer and others on an early-morning tour of Paris, then gleefully told his chief architect it was time to resurrect their plans for Germania. 'Berlin', he said, 'is to be given the style commensurate with the grandeur of our victory.'

On 6 July 1940, Hitler had returned to Berlin for a triumphant parade through the city to rival anything witnessed in Ancient Rome. Over a quarter of a million ecstatic Berliners thronged the streets, cheering, waving, swastikas lining the procession. Berlin was awash with colour: the deep red of the flags, the brilliant blue of the summer sky, the vivid sunlight reflecting on the bright walls and glass of the buildings. Berliners were delirious; twenty years earlier they had faced defeat, disaster and despair, but under Hitler Germany had been transformed. Never had victory tasted so sweet; never had Germany's future looked so bright. Their Führer had brought them this. His vision, his brilliance, his belief. His will.

Five years on, such scenes seemed to belong to a different age entirely. Now Berlin was a city of monochrome. Of ruins. Of ghosts. A 1,000-Year Reich or Armageddon, Hitler had promised. It had always been a matter of black or white; one or the other. Either the German people had the will to win the struggle or they did not. On the first day of May 1945, the outcome was tragically clear.

It was Armageddon.

The final Red Army offensive had begun on 16 April 1945, thirty-five miles to the east of Berlin on the River Oder. Zhukov's

1st Belorussian Front contained no fewer than nine armies: 908,000 men, 3,155 tanks, 16,934 artillery pieces, 7 million shells, nearly 100,000 vehicles supported by 3,290 aircraft. Against them were some 200,000 badly armed and mostly undertrained men and teenage boys, perhaps 500 tanks, 2,600 artillery pieces and 300 aircraft with almost no fuel. They didn't stand a chance, and everyone knew it.

Everyone except Hitler, who still refused to accept that the game was up. Nevertheless, it had been understood within his inner circle that on 20 April, his fifty-sixth birthday, the Führer would fly out of the capital and continue the fight in what was being termed the 'Alpine Redoubt' – a roughly triangular area between Bad Reichenhall, Berchtesgaden in Bavaria and Salzburg in Austria. Most in the Führerbunker were delighted about this; there were still perhaps as many as fifty people down there and almost all had been permanently housed in this concrete mausoleum since Hitler had moved in back in March. It had been built in the garden of Albert Speer's enormous Reichskanzlei and, strictly speaking, was two bunkers rolled into one. The first part, the Vorbunker, had been constructed as early as 1936 and covered some 300 square metres. It contained fourteen rooms of 10 metres square each. The second part had been built on Hitler's orders in 1943 after RAF Bomber Command made several raids on the capital. It was 2.5 metres deeper at 8.5 metres below ground and connected by a single staircase. There had always been a touch of the puritan about Hitler, despite his love of outsize objects, and the spartan nature of the Führerbunker reflected this. There was none of the parquet flooring, wood panelling and touches of luxury that singled out some of his earlier bunker complexes. Ventilators pumped in fresh air, but damp was a constant issue. And it was concrete, painted grey, subterranean, fetid, lit by artificial light, uniform and sparse. The Führerbunker was grim. In this second part of the complex Hitler had four rooms for his personal use and that of his mistress, the thirty-three-year-old Eva Braun, and there were also rooms for Martin Bormann, his secretary; Dr Theodor Morell, his doctor; Otto Günsche, his aide-de-camp; and Sturmbannführer Heinz Linge, his valet. Everyone else – secretaries, bodyguards, officers, even generals – was in the Vorbunker.

Even in this subterranean concrete crypt they had heard the guns getting closer, and by 19 April, with the Oder Front completely collapsed, the Red Army was nearing the city. That afternoon Krebs informed Hitler that the Russian tanks had broken through to the north of Berlin. This prompted an eruption of rage from Hitler, who exploded at the incompetence of his generals. Clearly, there was only one thing for it, he told Krebs and others now being berated. He would have to take direct command himself. And in such circumstances there could be no thought of flying out. Rather he would stay here, in Berlin. And if Hitler remained there, then most of those around him would have to do so too. As was all too obvious, the time for dramatic military reverses had passed. The Führerbunker had always felt rather like a tomb; it appeared that it might well become one for real. And so instead of celebrating Hitler's birthday at his beloved Berghof, his home near Berchtesgaden, they would be stuck in the ruins of Berlin contemplating their imminent demise. An understandably funereal mood swiftly descended on those trapped there.

The Führergeburtstag, Hitler's birthday, was a sacred date in the Third Reich's calendar and had, over the years, been a cause for widespread celebration. For Hitler's fiftieth birthday, for example, in 1939 Martin Bormann had overseen the building of the Kehlsteinhaus – the Eagle's Nest – high in the mountains above the Berghof. Its construction had involved building the highest road in Europe; it was a triumph of German engineering. Normally, Hitler had been inundated with messages and gifts from around the world. There had been parades and great celebrations. But the Führer understandably did not want a party on this occasion. 'Sadly,' noted Martin Bormann in his diary the following day, Friday, 20 April 1945, 'not exactly a birthday mood.' Hauptmann Hans Bauer, Hitler's personal pilot, agreed. 'A grim and sad affair,' he noted. Despite this, a number of senior Nazis trooped through the funereal atmosphere with their birthday wishes: Heinrich Himmler, the head of the SS; Reichsmarschall Hermann Göring, Vice-Chancellor and still Commander-in-Chief of the Luftwaffe; Feldmarschall Wilhelm Keitel, the head of the OKW, the Oberkommando der Wehrmacht – the German General Staff; Grossadmiral Karl Dönitz, Commander-in-Chief of the Kriegsmarine, the navy. Joachim von Ribbentrop had also presented himself. It had been von Ribbentrop, as Foreign Minister, who had effectively kick-started the war in 1939 with his pact with the Soviets over the partition of Poland. Back then Hitler had still been fit, vital and energized. Now, at fifty-six, he looked ten years older and shuffled like an old man, his back bent, his left arm, especially, afflicted with shakes he could not control. Those vivid pale eyes that once burned so bright were now sunken behind dark rings. The Führer was exhausted.

None of the visitors that day remained in Berlin. Dönitz, for example, headed straight back to Flensburg on the Baltic coast. Himmler went north-west too. Göring had abandoned his beloved home at Carinhall, to the north-east of Berlin, and fled to Bavaria; the Führer might have changed his plans, but the Reichsmarschall had no intention of dying in Berlin. Russian guns were getting closer. Everyone in the Führerbunker could hear them: a dull thud, a perceptible tremor, even 7 metres and more below ground.

Despite Hitler's decision to remain in Berlin, Martin Bormann had taken it upon himself to send much of the Führer's headquarters ahead to the Reichskanzlei in Berchtesgaden. This meant some of the staff and much of the paperwork being flown out while it was still just about safe enough to do so, but was also indicative of Bormann's hope that he could still persuade Hitler to leave Berlin. The Führer, however, was not to be swayed. Some 2.5 million civilians remained in the city and there was not the remotest chance it could be saved. Without question, the most likely way to spare lives was to surrender it right away. That, though, was simply not part of Hitler's thinking. Rather, his people would have to fight to the last. Willpower alone might still win the day. A counter-attack might prevail. No, a counter-attack would surely prevail. And this could maybe buy them time. In any case, it was an all or nothing situation; it always had been. The 1,000-Year Reich or Armageddon.

The prospect of Hitler being in direct command of any military situation was always to be feared because his decision-making was invariably the same and had been ever since he'd taken over as Commander-in-Chief of the Army in mid-December 1941: no retreats, and any setback to be restored by an immediate counter-attack of maximum ferocity. It had never proved very successful and had always cost untold lives. Since early 1943, more than two years earlier, it had inevitably ended in failure.

Overnight and into the morning of 21 April, chaos reigned as it became increasingly clear that the Red Army was now at Berlin's gates. Josef Goebbels, Reich Propaganda Minister but also Reich Commissioner for Berlin, announced that no man capable of bearing arms was permitted to leave the city. RAF Bomber Command was once again over as seventy-six Mosquitoes brought yet more destruction. Red Army troops of Marshal Ivan Konev's 4th Ukrainian Front had dramatically crossed the River Spree south of the city and were closing in on Zossen, the headquarters of the Heer – the German Army. The 9. Armee was also streaming back towards Berlin in disarray despite Hitler's orders for it to restore the Oder Front. Then, at 9.30 a.m., a massive Red Army artillery barrage announced the start of the Soviet assault on the city. This woke up Hitler. Unshaven and bleary-eyed, he demanded to know what was going on, and was shocked to hear that the Russians were so close already. Zossen was now about to be overrun; permission was asked to relocate army headquarters. Predictably, Hitler initially refused, before finally relenting just in the nick of time at around 1 p.m.

The Red Army was unstoppable, but Hitler continued to pore over situation maps and plot counter-attacks. Covering the Berlin area was Heeresgruppe Weichsel, commanded by General Gotthard Heinrici, while to the south was the newly appointed Feldmarschall Ferdinand Schörner's Heeresgruppe Mitte. These contained a number of armies, but in reality they were cobbled-together forces of woefully understrength divisions and regiments. The 9. Armee, for example, had been on the receiving end of the Red Army onslaught on the Seelow Heights overlooking the River Oder, the last natural defensive position before Berlin. It had been utterly overwhelmed by the enormity of the onslaught and by the 20th was in danger of being annihilated. General Wilhelm Burgdorf, Hitler's chief adjutant in the Führerbunker, suggested withdrawing 9. Armee to Berlin to help directly defend the city and reinforcing it with General Helmuth Weidling's LVI Panzerkorps. Hitler was having none of it, however. Rather, 9. Armee was to restore the front on the Oder at all costs. Looking at his maps, he then realized that Heinrici had III (Germanische) SS-Panzerkorps in reserve; this force, he decided, could be flung into the defence of Berlin against the northern flank of Zhukov's 1st Belorussian Front. Unbeknown to Hitler, however, most of III SS-Panzerkorps had already been sent to reinforce 9. Armee three days earlier; among the units hurried to the Oder was the 11. SS Freiwilligen (Volunteer) Panzergrenadier-Division Nordland, made up mostly of Swedes, Finns, Danes and Norwegians. The Nordland had already suffered some 15,000 casualties in 1945, roughly 100 per cent of its establishment strength. It was further reduced en route to the front, when it was hammered by Russian Shturmovik ground-attack aircraft. Soon after, the Nordland's meagre supply of vehicles ran out of fuel.

Ringing the commander of the Germanische Panzerkorps, Obergruppenführer Felix Steiner, in person, Hitler told him to counter-attack without delay. 'You will see,' he told Steiner, 'the Russians will suffer the greatest defeat in their history, before the gates of Berlin.' Steiner was expressly forbidden to allow any of his troops to fall back westwards; he was so shocked he could barely reply before the Führer called off. Only a few half-strength battalions of several hundred men each remained of his corps; Hitler was now re-labelling his meagre command an army group and telling him to plunge them into an enemy hundreds of times larger and better equipped in every regard. Minutes later, Steiner called back and spoke to Krebs, explaining that what Hitler was demanding was impossible. Krebs merely repeated the orders and told him to get moving.

While Konev's troops were swarming over Zossen and Zhukov's massed forces nearing Berlin, the Americans were sweeping across central and southern Germany and the British rapidly pushing north. The remnants of the Third Reich was being systematically crushed in a giant vice. Once again, Hitler was urged by Bormann and his remaining senior commanders that he should evacuate Berlin immediately. And once again he refused although conceded that anyone who wanted to leave the Führerbunker was free to do so. There were, though, only four Focke-Wulf Kondors available for the evacuation to Berchtesgaden, and it was unclear how many flights they might be able to manage before Berlin was closed to them. So began a frantic clamour for places. Some were not allowed to leave, however; Bormann, Krebs, Goebbels and all his immediate staff were among those who would be remaining with the Führer.

If Hitler had been functioning in a bubble of pure fantasy on 21 April, he was unable to ignore the reality as presented to him by his terrified generals the following afternoon during a conference in the Führerbunker. Down there, days and nights merged; Hitler tended not to go to bed until almost dawn then not rise again until one in the afternoon. On 22 April, Russian shelling had woken him early, at 10 a.m. Discombobulated, exhausted and stuffed full of Dr Morell's cocktail of drugs, he was hardly on peak form when the situation conference began at 4 p.m. When he asked for an update on how Steiner's counter-attack was getting on, there was a pause before his generals admitted that it had not taken place. And never would. Nor had 9. Armee restored the line on the Oder. Rather, it was now surrounded and only a few elements seemed likely to make it back to the city.

For a moment, Hitler did not speak. Then he quietly told everyone to leave except for Keitel, Generaloberst Alfred Jodl, Krebs and Burgdorf. Once alone with them, he launched into an uncontrolled tirade. He was surrounded by treachery, by incompetence. He had no more orders for them, he screamed. He suggested they turn to Göring for future instructions. Jodl, Chief of the Operation Staff of the OKW, then relayed this message, which was passed to the Reichsmarschall, now in Berchtesgaden. 'Even the SS goes behind my back and deceives me wherever they can,' Hitler later told Linge. 'Now I shall remain in Berlin and die here.'

There was a further week in the bunker until Hitler fulfilled this pledge, however. A week of mounting despair interspersed with bouts of irrational optimism. Of flashes of anger and then calm resignation. Of surreal conversations and even more surreal events. And of betrayals, both perceived and actual. The Third Reich had always been built on the very flimsiest of foundations, from its economy to its grotesque ideology. Hitler and those around him had, in many ways, created a fantasy world, and so it was hardly surprising that in its death throes the fantasy would be maintained to the last. The corruption, the irrationality, the warped ideology, the terrible strategic decisions, the malevolent violence meted out on the Poles and then the Soviet Union and the systematic annihilation of the Jews accelerated as total defeat loomed; they had all conspired against a 1,000-Year Reich. Combined with an inability to draw on the kind of global resources enjoyed by Germany's enemies, those odds had lengthened even further. In truth, Hitler's grand plan had always been an extremely unlikely proposition long before a single shot had been fired in this cataclysmic war; it had remained so even when he had been basking in the triumphs of the early Blitzkrieg years and dreaming of Germania. When his forces failed to rout the Soviet Union at their first attempt in 1941, the edifice began to crack badly. By the time the emaciated wreck of 6. Armee surrendered at Stalingrad in February 1943, the great retraction had begun. Whatever faint, lingering chance there was of a change in fortunes had vanished on the smoke-filled air – despite rockets and other scientific wizardry – long before Marshal Zhukov launched his final offensive on 16 April. And so in this fetid, ghastly, twenty-four-hour existence, Hitler and his remaining acolytes waited for the alternative, Armageddon, while the enemy guns approached ever closer, the ground trembling more violently and more consistently not just with every passing day but with every hour.

The Third Reich was rotten at its core because Hitler was. He'd surrounded himself with men equally corrupted and equally full of hate, anger and jealousies. Of course, they loathed one another; how could they not when they were all jockeying for power and the attention of their Führer? Göring had been asked by Jodl to take over the decision-making from Berchtesgaden and had anxiously asked for clarification and confirmation. He'd given a time limit for a response, but in the meantime Bormann had taken the opportunity to both poison Hitler's mind against the Reichsmarschall and also give the Führer a glimmer of hope. General Walther Wenck's 12. Armee was fighting the Allies at the Elbe, but could be urgently brought to Berlin instead. Combined with the retreating 9. Armee, Berlin might yet be saved. It was nonsense, of course, but Hitler grabbed it, as Bormann knew he would. No confirmation was sent to Göring, who accordingly announced he was taking over. Bormann then told Hitler this was a terrible betrayal, a lie Hitler again swallowed. Orders were immediately sent out for Göring's arrest.

People came and went. Planes flew from Gatow, to the west of the city, to Berchtesgaden for four days. Keitel and Jodl headed north to join Dönitz. On the evening of 23 April, General Helmuth Weidling had appeared in the bunker. The commander of LVI Panzerkorps, part of the dislocated and spattered 9. Armee, he had been out of communication since the 20th and Hitler had ordered his arrest. Rather courageously, he had made his way to the Führerbunker to protest his innocence. Impressed, Hitler rescinded the arrest and promptly put him in command of Berlin's defence instead. To fulfil this mammoth undertaking, he had fewer than 100,000 Waffen-SS and Wehrmacht troops, old men and teenagers. Against 2.5 million Red Army troops flush with fuel, fire and an immense arsenal of weaponry. Berlin was no Thermopylae. In any case, even those outnumbered heroes lost the battle.

On the 24th Albert Speer turned up, having made it through from the north. On arrival he was accosted by Bormann; the two loathed one another but Bormann was now friendliness itself. He implored Speer to try and persuade Hitler to leave. Speer did the very opposite, advising Hitler to stay and end it here in Berlin. 'Believe me, Speer,' Hitler told him, 'it will be easy to end my life. A brief moment and I am freed from everything, released from this miserable existence.' Speer then spent the night drinking champagne with Eva Braun, the Moët and Chandon bottles drawn from the extensive Reichskanzlei cellars. She had devoted herself to her beloved Führer for the past decade and had forgone the chance to stay away from Berlin. She told Speer calmly that she had returned to be with Hitler and end her life with him too. The following day, Speer was offered a limp handshake from Hitler. 'You're going then,' Hitler said. 'Good. Goodbye.'

Josef Goebbels, his wife Magda and their six children moved in, also to meet their end with Hitler. Life without Hitler, without the Third Reich, was unthinkable to both, although it was clear that Magda Goebbels was in a terrible state about ending not only her and her husband's lives but those of their children too. The prospect was eating her alive. Generaloberst Robert von Greim also arrived, along with the test pilot Hanna Reitsch. Von Greim had been needlessly summoned by Hitler to be told he was now in charge of the Luftwaffe, not that it really existed any more. They only got there by landing a Fieseler Storch on the wrecked runway at Gatow in the nick of time. Von Greim was wounded in the foot by a bullet fired at them as they hedge-hopped into the city; they eventually reached the bunker around 6 p.m. on 26 April. Later that evening, Hitler told Reitsch she would die alongside him and gave her a phial of cyanide. At this she burst into tears and pleaded with him to leave. She could, she told him, still fly him out. This, he told her, was not possible. 'By staying,' he said, 'I thought all the troops of the country would follow my example and come to the aid of the city. I hoped they would make superhuman efforts to save me and thus save my three million compatriots.' It was not, however, possible to achieve the impossible. There could be no triumph from willpower alone after all.

The next betrayal was that of Gruppenführer Hermann

Fegelein, Hitler's SS liaison officer. Fegelein had married Eva Braun's sister, Gretl, and this had helped make him a favoured player at the court of the Führer. However, his absence had been noticed on 27 April and Hitler wanted him back immediately. Erich Kempka, Hitler's chauffeur, knew that Fegelein had gone to his flat in Charlottenburg and so hurried to fetch him. He found Fegelein that evening with another woman, wearing civilian clothes, with bags packed and a stash of money. He was also drunk, and before heading off with Kempka rang Eva Braun and pleaded with her to intercede. She was unwilling to do so, and so Fegelein was brought back, under arrest, and put in a guarded room until he had sobered up.

Then came the news, via a Reuters radio report, that Himmler had offered to surrender to the Allies. Hitler had initially taken this calmly but then brooded on the matter, working himself up into an increasingly incensed lather. The refusal of Steiner to counter-attack, the flight of Fegelein, the news of Himmler – it all added up. The SS had betrayed him. This was treason. Himmler was out of reach but Fegelein was now back in the bunker. On Hitler's insistence, he was given a perfunctory court-martial by Burgdorf and then taken out and shot.

But Hitler's end was nearing. Red Army troops were now at Potsdamer Platz, barely a stone's throw away. After Fegelein's execution Hitler summoned his valet, Heinz Linge. He wanted Linge to have ready two blankets and enough petrol to cremate two bodies. He and Eva were going to kill themselves, he told Linge, and he wanted him to then carry their bodies up into the Reichskanzlei garden and burn them. 'Jawohl, mein Führer,' Linge stuttered.

The only people who wished to die were Hitler, Eva Braun

and the Goebbels. Everyone else wanted to escape and survive. But in the surreal atmosphere of the bunker mausoleum, the topic of conversation over tea on the evening of 28 April revolved around what was the most favoured way to commit suicide. It boiled down to cyanide or a bullet to the brain. It was then a question of individual preference.

Yet, before death, there was to be a wedding. Hitler had always been clear to Eva Braun that he could not marry her because he was already married to the German people. Now, though, at the end, he felt he was free to do so after all. He knew she wanted this and he was willing, in these last hours, to grant her that wish. After all, she had come back to Berlin to be with him. Goebbels and Bormann were witnesses and after the brief ceremony champagne and sandwiches were served for the bride, groom and guests. Eva, all who saw her agreed, had been radiant. Afterwards, Heinz Linge made great play of calling her 'Frau Hitler'. 'Her eyes lit up,' he wrote. 'She gave me a happy smile and for a moment laid her hand on my forearm.'

It was Sunday, 29 April. Hitler and his new wife would be married for barely thirty-six hours before they finally chose the moment to end their lives.

A lot of nonsense has been claimed about what happened next. There is, however, absolutely no doubt whatsoever that Hitler died by his own hand in the early afternoon of Monday, 30 April 1945. Hanna Reitsch did not fly him out at the last moment, although she and von Greim had managed to escape in an Arado 96 the day before. This was a Luftwaffe trainer plane and had been kept under a tarpaulin near the Brandenburg Gate. Miraculously, they managed to take off down the

Charlottenburger Chaussee that ran west with enough surprise and a steep enough climb to avoid being shot down. At any rate, Hitler was not spirited away, nor did he shave off his square smudge of a moustache, grease back his hair and live out his life in anonymity in South America. Those rumours were spread by the Soviet KGB, the post-war secret intelligence service, purely to wind up the Americans and British and to test the response. Of course Hitler killed himself. To suggest a last-ditch escape is to fail entirely to understand his character or the black-and-white, all-or-nothing proposition he had presented to the German people from the outset. If there could be no 1,000-Year Reich, there would be Armageddon. And Armageddon meant death.

Hitler dictated his last will and testament on the 29th and was up early – for him – the following day, having slept alone and fully dressed after he'd gone to bed the previous night. Bormann, Krebs and Burgdorf were asleep in the Führer's rooms with loaded pistols beside them in case the Russians burst in. A telephone conversation with Weidling confirmed that Berlin was lost, although fierce fighting continued. Hitler fretted that the cyanide capsules they had might not be real and so tested a capsule on his much-loved dog, Blondi. She died in convulsions soon after. So that had cleared up that particular worry. A last meal was then eaten at midday at which Hitler gave a monologue about the post-war world and his posterity. He recognized that his reputation was bound to take a battering in the short term but hoped that in the future he would be treated 'justly'. The precise time that Hitler and his wife retired to kill themselves is disputed, but it seems likely that Heinz Linge was probably right in claiming it was around 3.15 p.m. In any case, it hardly matters. 'Linge,'

Hitler told him, 'I am going to shoot myself now. You know what you have to do. I have given the order for the break-out. Attach yourself to one of the groups and try to get through to the west.' Linge asked him what he should now fight for. 'For the coming man,' Hitler replied. Linge saluted, shook his hand, then closed the door on him.

Linge did not hear any shots but did smell cordite and so, having called on Bormann, the two men, with Günsche following, went into Hitler's rooms where they found both Eva and Hitler dead on a sofa, blood spattered on the carpet. Eva's contorted face showed that she had died by cyanide, while Hitler had put a single bullet through his right temple. The method of killing oneself boiled down to personal choice, after all, as had been agreed a couple of days earlier. Now, while Bormann went to get help, Linge laid out the blankets and placed the bodies on them, then wrapped the cloth around them. It was Bormann who carried Eva out of the room before Kempka insisted on taking her; he knew how much she had hated Bormann and didn't like the idea of him carrying her out to be cremated. Linge took Hitler's head and shoulders and two SS bodyguards lifted his body. Both corpses were removed from the bunker, laid in a shallow depression and doused in the fuel that Linge had ordered Kempka to have ready. A strong wind had whipped up and their first attempts to throw a light on to the bodies failed. Russian artillery thundered and shells were falling nearby. Linge hurried back into the bunker and made a thick wick from fuel-soaked paper. Back outside, he lit it and threw it on Hitler's body. Linge reckoned that both corpses were still smouldering at 7.30 p.m. The carbonized remains were buried at the bottom of a shell crater the following morning.

*

It was now Tuesday, 1 May. Magda and Josef Goebbels had planned to kill themselves the previous day but had lost their nerve. Magda was beside herself, but both were still determined that they should die and that their six children should be spared the world that would surely follow. The secretaries still in the bunker pleaded with them to spare them, offering to look after them. But their parents believed that they would be saving them by ending their lives. And so, at around 6 p.m., Hitler's other physician, Dr Ludwig Stumpfegger, administered a sleeping draught then cyanide to each of them. Then, having murdered their children, Josef and Magda Goebbels finally took cyanide themselves. Their bodies were also burnt with the petrol that was left.

At around 11 p.m. that night the breakout from the bunker began, the survivors splitting themselves into groups and leaving at different times. Linge teamed up with Kempka and escaped the Reichskanzlei area via tunnels under the government district. Some made it, most did not and were picked up by Red Army troops. Bormann was killed while scampering along the railway tracks near Lehrter Station in the early hours of 2 May.

General Weidling finally surrendered the city – unconditionally – at 8.30 on the morning of Tuesday, 2 May. Hitler was dead and the Battle for Berlin was over. It was not, however, quite the end of the Third Reich; there were still more days of madness to play out before victory in Europe, and with it peace, could finally be announced.

CHAPTER 2

THE DUEL PART 1

The Surrender in Italy, *2 May 1945*

Kaltenbrunner always appeared to me to be a very reserved type, who was hard to get near as man to man. Heydrich was like that too, only more cynical. All the same, he had certain human qualities. He never succeeded in getting on the same level as the Reichsführer or the Führer, mentally. After Heydrich's death, I tried to transfer my friendship to him, as Heydrich's successor, because the Wolff–Heydrich friendship was one of the pillars of the original SS. I offered him my friendship, and even used 'du' to him, but he never made any use of my offer.

Obergruppenführer Karl Wolff

The unconditional surrender of all German troops in Italy was signed at 2 p.m. on Sunday, 29 April 1945, although it did not finally come into force until midday on 2 May. It was the first total capitulation of German forces on any major front and the news reached the Führerbunker in time for Hitler to hear the tidings before he put a bullet into his head the following day. Yet although this was the first surrender, as far as Obergruppenführer und General der Waffen-SS Karl Wolff was concerned, it was already several months later than he'd hoped and certainly at least ten days longer than needed to have been the case. Wolff was the joint second-highest-ranking member of the SS in Hitler's Reich and yet, much to his immense frustration, it had been the Wehrmacht commanders in Italy, with their ludicrous adherence of sworn loyalty to the Führer, that had scuppered his plans to end the slaughter. But while there might have been a grain of compassion behind the urgency with which he'd been pursuing the German surrender there, his prime motivation was unquestionably to save his own skin. He had correctly calculated that the sooner Germany surrendered in Italy, the greater the chance of him escaping the Allied gallows as a war criminal. Conversely, the longer it took, the less obvious would be his own impact on the ending of hostilities. And with it the chances of Allied mercy.

In many ways it was remarkable that he was still alive: paradoxically, his determination for self-preservation had led him to take a number of astonishing risks, not least because for much of the last few months he had been pitted against his nemesis and equal within the SS, Obergruppenführer Ernst Kaltenbrunner. Each had been trying to outwit the other in a deadly duel of survival – a game in which they instinctively understood that there could be only one winner. And so both had been playing increasingly desperate hands, pursuing outrageous schemes and plans – albeit supported by a cast of money launderers, art thieves, outcasts, hostages, spies, mass murderers and, it must be said, a few good men too. As two at the very top of the SS machinery, both Wolff and Kaltenbrunner had been complicit in unspeakable crimes, of aiding and abetting the annihilation of Europe's Jews and many more people besides. Yet, as the always shaky edifice of the Third Reich and its despicable ideology began to crumble before their eyes, the two men realized that they would be held to account once the Nazi regime – and with it the war – was over. Their only chance of survival was to plan for the future: by stockpiling funds and assets, gathering bargaining chips and invoking leniency from the Allies as men of peace and humanity should they ever be brought to heel. This, however, meant facing double jeopardy: if their plots were discovered, their fate would be a Nazi firing squad or worse. But if captured by the Allies, having done nothing to help bring the war to an end, the gallows surely awaited.

By the time of the surrender, Wolff had moved his headquarters to the Palazzo Ducale in Bolzano, a grand villa rebuilt during the fascist era on the orders of the dictator Benito Mussolini. The palazzo had long salons lined with fascist emblems and homages to Il Duce, but for Wolff it was a fine house that allowed him to live in the style to which he'd become accustomed; after all, even in these dark days there was no point in slumming it if one didn't need to. And Bolzano was ideally placed at the heart of South Tyrol; it was through the town that the main rail route and road from southern Austria and the Reich ran, a link through the Alps. The entire region was also achingly beautiful: an Eden of majestic peaks, lush mountain pastures, gushing streams and quaint, picture-box Alpine villages and towns. With its hidden valleys and ancient trails it was a place one could hide oneself in, but also a waypoint too, a link between northern and southern Europe. To the north of Bolzano the Brenner Pass linked Austria to Italy, making it the main supply route for the German armies to the south; through here almost every soldier, every supply of ammunition and weapons had passed since the Italian armistice back in September 1943. It was also an area betwixt and between: Austrian until it had become part of Italy after the end of the First World War, but then, following Italy's exit from the Second World War, absorbed into the Reich as the 'Alpenvorland', complete with its own Gauleiter – Nazi governor – Franz Hofer. It remained Germanic as well as Italian, the influences of both cultures apparent in the architecture and languages of its people.

But as the prime passageway from Germany and Austria into Italy it had also been a major target for Allied bombers. On 28 February 1945, for example, the US Fifteenth Air Force, operating from Foggia in southern Italy, had dropped its biggest-ever tonnage of bombs in a single day, and much of it had been directed at the railway station and marshalling yards at Bolzano. By this stage of the war, Italy was one of three main front lines. To the east lay the Red Army, by the beginning of March closing in on the German border and pressing the Third Reich's allies and territories to the south-east. In the west the Americans, British, Canadians and French were nearing the River Rhine. The Reich was being crushed, slowly but decisively, in a mighty vice. To the south, however, in Italy, the front had remained static through the winter, the German armies strung out across the leg of the peninsula amid the high peaks of the northern Apennine Mountains. With the onset of spring, and better weather, the Allied armies in Italy were sure to launch a major – and perhaps final – offensive. Wolff had hoped to bring about peace here before that battle was launched. And in so doing, halt the fighting. Many lives saved in return for his.

Thin-lipped, with a wide, receding forehead and pale-grey eyes, Wolff looked a little older than his forty-four years but none the less had a genial, almost gentle face. He was quick to smile, naturally charming, highly cultured and fiercely intelligent; not at all the cartoon-book villain. An infantry officer in the First World War, he had later studied law, then run his own advertising agency and had joined the SS in 1931, two years before Hitler took power, and steadily rose up through the SS hierarchy, becoming an increasingly close and trusted confidant of Reichsführer Heinrich Himmler. In June 1939 he had become his Chief of Staff, which meant also being Himmler's representative in Hitler's military headquarters. In early 1943, however, Wolff had incurred Himmler's wrath for divorcing his wife and marrying Countess Ingeborg Maria von Bernstorff; while having mistresses was deemed acceptable, divorce was not in the Nazi world, where the perfect home life was seen as an ideological aspiration that leading Nazis were supposed to adhere to themselves. At any rate, by the autumn of that year Himmler had forgiven him. With the Italian armistice in September 1943 and the German occupation of much of the country, the Reichsführer had sent him to be Höchster SS- und Polizeiführer in Italy – the 'highest' SS police leader.

In sharp contrast, his rival, Ernst Kaltenbrunner, most certainly did fit the bill of pantomime villain. Forty-one years old in the spring of 1945, he was tall at six foot seven and ruggedly handsome, but also cruel-looking, his cheeks crossed with duelling scars, a rather warped badge of honour from his university days. A lawyer by training from Vienna, Kaltenbrunner was Head of the Reichssicherheitshauptamt – the Reich Main Security Office, or RSHA. It was a post he'd taken over in June 1942, after the previous incumbent, Reinhard Heydrich, one of the cruellest of all the Nazis, had been assassinated in Prague. This meant Kaltenbrunner was in charge of both the police and the secret police, the Sicherheitsdienst – SD – better known by its cure-all moniker, the Gestapo.

Hitler had always maintained an approach of divide and rule and his immediate subordinates did the same. With Wolff and Kaltenbrunner as the only two men holding the same exalted SS rank, their rivalry was inevitable. This was also exacerbated by their differing nationalities; there were distinct factions within the Nazi hierarchy, and if two people rubbed each other up the wrong way it was likely to be because one was German and the other Austrian. Their situations were also different. Kaltenbrunner had the distinct advantage of a position near the apex of Nazi power and with greater levers of authority and the machinery of command at his fingertips. Wolff, by contrast, had the benefit of being in Italy itself and, arguably, of having a base comparatively far from Berlin. By early 1945 both were desperate to deliver the surrender in Italy, yet the rub, quite apart from the risks of going behind Hitler's back, was this: there could be only one successful negotiated surrender.

The key player for both Wolff and Kaltenbrunner was an American named Allen Dulles. A fifty-one-year-old prematurely silver-haired former lawyer and diplomat from New York, he had been part of the American delegation at the Paris Peace Conference following the end of the First World War, later becoming a legal advisor on arms limitations to the League of Nations. In this capacity he had met Hitler and Mussolini, among many others, during the 1930s. In the summer of 1941, before America's entry into the war, President Roosevelt had charged his old friend, William 'Wild Bill' Donovan, a former soldier, lawyer and winner of the Medal of Honor during the last war, with creating a new unit based on the British foreign secret intelligence service, the Special Operations Executive; this latter organization had initially been designed to foment resistance and carry out acts of sabotage against Nazi occupiers in Europe. Donovan's resulting creation was the Office of Strategic Services, the OSS, and even before it officially came into being in July 1942 he had recruited the smart and worldly Allen Dulles to be his main man in that most important of countries, Switzerland – for this neutral Alpine nation, bordering Germany, Austria, Italy and France, was another waypoint like South Tyrol. Here clandestine discussions could be held, deals could be done. What was impossible elsewhere was possible in Switzerland. And especially so in the German-speaking Swiss city of Berne. From Berne, Dulles had a direct line not only to Washington but also to Field Marshal Sir Harold Alexander, the Supreme Allied Commander in the Mediterranean theatre.

For senior Nazis, however, making contact with Dulles was not at all straightforward, involved immense risk and was, frankly, impossible without a trusted go-between. These did not grow on trees. None the less, the previous year Wolff had begun the plot to save his neck when he'd put out tentative feelers to the Vatican to act as a potential liaison with the Allies, although nothing much had come of it. He'd also consciously begun creating a portfolio that would stand him in good stead once the war was over by deliberately reining in anti-partisan operations in northern Italy and showing leniency to striking Italian workers.

Instead it was Kaltenbrunner who was first to attempt to make contact with Dulles via one of his SS agents, Sturmbannführer Wilhelm Höttl. A fellow Austrian, Höttl had been an ardent Nazi as a teenager, joining the SS aged just sixteen. Clever and cunning, he'd been recruited by the SD in Vienna, although it was not until Kaltenbrunner was in charge of the RSHA that Höttl's career took off. By 1944 he was head of the Italian desk for the SD's foreign intelligence and had won plaudits for helping to engineer the rescue of Mussolini from captivity in September 1943. He had also been directly involved in the arrest of Mussolini's son-in-law and former Italian Foreign Minister, Count Galeazzo Ciano, who was subsequently executed in January 1945. For this, and for his loyalty, Kaltenbrunner had promoted him to Sturmbannführer before he'd turned thirty, which was unusual. However, Höttl's biggest role had been building up contacts in Hungary, vital once the Nazis occupied the country in March 1944 and which directly helped seal the fate of Hungary's 725,000 Jews. Höttl's contacts and information were passed to his fellow Austrian in the SS, Adolf Eichmann, who had overseen the Hungarian Jews' deportation to Auschwitz, where almost all had been murdered in the gas chambers.

Yet while Kaltenbrunner had identified Dulles as his route to the Americans ahead of Wolff, it was his rival who managed to reach the OSS man first. This had only come about because, at the end of January 1945, Wolff had recognized that he needed to accelerate his plans. This, he claimed, had been prompted by a conversation with his friends in the Leibstandarte, the 1. SS Panzer-Division, who told him that during the fighting in the Ardennes that December they'd been promised 3,000 aircraft in support but had not seen a single one – only superior Allied fighters and bombers. 'It was only at the end of January that I realised the rottenness of our position,' he said. 'After that, I grew very impatient.'

On the very same day at the end of February that Allied bombers were pummelling Bolzano, Wolff was holding a secret meeting at his previous headquarters on the shores of Lake Garda. Those attending were Standartenführer Walter Rauff, head of the SS in Milan, and, earlier in the war, the inventor of the mobile gas chamber; Eugen Dollmann, an art historian and German ambassador to the Vatican; and Gruppenführer Wilhelm Harster, an SS general in the SD who had been personally responsible for rounding up many of the Dutch Jews, including the teenage diarist Anne Frank. He was now head of the SD in Italy and based in Verona. Perhaps the most important player there, however, was Baron Luigi Parilli, a wealthy Italian industrialist with connections in Switzerland who suggested to Wolff that he try and make contact with Allen Dulles. This, Parilli, suggested, might be achieved via Dr Max Husmann, who ran a private school in Switzerland and who was fabulously well connected. Nor was that all, because

Eugen Dollmann knew Dr Gero von Schulze-Gaevernitz, a German-born American businessman based in Switzerland who happened to be Dulles's right-hand man. These were precisely the connections Wolff urgently needed. A plan was hatched: Parilli and Dollmann would travel together to Switzerland and attempt to make contact with Dulles.

Dollmann and Parilli took a train into Switzerland on 3 March having made contact with von Schulze-Gaevernitz, who in turn informed Dulles. The OSS men then sent emissaries to meet Dollmann and Parilli. The message was simple: only unconditional surrender of all German forces in Italy would be considered. Furthermore, as an act of good faith, Dulles demanded that Ferruccio Parri, an Italian resistance leader, and Antonio Usmiani, an Italian agent who had been working for Dulles, be freed from SS captivity in Verona. This was a clear test to see whether Wolff was serious.

Three days later, on 6 March, Wolff sent his reply. Parri and Usmiani would be freed and sent to Switzerland and he accepted the terms of unconditional surrender. Both men were freed immediately. Furthermore, Wolff was willing to travel to Switzerland himself and meet Dulles in person. This he planned to do on 8 March. It had been impressively fast work on Wolff's part to release the two prisoners and set up the trip to Switzerland; it was also very high-risk. Wolff could easily be recognized at any point of the journey; he was hardly an unknown figure.

Wolff was taken by car to join a train that passed over the border via the Gotthard Pass. There, however, the snow was so deep that the train could go no further; Wolff had been lying low in a compartment with the blinds pulled down but now he and his small party had to disembark and walk several hundred yards through the snow to a waiting train on the far side of the drifts. Luck was with him, however. No one seemed to recognize him and he and his delegation secured another private compartment. With the blinds down, they rolled on to Zurich.

As it happened, Dulles had been in two minds about whether to see Wolff, aware that the Soviets, their current allies, were vehemently opposed to separate peace deals. 'If Wolff was trying to trick me, the consequences could be unpleasant,' noted Dulles. 'I could see the headlines: "Envoy of President Roosevelt receives highest SS officer."' On the other hand, the opportunity to confer with such a high-ranking figure, especially since Wolff appeared to be genuine in his intentions, was too good to pass over. And so, using one of his safe houses, at Genferstrasse in the heart of Zurich, Dulles decided that meeting Wolff face to face was a gamble worth taking. First, though, he wanted to make Wolff sweat a little, insisting on seeing Usmiani and Parri first and then keeping the German waiting at Max Husmann's Zurich apartment. As the hours passed, Wolff became increasingly agitated.

Eventually, Wolff was hustled into a car and taken to the safe house. 'I control the SS forces in Italy,' Wolff told him, 'and I am willing to place myself and my entire organization at the disposal of the Allies to terminate hostilities.' Those forces, however, did not include the Wehrmacht – non-SS – troops under the command of Feldmarschall Albert Kesselring, Dulles pointed out. How was Wolff going to bring them all to heel? Kesselring, Wolff assured him, was an old friend and could be brought round. What's more, Wolff told him, the all-important Brenner Pass fell under his jurisdiction. Further pledges were made: to release Italian Jews being held in the concentration camp near Bolzano and to stop all further actions against partisans.

'Gentlemen,' Wolff told Dulles and von Schulze-Gaevernitz, 'if you can be patient, I will hand you Italy on a silver platter.'

With this first – encouraging – meeting over, Wolff planned to head straight to Bolzano and do his best to persuade Kesselring to fall in with his plans, but then things started to dramatically unravel. A message arrived that Kaltenbrunner wanted to see him urgently in Innsbruck; that did not bode well. Then, on the return trip, Wolff was travelling back towards Lake Garda when his car was strafed by an Allied fighter plane; he was lucky to survive. Worse was to follow, for on safely reaching his villa at Lake Garda he learned that Kesselring had been summoned to Berlin and the rumour was that Hitler was about to appoint him to command all German forces in the west. That would mean he would be leaving Italy and a replacement, very possibly little known to Wolff, taking over.

Meanwhile, Wilhelm Höttl had also made contact with Dulles, although what Kaltenbrunner was offering was not a surrender in Italy but one in Austria. The implication, however, was that German forces in Italy, directly south of Austria, would very swiftly collapse and follow suit once Austria had thrown in the towel. Dulles was certainly intrigued, but while Wolff had used legitimate contacts as go-betweens, Höttl was an SS officer, had a despicable past, and there was no reason at all to remotely trust him. So instead Dulles sent representatives to meet him. At this meeting, Höttl repeatedly stressed that he was a peace envoy sent directly from Kaltenbrunner and that his boss would deliver the unconditional surrender of Austria. He also offered his own services to the OSS; Wolff and Kaltenbrunner weren't the only two looking to save themselves once the war was over.

*

While, on the face of it, Wolff appeared to be one step ahead of Kaltenbrunner in his contacts with the Allies, the RSHA chief had been stockpiling immense amounts of cash for a post-war world in which money could well buy him out of trouble. Twenty miles north-west of Bolzano, down a long Alpine valley, lay Merano, a small spa town popular before the war for its mountain sports, which had been home to a number of Jews, most of whom had since been arrested and deported. Since early the previous year, it had also been the headquarters of an outrageous money-laundering operation. In fact, there were warehouses next to Merano's racecourse now stuffed with boxes full of counterfeit British and US banknotes.

The location of Merano – between Innsbruck and Austria to the north, Switzerland to the east, and with Verona, Lake Garda and Bologna all as local satellites – made the town the ideal place from which to run a money-laundering operation. To launder money, the ability to distribute it and spread it to the four winds was essential, but equally important was to keep the enterprise away from too many prying eyes. Kaltenbrunner was mostly in Berlin, but Merano was surrounded by mountains and isolated. Here another of his creatures could mastermind the entire operation with comparative impunity.

Forging British banknotes had originally been devised by the SD back in 1940, although the counterfeiters initially struggled and by the time of Heydrich's assassination in Prague in June 1942 the operation had already been wound down. Under Kaltenbrunner, however, counterfeiting British notes was revived as Operation BERNHARD. The aim was no longer to flood the British economy but rather to use the money to finance secret intelligence operations. And this time the counterfeiters were of an entirely higher calibre: Jewish prisoners at Sachsenhausen concentration camp to the north of Berlin who were superb at the art of forging banknotes. By 1943, some 140 prisoners were producing tens of millions of pounds' worth of notes from six flat-bed printing presses. By May 1944, Kaltenbrunner ordered them to start producing US dollars as well, not exactly for intelligence operations but for his own personal use, whether that might be a last stand in the Alpine redoubt – certainly his cover story – or, more realistically, to accumulate a vast private fund for a rainy post-war day.

Running the laundering of this extraordinary counterfeiting operation was another unscrupulous rogue called Friedrich Schwend, part of the mosaic of corruption, criminality and deceit that marked the Nazi regime. Like Kaltenbrunner, Schwend had been only too willing to cast ideology aside in favour of looking after number one and was proving adept at adapting his skills to self-preservation. Schwend was thirty-eight, a former pre-war car engine salesman and a smooth-talking charmer who had been working for the Abwehr, the Wehrmacht's intelligence service – rather than the SS-run RSHA – at the start of the war. Repeatedly getting himself into trouble, he was caught out by his superiors selling unauthorized but bogus German U-boat plans to the British for cash, captured by Italian secret intelligence agents, turned back over to the Germans at the Brenner Pass and flung in prison at Klagenfurt in the Austrian Alps.

Kaltenbrunner learned about Schwend from none other than Wilhelm Höttl, who suggested this canny rogue as just the man for overseeing a money-laundering operation. That Schwend had fallen foul of the Abwehr was no disqualification for working for Kaltenbrunner; quite the opposite, in fact. Releasing Schwend from his incarceration, the RSHA boss instructed him to run the entire laundering operation of forged banknotes, giving him, frankly, astonishing levels of latitude so long as he successfully and swiftly spread the notes as far and wide as possible. Incredibly, Schwend even negotiated for himself a 33.33 per cent cut of every pound sterling he brought into circulation.

In very swift order, Schwend established his small operation under the entirely fake name of 'Stab. 4 Deutsches Panzerkorps', initially at Abbazia and Trieste before realizing that Merano offered a considerably better, more discreet location. Taking over the Schloss Labers, a grand – but not too grand – villa perched among vineyards on a hill overlooking the town, and protected by a small squad of SS police troops, Schwend got down to building a fortune. With the forged notes he bought houses, hotels, ships, cars and shares in a number of companies. Some of it was used for bribes and he also sent plenty to vaults in Zurich. He developed a dense network of couriers and agents, including Jews. Jack Van Herten, for example, was a Dutch Jew operating under the cover of the International Committee of the Red Cross. In reality, he was smuggling Jews to the Middle East but at the same time passing on laundered money for Schwend. And Schwend also took over those warehouses at the Merano racecourse, hiding counterfeit notes in race boxes that were then distributed to Holland, France, Denmark and elsewhere. It was a huge operation and Schwend was making millions. But Kaltenbrunner was making even more. And right under the nose of the Höchster SS und Polizeiführer in Italy, Karl Wolff.

Yet Wolff had been creating his own insurance policies too, not through laundered money but art. Priceless works of art.

Some of the world's greatest masterpieces. SS Standartenführer Professor Alexander Langsdorff was an archaeologist and art historian and had been appointed head of the Kunstschutz in Italy, a Nazi organization set up to 'protect' great works of art as war ravaged the country. And, as an SS colonel in Italy, he reported to Wolff.

Art was one of Hitler's great passions – and particularly the art of the Renaissance; he had little truck with modern art, which had been denounced by the Nazis as 'degenerate' and banned from public show. Back in 1938, the Führer had visited Florence and the world-famous Uffizi Gallery, and had been so impressed by what he'd seen that he determined to create his own version. The Führermuseum would be specially created in Linz, his home town in Austria. It was to be his lasting artistic legacy to the German peoples and seal his place as one of the world's great patrons of the arts. And, fortunately for Wolff, Italy was brimming with works by some of the Führer's favourite artists: Botticelli, Cranach, Rubens, Michaelangelo and Raphael, to name but a few.

At the start of the war, many of Florence's art treasures, some 11,000 in all, had been moved to a number of palaces and villas in the nearby Tuscan countryside. By June 1944, however, as the war had finally moved north of Rome, Mussolini, now head of the puppet Repubblica Sociale Italiana – the RSI – insisted that these priceless works be moved again for safety. Standartenführer Langsdorff was to work alongside Florentine officials to ensure that the move took place right away. But working 'alongside' meant no such thing. Rather, and against the wishes of the Italians, who had intended to ignore Mussolini and keep them safe in Tuscany until the front passed, Langsdorff oversaw the movement of the art himself, using purloined vehicles and SS police troops. The Italians were assured that the art belonged to Italy and Italy alone; but it was now in German, not Italian, hands.

And the works of art fell into Wolff's hands, because on 21 July 1944 Langsdorff arrived at Lake Garda and asked for his boss's help in ensuring that these treasures were not handed over to Nazi officials in the Reich; he was aware that many of the works destined for the still-planned Führermuseum had been sent for safekeeping to the salt mines near Altaussee in Austria and did not want the same to happen to Italy's masterpieces. Wolff was far too canny an operator not to know a gift laid at his feet when he saw it. Immediately, he ordered Langsdorff to bring as many art treasures north as possible. Instructions from the Italians were to be ignored; instead, they would be taken to South Tyrol. Here Wolff could keep them under his direct control in secret locations undisclosed to the Italians and used entirely to his advantage: to curry favour either with the Führer or the Allies, depending on how the situation panned out. Langsdorff stored the art in two places deep in South Tyrol known only to him and Wolff.

Yet at the end of January 1945, Wolff received a direct order from Martin Bormann, Hitler's personal secretary. 'Based on the Führer's orders, the existence of all confiscated works of art, especially paintings, objects of artistic interest and weapons of artistic importance in Greater Germany and the Occupied Territories', Bormann instructed, 'is to be reported to the Führer's advisors in such matters; who, on consideration of the individual cases, will send a report to the Führer through me, so that the Führer can himself decide what use he will make of the acquired articles.' Wolff also then received a further direct order from Himmler to send the art specifically to the salt mines at Altaussee, where much of the planned Führermuseum art was now being stored. Wolff knew that he had to keep control of these treasures so told Himmler he did not have the vehicles or fuel to transport them to Austria; he also made sure that he and Langsdorff were the only two Germans to know both the inventory of the artworks and where they were located. Hitler and Himmler had only a vague idea of what had been collected, so Wolff was able to successfully stall these instructions. He did, however, make a detailed, photographed inventory as an extra level of insurance: either as proof of his attempts to save the art or to present to Hitler on his fifty-sixth birthday on 20 April 1945.

Meanwhile, in the middle of March, Wolff travelled to Switzerland again for a second meeting with Dulles. The stakes were now being ramped up considerably; Wolff had already issued his orders forbidding all violent operations against partisans, which had been reported back to the OSS chief via the go-between, Luigi Parilli. This order alone could have been enough to set off alarm bells in Germany were it to be leaked. Wolff was also keenly aware that his hand would be significantly strengthened if he could get the army leadership in Italy to fall in with his plans, but Kesselring had now been posted to the west and his replacement not announced. A message reached Wolff from Dulles asking him whether he could agree a surrender without the army commander. 'If there is no other way,' Wolff replied, 'then I'm prepared to deal with this alone.'

Dulles was facing difficulties of his own. Moscow had found out about the negotiations and was demanding a presence at the table. Flying Soviet generals into Switzerland was next to impossible, however, because Switzerland didn't even have diplomatic relations with the Soviet Union. By meeting with Wolff, he was now going behind Russian backs. Yet meet him he did, at Ascona on the Swiss–Italian border, on 19 March and with Field Marshal Alexander's American Chief of Staff, General Lyman Lemnitzer, also present along with British General Terence Airey. This was the first time in the entire war to date that Allied and German generals had met on neutral ground. Wolff brought news that General Heinrich von Vietinghoff, former 10. Armee commander in Italy, was now Commander-in-Chief in Italy, which he thought boded well; he got on with him. Wolff was also relieved to hear that the negotiations now had an operational name: SUNRISE. It was proof, against all the odds, that these talks were palpably leading somewhere. Wolff told the Allied contingency that Kesselring still had an important part to play, more so now that he was Commander-in-Chief in the west.

'I have laid the ground work with Kesselring,' Wolff told them, 'and what is more, I have a perfectly legitimate reason to visit him. There are many unfinished matters affecting the Italian theatre which I need to discuss with him.'

'And what about Kaltenbrunner?' Dulles asked him.

'We both know that Kaltenbrunner is trying to develop his own line through Switzerland for peace negotiations,' Wolff answered. 'But I implore you, do not let him ruin our plan with a competing one.'

As it happened, Dulles had no intention of pursuing talks with Kaltenbrunner. By now the Allies were growing increasingly concerned about intelligence reports suggesting the Nazis were preparing a final redoubt in the Alps, which might cost many more casualties. Kaltenbrunner was linked with this, and made Wolff's acceptance of unconditional surrender appear even more attractive. 'Everything possible', Wolff stressed to them, 'must be done to prevent such last-ditch resistance.'

Two days later, Wolff drove up through the Brenner Pass and on to Bad Nauheim, where on 23 March he reached Kesselring's headquarters to the news that the Allies had begun crossing the mighty River Rhine. Despite this seismic development, Wolff was able to talk with Kesselring. 'He seemed quite ready to fall in with our plans,' said Wolff, 'provided that the thing was done openly, either with the consent of the Führer or after his death. He didn't want any conflicts, or anything that would mean breaking his oath.' That was the rub, but Wolff believed he could work around Kesselring's concerns and offered placatory words that seemed to do the trick. After hearing Wolff's assurances, he promised to order von Vietinghoff to fall in behind the plans. Relieved, Wolff immediately sent a signal to Dulles. Perhaps there would be a surrender in Italy within a matter of days, and before General Mark Clark's Allied armies launched their spring offensive.

Yet while there was no question that Wolff had by now stolen the march on Kaltenbrunner in terms of a direct line of contact to the Allies, his rival was closing in on his activities. In Gruppenführer Harster Kaltenbrunner had a mole in Wolff's camp and through him had learned of the meeting with Dulles. This he in turn reported to Himmler. While Wolff could ignore summons from Kaltenbrunner he could not disregard those from his boss, still the most powerful man in the SS. What's more, Himmler wanted Wolff to fly to Berlin. At precisely this moment when Wolff seemed on the cusp of securing an early surrender in Italy, he now faced the wolves moving in on him at the very heart of the shattered remains of the Reich.

CHAPTER 3

THE DUEL PART 2

The Surrender in Italy, 2 May 1945

I have at least been able to conclude the negotiations under the best conditions possible with the Anglo-American – admittedly in the presence of a Russian, but he simply stood there and neither signed nor spoke a single word. I have managed to save a lot of my men; they won't go to Siberia or to the Balkans or to North Africa or heaven knows where else; and I could probably do the same for many of the others. The question is whether you will be able to answer to history or to our enemies for continuing the fight after our lines have collapsed. Particularly now that the death of the Führer has become known and released you from your oath, it is your duty to refuse to transfer this oath to any other person. No oath of personal loyalty is transferable, anyway. I am not in the least interested in Herr Dönitz. I feel in no way bound to obedience to Herr Dönitz. Herr Dönitz means less than nothing to me. Whoever goes on fighting now is the greatest of war criminals; to go on is irresponsibility itself.

Obergruppenführer Karl Wolff to Generalfeldmarschall Albert Kesselring in the early hours of 2 May 1945.

Wolff flew straight from Bad Nauheim to Berlin, arriving into Tempelhof at around midday on 24 March, nerves a little rattled after his plane had once again been shot at by marauding Allied fighters en route. His summons took him to No. 4 Bleibtreustrasse, which, ironically, meant 'Stay Loyal Street' and was near the Kurfürstendamm. The address was the apartment of Gruppenführer Hermann Fegelein, who had taken over from Wolff as SS liaison officer to the Führer.

Waiting for Wolff was not only Himmler but also Kaltenbrunner. The Reichsführer immediately berated Wolff for contacting Dulles without his approval and then Kaltenbrunner waded in, taking over as chief interrogator. It quickly became clear to Wolff, however, that they did not yet know about the second meeting at Ascona, and so he was able to retreat behind his cover story: that Hitler himself had encouraged him to make contact with the Allies through channels in Switzerland back on 6 February. Peace had not been discussed, Wolff told them, but rather he'd proposed a prisoner swap, particularly of Max Wünsche, a highly decorated Obersturmbannführer in the Waffen-SS. It was all too clear that Kaltenbrunner was itching to arrest him on the spot, but without Himmler's say-so he could not make the move. Instead, Himmler told Wolff he wanted him to go with Kaltenbrunner to the Burg Rudolfstein, near Hof in Bavaria, the following day, 25 March, to talk with Brigadeführer Walter Schellenberg, the head of the SD. The icy atmosphere of that long drive can only be imagined, but once at Burg Rudolfstein Wolff was shown the statements Schellenberg had received from Gruppenführer Harster. Later, Harster, the head of the Italian SD, arrived in person. Schellenberg's Swiss-Italian specialist, Standartenführer Eugen Steimle, was also brought in but Wolff stuck to his line: the talks in Switzerland had been only about possible prisoner exchanges and exploring channels for potential peace feelers; as both Schellenberg and Steimle were junior in rank and Kaltenbrunner had no further detailed information in his grasp, Wolff was able to avoid any slip-ups. Wolff also suspected that Kaltenbrunner was looking to take any peace initiative out of his hands and put it in his own. The following day the grilling finally ended. Wolff was allowed to return to Italy but warned by both Kaltenbrunner and Himmler not to travel to Switzerland again without their express permission.

There was a further close shave, however. The drive back to Berlin from Burg Rudolfstein was a long one and Kaltenbrunner, a notoriously reckless driver, was at the wheel. Suddenly he lost control, skidded and rolled the car twice. Miraculously, neither man was badly hurt, but over the past three weeks Wolff had been strafed in his car, shot at in his plane, and now survived the overturned car he was riding in. And what's more, he managed to escape back to his fiefdom in Italy, visiting his wife and children en route at Wolfgangsee in Austria; he planned to bring them to South Tyrol. He was then back in Italy on 29 March, comparatively safe for the moment, and without either Kaltenbrunner or Himmler knowing he'd made a second visit to see Dulles just a few days earlier. He had the luck of the devil with him.

There was no doubt, however, that Wolff was now a marked man. A day after his return Himmler rang him personally, having heard about his intention to bring his family south. 'That was a grave mistake,' Himmler told him. 'I took the liberty of correcting it. Your wife and your children are remaining at Wolfgangsee. There, they are under my protection.' Coming from Himmler, this was the kind of conversation to make Wolff's blood run cold; he had been due to meet again with Dulles on 2 April, but it was now out of the question with Himmler and Kaltenbrunner breathing down his neck and General von Vietinghoff, the new commander in Italy, proving slow to act alongside him.

Meanwhile, the Soviets were accusing the United States of pursuing a German surrender that violated earlier agreements between the Allies. The 'Berne Incident', as it was being referred to by Moscow, was becoming the first significant acrimonious altercation between the Americans and the Soviets, with the Russians angrily accusing the Allies of negotiating with the enemy behind their back. Stalin even wrote to President Roosevelt in person, accusing him of allowing the Germans to open up the front to the Western Allies to the detriment of the Red Army. 'I thank you for your frank expression of the Soviet point of view regarding the incident in Berne,' Roosevelt replied on 12 April, 'which appears to have run aground without any meaningful results.' It was one of the last letters he wrote; the President died the very same day.

Operation SUNRISE did appear to be dead in the water, what with Soviet outrage and the death of the President, combined with the closer scrutiny of Wolff and his family, effectively now hostages to Himmler. Despite this, the lines of communication remained open to Dulles via Luigi Parilli; Wolff sent a message of condolence to Dulles about the death of Roosevelt and before this a plan had been hatched to have an Allied radio operator planted in the SS in Italy. In the first week of April, Václav Hradecký, a young Czech, safely crossed the Swiss border and, incredibly, was then installed in an attic room in the headquarters of the Milan SD. Like many Czechs, he was a fluent German speaker; he had survived Dachau, then escaped to Switzerland and there joined the OSS. The only two men allowed access to Hradecký's garret room were Parilli and a trusted SS officer called Guido Zimmer. Hradecký's first signal was picked up by Dulles's team on 14 April. Wolff hoped that by agreeing to this plan he would further gain Dulles's trust and convince him of his sincerity. He was, though, taking a grave risk.

By this time, the battle was once again raging to the south in Italy. General Mark Clark's offensive had begun at 1.50 p.m. on 9 April as 825 heavy bombers had flown over the German front line and dropped a staggering 175,000 fragmentation bombs. Wolff had repeatedly told Kesselring, von Vietinghoff and, of course, Dulles and the Allies, that with every passing day unnecessary lives were being sacrificed. Now, with the full weight of two Allied armies bearing down on the Germans as they desperately tried to cling on to their positions in the Apennines, many more lives most certainly were being lost. Whatever motives Wolff may have had for wanting an early and swift surrender, his warnings were proving all too tragically true.

Hiding out in his villa headquarters at Fasano on Lake Garda, Wolff was sending missives to Dulles but also to von Vietinghoff and the latter's new Chief of Staff, Generalmajor Hans Röttiger, with whom he got on well and who was also entirely in agreement over the urgent need to conclude a surrender as soon as possible. Von Vietinghoff was dragging his feet, however, making unrealistic demands over the terms of surrender; he seemed to be singularly incapable of understanding that the only acceptable terms to the Allies were those without any conditions whatsoever.

And then, on 13 April, Wolff was suddenly summoned once more by Himmler. Wolff told him that leaving Italy now was impossible: the front line was collapsing and there were now urgent matters arising that required his immediate attention. Furthermore, Mussolini needed to be reined in once more. Yet two days later, on 15 April, Himmler's request became an order. When Wolff informed Dulles, the American advised him to escape; he even offered him asylum. Wolff could not do this, however, because his family were now Himmler's hostages. Giving a letter to Parilli to pass on to Dulles, Wolff pledged to see the surrender through to its conclusion, but if he was arrested and executed he hoped the OSS chief might defend his honour. He had not been negotiating out of self-interest, he wrote, but 'out of the conviction and hope of saving, as far as possible, the German people'.

Kaltenbrunner, meanwhile, had also decided that hostages might offer a little bit of leverage in these days of the crumbling Third Reich. Throughout Germany were a number of high-profile prisoners, *Prominenten*, as they were termed. At the beginning of April Kaltenbrunner drew up a list of 139 men, women and children and ordered them all to be brought together. They were of seventeen different nationalities: there were Germans, French, British, Soviets, Czechs, Danish, Italians, Hungarians and even Greeks among them. They included the former French Prime Minister, Léon Blum, Admiral Miklós Horthy of Hungary, Colonel 'Mad Jack' Churchill, a British Commando officer, and even General Franz Halder, the former

Chief of Staff of the German Army and the architect of the Blitzkrieg in the west back in 1940. General Georg Thomas, the former head of the Economic Department of the OKW, was also on the list, as were a number of those now categorized as *Sippenhaft* – family members of disgraced Germans, such as the wife and children of Claus von Stauffenberg, the man who had attempted to assassinate Hitler the previous July.

It was an astonishingly eclectic bunch of VIP prisoners, now brought together by Kaltenbrunner. They were to be sent first to Innsbruck and from there to South Tyrol, where they would be hidden away in a remote mountain resort and guarded by the SS. And from there they could be used as a bargaining chip under the threat of execution, which, if necessary, Kaltenbrunner fully intended to carry out.

Yet while the *Prominenten* were being corralled and transported southwards towards the Alps, Wolff was heading back to Germany, unable to ignore Himmler any longer. Flying into war-torn Berlin on the evening of 16 April, he then had to drive seventy-five miles north to Hohenlychen. Himmler, like Wolff and Kaltenbrunner, wanted to survive and so had escaped the shattered wreckage of Berlin and the Führerbunker; ideology, for these most senior SS men, played second fiddle to personal survival.

Wolff was perfectly aware that this might well prove to be the last journey of his life. The closer each day took them to the end of the war, the greater his personal danger. These were desperate times and he was dealing with desperate men; dangerous men. Hohenlychen had originally been built at the turn of the twentieth century as a sanitarium for children suffering from tuberculosis, but since the advent of the Nazis it had been taken over by the SS, becoming one of its main medical facilities. Giant red crosses had been painted on the roofs, giving Himmler and his staff a sense of security that had been entirely lacking in Berlin.

To Wolff's huge relief, Himmler was in amiable form and the two had a convivial lunch together. The Reichsführer seemed to accept Wolff's assurances that he'd not veered from the path of loyalty nor done anything other than that sanctioned by Hitler. The atmosphere changed, however, the moment Kaltenbrunner arrived and asked to see Himmler alone, to which the Reichsführer agreed. When Wolff was later called to join them, Himmler's mood had palpably darkened. Then Kaltenbrunner accused Wolff outright of treason; Wolff denied it, but Kaltenbrunner pressed the point. The exchange became increasingly heated. Three of the most powerful men in the Third Reich, together in a single room in a remote hospital way to the north of Berlin: two snarling at one another, the third, Himmler, listening with an ever more displeased expression on his face. Wolff clearly knew his grip was slipping, so now feigned outraged indignation and demanded they go immediately to see Hitler himself. It was the last card he had left to play. All three, he proposed, should drive to the Führerbunker. Himmler was having none of it; he was not prepared to risk heading back to Berlin but ordered both Wolff and Kaltenbrunner to go without him.

Incredibly, that's exactly what they did; the two men sat side by side in the back of a Mercedes all the way to Berlin. It was around 3 a.m. on 18 April when they reached the Führerbunker, but before they descended the steps Wolff turned to his rival and warned him to think twice before using the Dulles meeting as evidence of treason. Do that, he threatened Kaltenbrunner, and he would tell Hitler that both he and Himmler had known all about it but had hidden it from the Führer. 'If they hang me,' Wolff said, 'my place will be between yours and Himmler's.'

In the bunker Hitler kept them waiting, but when he did summon both men he confronted Wolff immediately. Himmler and Kaltenbrunner, he said, had already shed light on his negotiations with the enemy. 'I am happy to be able to report to my Führer,' Wolff replied, 'that through Mr Dulles, I have been successful in opening the gates to the White House in Washington and the door to the Prime Minister in London for talks. I request instructions for the future, my Führer!' This, of course, was pure bluff, but it earned him a stay of execution. They were dismissed but told to wait for a further summons later.

Long hours followed in which Wolff's fate hung by a thread. Then, at 5 p.m. on 19 April, the day before Hitler's fifty-sixth birthday, the Führer took the two men for a walk in the Reichskanzlei garden for some much-needed air; no Allied aircraft were overhead and the city was mercifully quiet. Hitler now explained his take on their current situation. He expected the Americans and Russians to fall out and their shaky alliance to collapse. This, he told them with emphatic certitude, was inevitable. Therefore he had decided that Wolff should carry on talking to Dulles as a means of buying the time necessary for this collapse of Allied relations to happen.

Wolff was off the hook. He'd called Kaltenbrunner's bluff and it had paid off – spectacularly. 'Actually,' commented Wolff a short time later, 'what I had done, opening negotiations with the enemy without the assent of the Führer, could be interpreted as high treason that might have led to a court martial and execution, or, at any rate, imprisonment. Thank God I was held in such personal esteem that they did not do the first and they did not have the courage to imprison me either.'

Having left Italy a few days earlier, wondering whether he'd ever return or even whether he'd survive the next few days, now he was back and with a clear path to finalizing negotiations with the Allies. Kaltenbrunner could no longer touch him. Yet the battle in Italy was still raging, ever more numbers of young lives were being cut short and with every passing day the effectiveness of Wolff's intervention was waning; and the less influence he was able to bring to bear, so the chances of clemency were diminishing. By this time, the final Battle for Berlin had begun: the Red Army was now bearing down on the capital of the Reich, the Western Allies were advancing deeper into Germany from the west, and if Wolff was not able to act fast, the danger was that German troops would surrender unconditionally elsewhere before they did so in Italy. That, he knew, could not be allowed to happen. His life depended on it.

On 22 April, three days after arriving back in Italy, he was invited to a conference called by Ambassador Rudolf Rahn at von Vietinghoff's headquarters near Verona. Wolff was reluctant to go, worrying that another of Kaltenbrunner's spies might also be present, yet Rahn had called it to try and accelerate a surrender; Wolff was the key to this and so he grudgingly agreed to go. All the German senior commanders were there: von Vietinghoff; his Chief of Staff, General Röttiger; General Max von Pohl of the Luftwaffe and Gauleiter Franz Hofer as well as Wolff and Rahn. It soon became clear, though, that while everyone agreed that it was time to end hostilities in Italy, they all had different ideas about how that should play out and what would follow. Von Vietinghoff was insisting on clinging to an honourable surrender while Hofer demanded that South Tyrol be separated from the rest of Italy and subject to different terms. Wolff continued to stress that unconditional surrender meant surrender without any terms at all, but von Vietinghoff and Hofer seemed deaf to this. Eventually, however, it was agreed that Wolff should travel to Switzerland for one more face-to-face meeting with Dulles, and this time with two senior officers in tow – Oberst Victor von Schweinitz of von Vietinghoff's staff and Obersturmbannführer Eugen Werner, one of Wolff's adjutants.

With the ongoing help of Baron Parilli they safely reached Lucerne in Switzerland on 23 April, only to learn that there would be no meeting after all. The new American President, Harry S. Truman, had been put under severe pressure from Stalin to quash any separate peace treaty in Italy, so Dulles had been ordered not to resume talks with Wolff. This, however, was not explained to Wolff and his delegation, who instead were given vague intimations that not all was well higher up the Allied chain but urged to be patient.

Patience, however, was one virtue that was deserting Wolff, and on 25 April he sent a message to Dulles that he was needed back in Italy; he'd already been gone several days and felt it was dangerous to be absent for any longer. Behind the scenes, Field Marshal Alexander had been lobbying London and Washington to allow the talks to proceed, but Dulles felt his hands were tied without express authorization to continue SUNRISE. At this point, Max Waibel intervened. A Swiss army officer, Waibel was head of the Swiss Intelligence Section 1 and had become a key mediator between Dulles and Wolff. 'Here we have the German negotiators ready to offer an unconditional surrender,' he appealed to Dulles, 'and the Allies don't even want to receive them! Do you want to end the war having them kill everyone?'

Dulles agreed, but Wolff had already headed back to Italy, leaving von Schweinitz and Werner in Lucerne to continue negotiations. Having slipped back over the border at the Reschen Pass, Wolff then stayed the night at Villa Locatelli at Cernobbio, an SS command post near Lake Como. The following morning, 26 April, however, partisans had surrounded the place and were baying for blood; the day before, Mussolini had fled along with his mistress, Clara Petacci, and Alessandro Pavolini, the head of the Italian Fascist Party, heading to Switzerland. Northern Italy was being overrun; while Wolff had been away both his and von Vietinghoff's headquarters had moved to Bolzano. It was clear that the end in Italy was rapidly approaching, with or without Wolff's input.

With his villa besieged, Wolff now telephoned Walter Rauff but he didn't have enough men nearby, so then he called Max Waibel. Once again Waibel saved the day, swiftly sending an OSS agent with vehicles, men and money to bribe the partisans to let Wolff slip back across the pass into Switzerland once more. Waibel and the American, Gero von Schulze-Gaevernitz, were waiting for him at the border. 'I will never forget what you have done for me,' an exhausted and emotional Wolff told Waibel. Smuggled north, he then crossed into Austria and headed south back via the Brenner Pass, finally reaching Bolzano on 27 April, just as his rival Kaltenbrunner made his own last-ditch attempt to save himself. On this same day, the 139 *Prominenten* hostages were being brought to a mountain lakeside resort called the Pragser Wildsee, some eight miles south-west.

Confusion and disorganization reigned, however, as the

Pragser Wildsee was still being used by the Luftwaffe, who had been given no warning about the imminent arrival of the *Prominenten*. Instead the hostages were debussed at Niederdorf, a sleepy Italian but distinctly Germanic-looking town of traditional wooden houses, hotels and inns signed with gothic lettering and a small square at its heart. An SS officer, Obersturmbannführer Friedrich Bader, was in charge of the *Prominenten*, but it was a different man, Obersturmführer Edgar Stiller, who was in command of their movements and who now had to find overnight accommodation for them all. Bader was well aware that they were Kaltenbrunner's bargaining chip; Stiller, on the other hand, was from the SS-Totenkopfverbände, the wing of the SS responsible for administering the concentration and death camps. The tension was palpable; both officers were frustrated by this enforced and unscheduled halt. Neither knew the whereabouts of Kaltenbrunner and communications with Berlin were down, the capital now being pressed on all sides by Red Army forces. The SS men were also both comparatively junior officers but had in their charge some very senior personnel, including the German Wehrmacht generals. Stiller was obviously nervous, aware that the war was almost over; Bader, by contrast, was an ideological Nazi and quite prepared to execute them all; in fact, it seemed he was hoping to be able to do so. Lodgings were found in the Rathaus, the town hall, and in the various hotels and *pensioni*, but keeping control of the hostages was increasingly challenging; a number of the SS guards began drinking, and as they consumed more so the tension grew.

Among the hostages at the Hotel Bachmann was Sigismund Payne Best, a British MI6 officer who had been captured by the Gestapo during the Venlo incident in Holland in November

1939 – a German sting on the British Secret Intelligence Service masterminded by Walter Schellenberg. Payne Best had been a prisoner ever since. Now, however, he was sharing a room with General Alexander von Falkenhausen, the former German Governor of Belgium who had been implicated in the von Stauffenberg plot the previous July, and also General Georg Thomas. While serving in the OKW, Thomas had been the architect of the Hunger Plan, which, had it been enacted, would have cost the lives of up to 30 million civilians in Ukraine and elsewhere in the Soviet Union. A British spook and two Nazi generals made an unlikely trio.

That first evening, Payne Best headed downstairs to try and find out what was going on and discovered that two of the SS guards were already drunk. Both were Totenkopfverbände and one had been a quartermaster at Dachau, the first of the Nazi concentration camps. Payne Best, who spoke fluent German, sat down with them and soon the three men were chatting amicably.

'I shall put in a good word for you when you fall into the hands of our troops,' he told them.

'Yes,' said the quartermaster, 'I know you're my friend and would help me – if you were alive.' He then produced orders from his breast pocket. 'Here is the order for your execution. You won't be alive after tomorrow.'

Payne Best doubted that the orders would be carried out, but the two guards were insistent. Bader, they said, always carried out his orders and meant to fulfil this one too.

'Shoot 'em all down,' slurred the other, fumbling at the catch of his pistol. 'Bum, bum, bum – bump 'em all off is best.'

Payne Best asked whether they would really gun down a man with whom they had just shared a drink.

'Ja, Herr Best,' said the quartermaster, 'but what can I do?'

Fortunately for Payne Best and the other hostages, General Georg Thomas and General Bogislaw von Bonin, who had been imprisoned for ordering a retreat earlier that year, had managed to slip away and put in a call to von Vietinghoff's headquarters, where von Bonin had spoken to General Röttiger, who had promised to act. After discussing the situation with von Vietinghoff, they agreed to order the Luftwaffe to immediately leave the Pragser Wildsee and also rang through to Hauptmann Wichard von Alvensleben, who served on von Vietinghoff's staff and who, coincidentally, was only a few miles away in Sexten scouting for a new headquarters. Von Alvensleben now immediately drove over to Niederdorf and met with Stiller, who quite openly confessed the terrible dilemma he was in over the fate of the *Prominenten*. It was now getting late on 27 April, so von Alvensleben hurried back to Sexten to report the situation but determined to return first thing the following morning.

Overnight a few more hostages had made good their escape, but when von Alvensleben returned to Niederdorf he found Bader in no mood to back down; the escapers had, if anything, stiffened his resolve to carry out the executions. After von Alvensleben had called up urgent reinforcements, he then had to wait for forty-five very tense minutes until fifteen Wehrmacht troops, most of whom were NCOs and experienced soldiers, reached Niederdorf. So began a stand-off, the SS men in and around the Bachmann on the northern side of the square, the Wehrmacht on the other. Realizing that the SS men might open fire at any moment, von Alvensleben rang through to Armeegruppe headquarters to ask permission to shoot if necessary. By chance, Wolff was standing next to Röttiger when he called and so spoke to the young captain himself. Yes, he said, von Alvensleben had the authority from von Vietinghoff to open fire but told him to order the SS men to withdraw.

This, however, was not enough to persuade Bader or even Stiller to back down. Anxious moments followed, with increasingly irate yells being exchanged across the town square. In the end it was Sigismund Payne Best who managed to persuade the SS that the Wehrmacht troops outgunned them and that they should lower their weapons. At last, they did so. The *Prominenten* siege was over. Von Alvensleben and his men rounded up the hostages and took them to the Pragser Wildsee, the threat of execution now mercifully lifted. Kaltenbrunner's scheme had achieved nothing except worsen the case against him.

Back in Bolzano, Wolff was still desperately trying to seal the unconditional surrender of German forces in Italy; on 27 April, the same day he reached Bolzano, he learned that the Allied Combined Chiefs of Staff had reversed their earlier instructions and now authorized the signing of the surrender. With this news, and with Mussolini captured that day by partisans and German troops streaming north in retreat, there should now have been no further impediment at all. The following day at around noon – and with Mussolini subsequently gunned down – Field Marshal Alexander's personal C-47 Dakota took off from Annecy, south of Geneva, with von Schweinitz and Werner on board and accompanied by Major Hanley of Lemnitzer's staff and Gero von Schulze-Gaevernitz. From there they flew over Mont Blanc and Corsica to Alexander's Supreme Allied HQ at Caserta, to the south of Rome. There they met with Generals Lemnitzer and Airey, but also with two Soviet representatives, Major-General A. P. Kislenko and his interpreter,

Lieutenant Uraevsky. The Germans had Wolff and von Vietinghoff's authority to sign, but they still tried to negotiate – over whether German officers could maintain their sidearms, how long troops might spend in prison camps following the cessation and various other minor points. There were also details to thrash out over the actual practicalities of the end of hostilities. None the less, at 2 p.m. on 29 April 1945, in the solemn setting of the ballroom of the Reggia, the former Royal Summer Palace in Caserta, the signing ceremony began. It was a vast room, one wall dominated by a huge situation map that showed the whole area of the Mediterranean.

Overseeing the procedure was Alexander's Chief of Staff, Lieutenant-General Sir William Morgan.

'I understand that you are prepared and empowered to sign the terms of a surrender agreement,' he said to the Germans. 'Is that correct?' Von Schulze-Gaevernitz translated.

'Ja,' answered von Schweinitz.

'Jawohl,' replied Werner. But then von Schweinitz added a final caveat: he was, he said, going beyond his authority. 'I presume that my Commander-in-Chief, General von Vietinghoff, will accept, but I cannot be entirely responsible.'

General Morgan was having none of it, however. The surrender, he stated, would be signed now and would come into effect at 2 p.m. on 2 May, allowing forty-eight hours for the news to be relayed to all German and pro-Axis Italian forces in Italy. It was 2.17 p.m. when Morgan closed proceedings, the first unconditional surrender of German forces in the war now signed, the ink already dry.

As von Schweinitz had intimated, however, their signatures might not be enough, and in the intervening time two things had happened. Firstly, Italy had now been added to

Kesselring's command of OB West, and secondly, Gauleiter Franz Hofer had got in touch with the field marshal and, as Wolff put it, 'poisoned his mind'. What had outraged Hofer was that the surrender had been signed without his say-so. When Kesselring heard the news he was likewise incensed. 'Without ringing me up,' said Wolff, 'or asking me what was happening, he summoned Vietinghoff, gave him a tremendous dressing down and relieved both him and Röttiger of their commands.' Kesselring could do nothing about Wolff, who was an SS general, not Wehrmacht, but instead rang Berlin to tell them of the betrayal and also informed Kaltenbrunner, who had left Berlin and emerged at Innsbruck in the heart of the Alps; he was frantically preparing for flight – even more so now he had lost grip of the *Prominenten*. He did, however, have Otto Skorzeny, a Waffen-SS colonel with a squad of troops at his command, and it seems Kaltenbrunner considered using them to head to Bolzano and arrest his nemesis. In the rush of escalating events, however, Skorzeny never did receive these orders; in any case, Wolff already had a large number of troops protecting the Palazzo Ducale for just such an eventuality.

Regardless of potential arrest warrants or even assassination attempts, Wolff had to act fast. Kesselring had always taken his oath of allegiance to Hitler seriously, but this was ridiculous. The surrender had been signed. The game was up, and most certainly so in Italy. Despite this, von Vietinghoff and Röttiger were replaced by General Friedrich Schulz and Generalmajor Fritz Wentzell, although they were still at army group headquarters in Bolzano. As soon as Schulz and Wentzell arrived, Röttiger had both locked up and guarded while Wolff in the meantime sent a message to Dulles via Hradecký, now in his attic at the Palazzo Ducale. Dulles and

Wolff arranged for von Schweinitz and Werner, who had been flown in from Switzerland, to cross at the Reschen Pass back into South Tyrol and so avoid the Brenner route, where Kaltenbrunner's men were waiting to intercept them and the surrender documents. Wolff could only get his hands on a rather clapped-out old car to fetch them, but eventually they safely reached Bolzano in the early hours of 1 May.

Then came the stunning news of Hitler's suicide in Berlin. 'There were tears in our eyes,' said Wolff, 'because after all the difficulties we had been through and all the wrestling we had had to do with so many people, fate had been kind to us.' Yet despite this Kesselring still refused to budge; he could not sanction any surrender until the new head of state, Grossadmiral Karl Dönitz, had authorized him to do so. For Wolff this was the last straw, but it prompted another round of anguish from the commanders in Italy: Schulz and Wentzell were released and agreed that the situation was hopeless, but still wanted authority from Kesselring. So too did General Joachim Lemelsen of 14. Armee and General Traugott Herr of 10. Armee. Even General von Pohl was wavering. The clock was ticking inexorably, while Alexander was sending messages asking for confirmation that the 2 p.m. deadline on 2 May would be met. Then news reached them that orders had been sent out for the arrest of von Vietinghoff and Röttiger, so Wolff immediately ordered his own troops and a number of tanks to surround them, with instructions to defend them to the last.

Finally, at around 2 a.m. on the morning of 2 May, Wolff and Kesselring spoke by telephone. Both men were seething. 'You are tearing all my defensive plans to pieces,' Kesselring railed, 'and causing the whole carefully built edifice to totter!' This was a grotesque claim; the entire Nazi state was facing

Armageddon. Had Kesselring not looked around at the wreckage of a totally broken state? The edifice wasn't tottering; it was already in a heap of rubble and ruin.

'Three times in these past months', Wolff retorted, 'I have offered my help and that of my armies, to you and to the Reich, and if you had made use of this offer, a lot of human blood need not have flowed and a great deal of destruction would have been avoided.' This was indisputable; Wolff's own motives were neither here nor there. The arguments raged through the night. Wolff pleaded, cajoled and threatened. If Kesselring didn't act now, Wolff told him, he would be one of the biggest and worst war criminals of all time. 'That is what I have to tell you,' said Wolff. Kesselring eventually called off, but half an hour later rang back. The surrender, he told Wolff, would stand.

And so at 2 p.m. that very same day, the war in Italy was finally over.

Wolff had delivered the surrender in the nick of time and was also now safe from Hitler, who was dead, and from Himmler, who was about to go on the run, and from Kaltenbrunner, who by now was already making good his escape. Wolff had avoided a Nazi firing squad for treachery, but whether he had done enough to escape the Allied gallows was still unclear. For the moment, though, and in the chaos of those early days of May, he remained in Bolzano, while Allied aircraft with loudspeakers flew up and down the valleys telling German troops to lay down their arms. On 3 May, men from the 85th 'Custer' Division reached Trento, to the south of Bolzano, then pushed on north, hurrying to join up with American soldiers from the Seventh Army, moving south from Austria. Whatever plans there had been for a Nazi Alpine redoubt had also crumbled to nothing.

As the Custermen pushed on north, only a handful of them could be spared for policing and so they agreed that a number of German Feldgendarmerie – the military police – would help with such duties. In Bolzano there was now the bizarre sight of Americans and Germans operating side by side, directing traffic.

Wolff, meanwhile, remained where he was in the Palazzo Ducale and even invited the negotiating team from Switzerland to join him. Dulles declined, but von Schulze-Gaevernitz accepted, arriving on 9 May, and was astonished by the calm and peaceful scenes he discovered, and even more by the armed SS guards still protecting the palace. Wolff also told von Schulze-Gaevernitz that he had the Florentine art treasures safely stored in what he assured him was another act of selflessness.

Von Schulze-Gaevernitz left Bolzano on 12 May; the next day was Wolff's forty-fifth birthday and so he decided to have a party. After all, the cellars were still full of prosecco and wine. It was in full swing when American troops of the 38th Division arrived, and only then were the guests rounded up and finally taken away, Wolff included. It was a damp squib to the end of his party but he had, at least, had a chance to raise a glass and congratulate himself on what he'd pulled off.

Wolff cooperated with his captors at every turn, not least in the recovery of the art which, he made pains to point out, he had refused to give to Hitler's officials despite orders to the contrary. Standartenführer Langsdorff was still holding a mass of works at the Castello Neumelans at Campo Tures, while another stash had been locked up in the cells of the police station at the tiny and unsuspecting village of San Leonardo, north of Merano. Here Caravaggio's *Bacchus* was recovered, as well as paintings by Titian and Rubens and Cranach's masterpiece *Adam and Eve*. With the safe recovery of these priceless works of art, many taken from the Uffizi, Wolff had honoured another promise to the Allies.

In contrast, Kaltenbrunner's schemes had delivered nothing at all to the Allies and he was now on the run in Austria. Gathering a stash of counterfeit money, he had headed to Altaussee, where much of the other art stolen by the Nazis was being stored. This small, quiet village, nestling on the shores of a lake and surrounded by towering mountains, was quite a focus for Austrian Nazis. Not only did Kaltenbrunner have a place here, so too did Adolf Eichmann, the man responsible for sending so many of Europe's Jews to the death camps. Kaltenbrunner reached his house, the Villa Kerry, on 6 May, where he was reunited with his mistress, the twenty-four-year-old Countess Gisela von Westarp. She had borne him twins in Altaussee on 12 March that year.

It's unclear how much money Kaltenbrunner had with him, but it was a lot – at least fifty kilograms of gold, as well as $2 million in notes, a similar sum in Swiss francs, five cases of jewels and a stolen stamp collection worth 5 million gold marks. It was more than enough with which to escape forever. Like a pirate of old, he buried some of it in his garden at the Villa Kerry then set off on 7 May with his adjutant and two guides into the mountains, where he intended to lie low and then hatch a proper plan of escape.

Two days later, 9 May, with the war now over, the Americans reached Altaussee, although they were only five in number and led by Captain Robert E. Matteson of the US 80th Counter Intelligence Corps, the CIC. In Altaussee, Matteson and his men arrested a number of Nazis – although not Eichmann, who had already fled after giving his young son a farewell thrashing. It was Kaltenbrunner Matteson was after, however. The first lead came from Gisela von Westarp, who accidentally revealed that her lover had been in the village, and then, on 11 May, Matteson learned from a local that his target had been spotted on the aptly named Totes Gebirge – 'Death Mountains'. Accompanied by a squad of ten GIs and four Austrian former Wehrmacht troops as guides, they set off at midnight that same day and by first light had reached a narrow mountain plateau on which was perched a wooden hut.

As they approached, the hut looked deserted, with the shutters closed and no apparent sign of life. There were no tracks outside either, and when Matteson tried the door he discovered it was bolted. But then he heard a sound from within. After banging furiously on the door, a window was opened and a man – not Kaltenbrunner – appeared, asking them what they wanted before hurriedly retreating back inside. Matteson now surrounded the entire hut and told whoever was inside to come out. 'For ten minutes', said Matteson, 'we kept repeating the call but with no results.' Not wanting to start shooting, he approached again and knocked once more. This time four men emerged, one of whom was unmistakably Kaltenbrunner: his height, his scars, his immediately recognizable face – all were giveaways. So too were the identity discs left in the ashes of the fire inside. For Kaltenbrunner, the game was up.

Another who had been at Altaussee was Wilhelm Höttl. Unbeknown to his boss, he had already been earmarked as a spy by the Americans for the already emerging post-war world. Although arrested, he became a witness for the prosecution during the war trials, worked for the CIA and later opened a school, wrote several books and died in 1999, aged eighty-four.

Frank Hofer was also arrested and imprisoned, but in 1948 managed to flee and returned to his pre-war life as a salesman in Mülheim. He died a natural death in 1975, aged seventy-three. Friedrich Schwend was also arrested and turned by the CIC. Like Kaltenbrunner, he had buried huge amounts of cash, most of which was recovered by the Allies. He later escaped to South America, where he too was later, briefly, recruited by the CIA.

There was no turning of Kaltenbrunner, however. He became one of the key men put on trial at Nuremberg, was found guilty of war crimes and hanged on 16 October 1946. By contrast, Wolff did save his neck, although only by playing such a dangerous game and taking so many outrageous risks. And so, in his deadly duel with Kaltenbrunner, he most emphatically won the day. His efforts to bring about an early surrender, as he had calculated, did work in his favour. Like Höttl, he was a witness for the prosecution during the war trials and was released in 1947, a free man, despite being second only to Himmler in the SS hierarchy. Later, in 1962, thanks to information emerging from the Adolf Eichmann trial in Jerusalem, Wolff's own part in the Holocaust came to light as it became clear he must have known what had been going on. Specifically, he was charged with masterminding a transit camp in northern Italy – at Bolzano, in fact – where more than 6,000 Italian Jews had passed en route to the death camps. Wolff had managed their arrival, detention and subsequent dispatch on his watch. He was tried, convicted and sentenced to fifteen years, but once again he wriggled free, let out in 1971 on 'health grounds'. He lived out the rest of his life peacefully and even returned to South Tyrol, where he was feted as something of an honoured guest. He died on 17 July 1984, aged eighty-four.

Karl Wolff had outlived and outfoxed them all.

CHAPTER 4

MONTY'S MEN

Lüneburg Heath,
3–4 May 1945

daily express from moorehead montgomery field headquarters may fourth take one stop here on a wild stretch of heath just south of luneburg at precisely six twenty five pm today montgomery signed peace with germany stop five german officers walked into the tent and stood behind their chairs at a table over which a grey army blanket had been thrown stop presently montgomery arrived and as he took his place at the end of the table the five germans saluted and in silence they sat down together stop montgomery took out his spectacles and in a slow careful voice dash his voice is never strong at any time undash read out the following terms of surrender stop.

STANDING IN THE GROUNDS OF A VILLA in Häcklingen in Lower Saxony some thirty-five miles south-south-east of Hamburg, the tents and caravans of Monty's entourage were bursting with the anticipation of the war's end. Monty's TAC HQ, his travelling headquarters, had moved to the Lüneburg Heath on 1 May, taking position on top of a hill called the Timeloberg, primarily to ensure that the No. 10 wireless set worked properly at a higher elevation. The spot also offered views over the country that his armies had conquered.

TAC HQ, a caravanserai of officers, dispatch riders, signallers, cipher specialists, cooks, batmen and security and defence troops, had disembarked in Normandy the previous June, following the army's advance and ensuring that the British Field Marshal was in touch with his forward units away from the larger, busier Main HQ, where he felt he would not have the freedom, space and solitude to think clearly. This was to be TAC HQ's final location – and while there had been the odd château and Schloss along the way, one of which Monty would earmark for future use as a British Army on the Rhine HQ, it was nevertheless his customary style to camp in the gardens. Determined to avoid any echoes of château generalship, and playing to his carefully crafted austere self-image, it was no affectation. His aide-de-camp, Johnny Henderson, tried to ensure that the tents were laid out in the same formation – the same, it was suggested, as at El Alamein – wherever the TAC

HQ ended up. Routine mattered to Montgomery; he liked things just so.

The method may have been the same, but the British Field Marshal's campaign was not ending with the bang that he had hoped for. Supreme Allied Commander General Ike Eisenhower had decided to divert the Allied armies away from Berlin, a decision which had been greeted by Montgomery with initial consternation and then bitter after-the-fact argument; but it had been made unilaterally and presented as a fait accompli, thus ceding the ultimate symbolic victory over Nazism to Stalin's forces and the Soviet Union.

Ike may have given Stalin what he wanted, but he had also done what the Western Allies, particularly the USA, needed. Eisenhower's trust in Stalin was not to be rewarded, but that was not the immediate point: the war against Japan was far from over, and American nerves about the necessary manpower for the fighting in the Far East meant that not expending lives in the European theatre was central to Ike's thinking. By April the US Army had begun to run out of replacements, and their planners, with the prospect of invading the Japanese islands on the horizon, were cutting their cloth accordingly and throttling back on the numbers of men they were sending to Europe.

General Omar Bradley, commanding the US 12th Army Group, had offered dire predictions of casualties should the Western Allies make for Berlin. His mood reflected the anxiety in Washington. Eisenhower justified his decision in terms of the resources to deal with a possible Nazi redoubt in the Bavarian Alps and claimed that Berlin was a purely political rather than military objective. Tension had long existed within Supreme Headquarters Allied Expeditionary Force – SHAEF – about how victory would be achieved, either by destroying Germany's armies or seizing her cities. Ike elected to choose the former, so it would be Soviet boots on the ground at the Reichstag.

By the beginning of May, the epically costly Battle for Berlin was finally won. The Reichstag was in Soviet hands, and while the battle raged around him Hitler had fired his own personal starting pistol for the German surrender. Berlin wasn't worth any more British, American or Allied soldiers' lives. They would be needed elsewhere.

That the Germans had almost completely abandoned resisting the Western Allies by the time Eisenhower made his decision, yet were still fighting Soviet forces for every inch of German soil, suggests that perhaps an American push on Berlin might not have been the bloodbath the Red Army found itself in. At least Ike had spared himself and the US Army the agony of finding out. Monty, keenly aware of fading British influence, felt that being in on the kill in Berlin was a political and military necessity, but could not contradict his boss. Therefore, come early May, 21st Army Group was committed to a race to the Baltic, trying to reach the Danish border before the Soviets. Missing out on the ultimate victory had soured the end of the hard trail from Normandy, and Montgomery on his hill overlooking the vast heath was lumping rather than liking it.

This was TAC HQ's twenty-sixth stop since first setting up in Creully in June the previous year. Designed to be ready to move at a moment's notice to the next location, here, on Lüneburg Heath, was the end of the long trail from France.

At the core of TAC HQ were seven caravans, begged, borrowed or, more accurately, stolen during the British Army's campaigns across the Mediterranean theatre. Three of them were designated for Monty's personal use, the oldest of these being Field Marshal Claude Auchinleck's Eighth Army caravan, which the Auk had in turn liberated from the Italian Generale Annibale Bergonzoli in 1941 after Operation COMPASS. Another caravan, also Italian in origin, had supposedly been used by the great adversary Erwin Rommel himself and would, if and when they visited, be handed over to the King or the Prime Minister for their use. The third was a vehicle that had been converted by his staff as a gift into a map room. There was a sergeants' mess and two officers' messes; Monty ate in the 'A' Mess.

The men of 21st Army Group had crossed the Rhine in March, and the spring had been an unpredictable and bitter slog into the heart of the Reich. Even though the Field Marshal was the most recognizable senior officer within the British Army, he knew that with the end of the war he might find himself devoid of purpose, without function. The moment could only be bittersweet, surely?

By now, units in the British van had rendezvoused with the Soviets; a meeting less cagey for the soldiers than for their officers, perhaps. The British 6th Airborne Division had made it to the Elbe port of Wismar on the Baltic coast on 1 May, thus defining a line across the German–Danish border to keep the Soviets out of Denmark. The paratroopers and glider soldiers had come some 400 miles from where they had landed at Wesel, making their way via Osnabrück, Minden, Wunstorf, Celle, Uelzen and on through Lüneburg.

Much of their time was spent dealing with Germans who had decided they were better off surrendering to the Allies than to the Soviets. When C Company of the 1st Canadian Parachute Battalion did finally encounter the men of Soviet III Tank Corps making their own dash for Wismar, they met an officer in a jeep who had, the War Diary states, 'come far in advance of his own columns, and was quite put out to find us sitting on what was the Russians' ultimate objective'. B Company then made 'the first contact with numbers of troops . . . to the North of Wismar, with Lt. P.G. Insole doing the handshaking and Vodka-drinking on behalf of the Battalion'. The situation was resolved by 6th Airborne's commanding officer, Major-General Eric Bols, who made it quite clear to his opposite numbers that Wismar was now firmly in British hands, pointing out that he had anti-tank guns and artillery batteries standing by and that he wouldn't be afraid to use them. Ending this war meant no one had an appetite for starting another one, and the Soviets backed down.

The 5th Battalion, King's Own Scottish Borderers had been fighting in Bremen and knew that the end was near. The combat in the city itself the day before had been relatively light and the battalion had captured the oil refineries and docks, 'innumerable policemen', 200 enemy troops, the Junkers aircraft factory, one unfinished destroyer and two incomplete submarines – exactly the kind of assets Hitler had wanted destroyed as Germany fell. Despite some light shelling overnight, the Jocks reported an apparent cessation of enemy activity on 30 April. Lieutenant-Colonel Hugh Batchelor, the 5th KOSB's commanding officer, took time to tot up the score:

> (A) No. of prisoners taken from 25 Mar to 30 Apr 45 from time Bn crossed the Rhine 16 Officers and 1250 O.Rs.
> (B) No. of casualties incurred by this Bn in same period. 13 Officers and 127 O.Rs. (includes 1 and 36 killed)

Even though the war was winding down, the cost of the continued fighting was ever present.

Outside Hamburg on 27 April, 1st Battalion, the Royal Tank Regiment lost its last tank of the war, 'probably the last in 7th Armoured Division'. The tank, in C Squadron, had been bazookaed with a Panzerfaust, but mercifully there were no casualties. They had been rounding up the Volkssturm, the national militia raised from the remaining populace, one of whom, an 'optimist' in his sixties, was carrying a prophylactic. The fighting continued over the next couple of days, the battalion's squadrons engaging occasional targets, patrolling aggressively, taking prisoners. But there were clear signs that the Germans had had enough. On 1 May at 19.45 a black staff car containing a representative of the Hamburg Garrison appeared, flying a white flag; he was 'conducted blindfold to Divisional HQ'.

The following morning, 2 May, orders were given not to shoot at the enemy, and the battalion was alive with rumour about the city's imminent surrender. At midday the commanding officer, Lieutenant-Colonel O. R. C. Hobart, attended a conference about the planned occupation procedures. And at five o'clock the diary got a glance of how things were beginning to end:

> Staff cars with negotiators for the surrender of Hamburg came through the lines to Divisional HQ. Later it was also discovered that these saw the Commander 21st Army Group concerning the surrender of the forces opposing the 21st Army Group.

With no obvious front line, and the Germans resisting or surrendering sporadically, the fighting had been bitter and scattershot. Not surprisingly, men were keener than ever not to lose their lives in the dying moments of the war. Furthermore,

21st Army Group was full of replacements, brought in to make up the dwindling numbers, particularly in the infantry, which had borne the brunt of the casualties. Many had come from the Royal Air Force, which had a surfeit of personnel: pity the lad who had joined the RAF in the hope of flying who now found himself in a German ditch being mortared. With their rushed basic training these replacements were known as 'six-week killers', often in their teens and their thirties. The old sweats would do what they could to help, but very often the new men, lacking battlefield smarts, could be gone as quickly as they arrived.

The manner in which many units now campaigned reflected the anticipation of the war's end. The British had fought the Second World War with the aspiration of expending 'steel not flesh', leaning on machinery and munitions to take the strain of defeating their enemies rather than manpower. In the war's final months, once across the Rhine and into the Fatherland, this style came to the fore, not just in the kind of vast preparatory bombardments favoured by Montgomery and his planners, but by artillery strikes and concentrations – 'stonks' – on pretty much anything. The war was ending and ammunition was plentiful, so it might as well be used on a pillbox if it saved British lives.

British determination to bring the war to an end had been further bolstered by the discovery of the camp at Bergen-Belsen on 15 April, but even so German resistance still lingered in pockets. Big battles may have been a thing of the past, but the enemy was still dangerous. Lurking in a ditch or a hedgerow, a youngster armed with a Panzerfaust or a machine gun and determined to die for the Fatherland could appear, or an entire town might surrender at the sight of British recce vehicles. For the first time the British troops were getting an impression of the enemy they had been fighting for six years. They were exhausted, ready for the end and unprepared to waste their lives, particularly on anyone disinclined to surrender.

Germany's cities lay in ruins under skies where aircraft roamed freely, looking for targets of opportunity. The Reichsbahn, Germany's rail system, had been attacked to the point of paralysis. Coal couldn't be moved to factories, disrupting production, and the Wehrmacht was unable to transport troops or supplies to its battlefields.

The gigantic offensives in the west and east had shattered the German armies, there had been a wave of suicides in the town of Demmin, set in motion by fears of what the Red Army might do in return for German atrocities in the Soviet Union, and now, with news of Hitler's death seeping out at the end of April, his spell was finally broken. Refugees of every stripe, Germans and those people from the countries the Nazis had conquered and put to work as slave labour, prisoners of war freed in the maelstrom of the Reich's destruction, all swarmed over the country. There was a vacuum in terms of power in Germany, but a surrender would and must come. On Allied terms though, and therefore unconditional.

Death at this stage of the war in Europe may have seemed futile, but it was still ever present, even for the men at the head of 21st Army Group. Monty's TAC HQ was staffed with young officers whose role as liaison officers – LOs – was to be his eyes and ears. The men tended not to be professional soldiers, but officers in only for the duration, some the sons of friends and acquaintances, others whose talent he had either inherited or spotted when he had come to fight in the desert in 1942.

TAC HQ and its band of LOs was a place of pets, pranks

and bets. Monty had accumulated quite the menagerie in Normandy, writing to Phyllis Reynolds, to whom he had entrusted care of his son David:

> I now have six canaries, one love bird, two dogs. The dogs are puppies, about ten weeks old. One is a fox terrier, given me by the BBC men in France; I have named him Hitler. The other is a gold cocker spaniel, brought back by Col. [Kit] Dawnay – who bought it from some girl in a girls' school!! I have named him Rommel – as his coat is the colour of golden sand from the desert. Hitler and Rommel both get beaten when necessary . . . both coming 'to heel well'.

For all his outward austerity, Monty was a gambling man, and liked to collect on bets. Notoriously among the Americans, in North Africa in 1943 he had won a B-17 Flying Fortress bomber for his personal use when he had bet General Eisenhower that he would be in Sfax by 15 April – he beat the deadline by five days, and to Ike's consternation insisted on taking delivery of the plane.

He also ran a betting book in his 'A' Mess, never laying any bets himself but happy to take them. Before D-Day, plenty of bets about the possible duration of the war and its outcome had been placed. Admiral Bertram Ramsay had bet £5 in January 1944 that the war would end before 1 January 1945. Monty was not to collect; Ramsay was killed in a plane crash on 2 January 1945. His Chief of Staff, Freddie de Guingand, had bet Monty that the monarchy would not exist in fifty years' time, suggesting an air of sporting levity, given that neither would have lived to see the outcome. General George S. Patton had bet Monty £100 that the British would be involved in another continental war within ten years. Again, Patton's death in December 1945 prevented Monty from collecting the vast sum of money he would have won.

Once the campaign was under way, at TAC HQ the betting ranged from the domestic to the strategic – various outcomes of the fighting, often serving as a barometer of Monty's mood about how the war was going. In November, fed up with what he saw as a lack of grip and strategy on Ike's part, Monty – who had been convinced there was a chance to win the war by Christmas if the Allies had taken bolder action – had taken a bet that it would not end until June the following year.

Monty himself was the subject of wagers, and with them the odd prank. His aide-de-camp, Johnny Henderson, got caught up in a wager about how often Monty needed to pee. Visiting a friend in the 60th Rifles, Henderson and the other men in the mess noted how often a friend of his needed to go to the toilet. Henderson remarked: 'Well, my man Monty has exactly the same habit.' And so a bet was laid on who would go to the toilet the most. Doing his rounds in the Field Marshal's staff car, Henderson made sure that he plied Monty with coffee and consequently won the bet, his driver keeping count of how often he relieved himself. Oblivious, when Monty asked Henderson to make sure that there was always plenty of coffee in the car – it was good for keeping out the cold – Henderson felt duty-bound to explain why it had been in such good supply. The Field Marshal was unimpressed.

Being an LO was therefore a job of rare status, access and privilege, but not without risk. They were given carte blanche to go wherever they wanted in 21st Army Group and beyond, and had their boss's authority to ask awkward questions. Setting off in jeeps, the men spent long days driving through the lines, dodging the enemy if they came across them. Carol Mather, who had first come to Montgomery's TAC HQ in the North African desert after being injured fighting with the SAS – Mather's brother Bill had recommended him – described the thrill of the job: 'one was right at the heart of the action; contrary to the usual perception, he was a very relaxed and easy master, but only if he trusted you. If he did not, you were out.'

Like many of the LOs, Mather's relationship with Monty had a certain paternal quality. They all spoke of Montgomery's dry, impish sense of humour and his indulgence of their own. Montgomery himself was everything his friends and enemies said he was: loyal, priggish, arrogant, trusting, cold, generous, cautious, caring, brilliant, obstinate, pig-headed, intolerant, gentle. Nevertheless they all agreed on one thing: his self-confidence. He was determined to do things his way, casting aside those he regarded as 'useless'. His dogged approach to argument and the almost intolerable tension he was apt to create with those whose judgement he didn't rate was balanced by his evident care for his men, his skill at managing those he trusted, and his ability to summarize and encapsulate problems and their solutions simply and clearly. Mather admired Montgomery greatly and ran some of his boss's most important errands – delivering Monty's orders to General Hodges at the beginning of the Battle of the Bulge, for instance, when the Americans were in chaos – but their relationship was to be ended by the perils of being an LO.

Flying in an Auster light spotter plane on 9 February near Grave in the Netherlands, Mather's aircraft was attacked by a Focke-Wulf FW190. The pilot, Flight Lieutenant Alastair McQueen, was killed instantly, and the plane was only successfully brought down by Mather working the brakes while

Major Richard Harden struggled with the controls. They crashed into a swamp and staggered away from the wreckage not knowing whether they were in Holland or Germany; 'all I knew is I was badly winded and one arm would not work'. Harden had cuts to his head, Mather had four bullet wounds, had lost a kidney and his 'left forearm is badly shattered', reported Monty. Appearing at his hospital bed a few days later, Monty asked Mather's doctor what the damage was:

'Tell me doctor, how many holes in him?'

'Counting the shrapnel – thirteen.'

'Thirteen, thirteen! Excellent, excellent!' said Monty and promptly left.

Mather was not to see him again until after the war in Europe had ended, when in July Monty refused to help him with his Army Medical Board reapplication. Mather had been lucky to survive, but two months later, in April, Major John Poston was not.

Aged twenty-five when he joined Monty, Major John Poston was one of the youngest but longest-serving LOs. He had come to Monty's HQ in the desert from the 11th Hussars as part of his inheritance of Eighth Army from Lieutenant-General William Gott, who'd been shot down and killed on his way back from the front to Cairo. Gott had taken on Poston as his aide-de-camp and Monty retained him. With a Military Cross to his credit he was a fighting officer, but he remained with Monty for the rest of the war. He was regarded as fearless, often connected with the 'liberation' of civilian items like pianos, and the maintenance of the party spirit once the Field Marshal had gone to bed. In his friends' estimation, 'he would have sailed with Drake'. Poston had his own caravan, which he had also 'liberated'.

On 21 April, Poston was returning from a typical foray into the German interior with Captain Peter Earle. It had been a tough day's driving to visit Major-General Pip Roberts's 11th Armoured Division's HQ, and rather than forcing their way back through queues of vehicles, with fighting all around and the uncertainty and edginess of Germany in collapse everywhere, they'd taken a recommended shortcut. The trip, they felt, had been a waste of time, but the shorter route home would go some way to make up for the journey.

Looking forward to the bottles of wine that would follow the debriefing with the Master, they were ambushed by a party of young German soldiers who had been bypassed by the British advance. A machine gun set up in the road opened fire on them. Trying to race on, Earle was hit in the arm, and they returned fire with their Sten guns until they ran out of rounds, whereupon Earle deliberately crashed the jeep into the machine gun, killing its crew. But there were more Germans. Poston was thrown by the impact into a ditch at the side of the road, and as Earle gathered himself he heard him cry, 'No, no, stop stop,' as one of the Germans plunged a bayonet into his chest, killing him there and then. At this point Poston was unarmed and had his hands up. His body was stripped of his watch and other valuables, and the Germans buried him where he was killed. Making sure that he had wiped clean the chinagraph markings on his map case, Earle was shot again, in the arm and hip, then taken prisoner and patched up by German medics in a barn, alongside Russian displaced persons and Belgian refugees. He had on him a letter from Monty stating that he was an LO for when he might appear unannounced in an HQ asking questions. That night he was asked if he was the Field Marshal's staff officer and if he knew where Monty was. He answered evasively and requested to be moved to the nearby British hospital at Soltau, which was under a white flag. This request was refused.

The following day, after being moved from the farm where he had initially been treated to a dressing station at which his wounds were attended to by a surgeon, Earle was freed by the Royal Welch Fusiliers. He had had to shout at the grim-faced, tin-hatted Tommy who appeared at the hospital window with his Sten gun that he was a British officer and that they mustn't shoot. He reassured the Germans as they were captured that the British wouldn't have shot the place up, but wasn't so sure he was right. Then, from his bed at 212 Field Ambulance, Earle had to wire TAC HQ: 'Regret to report JOHN POSTON killed at 1800 hrs.' On visiting him at the casualty clearing station, and hearing Earle explain bluntly that Poston had been 'bayonetted in a ditch', Montgomery pinned the ribbon of the Military Cross to his pyjama top: 'I am going to give you the Military Cross for your part in this gallant action: and I am going to do a very unusual thing; I am going to pin it now on to your pyjamas and we will have a photo taken for your wife.'

John Poston's death, running one of the Field Marshal's errands, shattered Monty. As far as he was concerned, Poston had been murdered. He locked himself away in his caravan and spoke to no one for two days. With a message of condolence from the Prime Minister, a funeral with a guard of honour from the 11th Hussars and a personally written obituary in *The Times* – 'I was completely devoted to him and I feel very sad: something has definitely gone out of my life' – TAC HQ bade farewell to John Poston, Monty weeping openly at his funeral. For a man who tried so ruthlessly to control his emotions, as well as fight the war in such a way as to minimize casualties,

Poston's death meant that the end, even in victory, was suffused with loss and the bitterness of war's true cost.

The surrender at Timeloberg began with a phone call.

On the morning of 3 May Colonel Kit Dawnay, Monty's assistant who in civilian life had been a stockbroker, took a call informing him that Lieutenant-General Miles Dempsey's HQ at Second Army had been visited by members of the Wehrmacht hierarchy, along with representatives of the Luftwaffe. A deputation from Dönitz's headquarters, his 'government', was coming to TAC HQ to talk surrender with Monty. Dönitz's authority was genuine – he had been named as Hitler's successor by the Führer – though not as a full-blown Führer, merely Reich President. Even in death, Hitler's ego overshadowed his successors.

Dönitz had been slavishly loyal to Hitler and, unlike others, been careful not to intrigue against him as the end came: Himmler had been busted for negotiating with the Swedes; Göring had fallen from favour for assuming that Hitler had absented himself from command decisions by becoming isolated in Berlin; Goebbels had stayed to the last, killing himself and his family a day after the Führer; Bormann had tried to escape Berlin and had perished in the carnage of the city; Speer had blown his standing with the Führer when, according to his own account, he refused the order to destroy German industry.

So it fell to Dönitz, whose optimism about winning the war had persisted to the end, to try to extricate what remained of the Third Reich from complete oblivion. After six years of total war, it was a tall order. Dönitz had sent a delegation because he felt, as the German head of state and even as Germany was being carved up by her enemies, that it was beneath him to negotiate with a mere Field Marshal. Narrowed down to a team of four, they were sent on to TAC HQ in a British car, with Captain Derek Knee from Dempsey's HQ translating, their impossible task to stall the surrender in order to keep as many Germans as possible out of Soviet hands. Even now the government in Flensburg, right on the Danish border, had got wind of Allied plans to divide Germany up into different areas of influence and wanted to get as many of their countrymen and women as they could into the British and American zones.

Leading the delegation, for whom Monty had ordered a Union Flag be raised at the entrance to his camp, was Generaladmiral Hans-Georg von Friedeburg, recently appointed Commander-in-Chief of the Kriegsmarine, his promotion coming as Dönitz was booted upstairs. Von Friedeburg was one of Dönitz's cronies; earlier in the war he had taken over command of the U-boat arm when Hitler had promoted Dönitz to head of the Kriegsmarine. With von Friedeburg were his flag officer, Konteradmiral Gerhard Wagner, Generalfeldmarschall Ernst Busch's Chief of Staff, General Eberhard Kinzel, and Major Hans Jochen Friedl from the OKW. Lieutenant-Colonel Trumbull Warren, a Canadian LO, described Kinzel as 'a magnificent looking officer about 6' 5' . . . complete with monocle – a real professional Prussian,' and Friedl as having 'the cruellest face of any man I have ever seen'.

None of the Germans spoke English, a small problem they had all overlooked. Montgomery and his men wore battledress, the British and DUKEX – Dominions, United Kingdom and Exile – soldiers' standard khaki wool two-piece, with Monty still sporting his famous two-badged beret. By contrast, von

Friedeburg and his party wore leather greatcoats and the peaked caps of their respective services, looking every inch the German officer class. The Germans were serving up clichés even at the end.

Perhaps with some measure of barely concealed glee, Monty asserted himself immediately and made them wait, sauntering down the five steps of his caravan as they stood to attention saluting, then returning their salute perfunctorily.

The German delegation stood behind the line Monty had asked his staff to draw in the ground for them to toe. German accounts refer to a stick instead, and that Feldmarschall Busch never got over the insult shown towards the delegation and his staff by Monty.

'Who are you?' Montgomery barked.

'I am Generaladmiral von Friedeburg, Commander-in-Chief of the Kriegsmarine, sir.'

'I have never heard of you! Who are you?'

'General Kinzel.'

'Never heard of you.' He turned to Friedl: 'Who are you?'

Friedl responded.

'Major? How dare you bring a Major to my headquarters!'

He made little effort to disguise how much he was enjoying being imperious in victory to his staff and reporters watching.

At this point Trumbull Warren whispered to Kit Dawnay, 'The Chief is putting on a pretty good act.' Dawnay whispered back: 'Shut up, you S.O.B., he has been rehearsing this for six years!'

'What do you want?'

Von Friedeburg attempted to then read a letter he was bearing from Dönitz's most senior general, Keitel, but his poor English and his nerves got the better of him. Knee translated instead. It was a tale of German woe that begged somehow for Allied sympathy; Heeresgruppe Weichsel, north of Berlin, was in tatters, and Keitel was asking for a stay of execution from the Soviets. Might they be able to surrender to the Western Allies instead? This suggestion received short shrift from Monty, who wanted nothing to do with the men facing the Soviets: 'Certainly not,' Montgomery said. 'Those armies are fighting the Russians, so they must surrender to the Russians. I am not going to have any dealings about anything on my eastern flank. That subject is closed.' He did then offer to readily accept any German soldiers 'with their hands up'; men simply surrendering themselves were welcome.

Monty knew he didn't have the authority to accept a western surrender, but because they had come to him first, authority or not, it was an opportunity to grab – and grab it he did. Months of being stymied by Eisenhower, a man he regarded as a great diplomat but not a soldier, had irked him since Normandy. He had to take his moment, as the Germans tried once more to parlay and squeeze special terms out of him. They asked again if he would withdraw to give the Germans space to escape the Soviet zone to the east.

But again he wasn't interested. Berating them for Coventry – 'You should have thought of this six years ago' – for the horrors of Bergen-Belsen, for starting the war, for bringing their own self-ruin, he made it clear that if there was not an unconditional surrender he would unleash further misery on them and their country. But then, in inimitable Monty style, he grabbed the initiative and got the enemy exactly how he liked them – off-balance. He made his play, asking if they would surrender all German forces between Lübeck and the Dutch coast, as well as those in Denmark, Heligoland and the German islands – in essence everyone he faced right now, rendering the German delegation speechless. They hadn't come with the authority to accept this kind of offer, yet here it was. So to ram his point home, Monty asked his staff for a map. On it he outlined his dispositions and the full state of play, delineating the exact situation the German forces found themselves in. It was pure Monty, a brilliant *coup de théâtre*, distilling and explaining a problem as succinctly as he could, displaying his intentions and outfoxing the enemy to boot.

Such was the disarray of the Wehrmacht that the German officers had had no real sense of just how bad things were. Monty invited them to think it over while they had some lunch. Von Friedeburg wept openly. The *Daily Express*'s Alan Moorehead, who had seen every aspect of the war from the desert to the Baltic, described it as 'embarrassing'.

Served a meal of British compo rations, the German delegation were pranked by the TAC HQ staff. A German-speaking officer, disguised as a mess sergeant, asked them what they thought of the food, apologizing that the day's supplies had not yet arrived and that the cooks were having to make do. The Germans said how much they liked it, only for the officer to reply that the lads wouldn't touch this muck. In the meantime, in the 'A' Mess, two blanket-covered tables were put together so that Monty could mark up the German positions again and lay out his next move. His staff were to be armed, but discreetly. Colonel Ewart would interpret.

After their meal, Monty met the delegation again, who were now full of lunch, brandy and coffee, and set about underlining the situation in greater detail. This time he was wearing his decorations and was less casual and more businesslike. Von Friedeburg wept again. There was no bargain to be struck. His plans to dodge the Russians and somehow deliver the fanciful solution his boss Dönitz wanted – and some influence over their destiny – had failed abjectly, as it only could when confronted by the precise and vengeful Field Marshal. Once the briefing was complete, Monty summed up what he wanted. His words were captured by the CBS correspondent Bill Downs: unconditional surrender in the areas touched on earlier. Once the Germans had surrendered – and only then – would he discuss 'the implications of your surrender: how we will dispose of those surrendered troops, how we will occupy the surrendered territory, how we will deal with the civilians, and so forth'.

He went on, his intent still chillingly clear now, eighty years later, heavy with the consequences of refusing to surrender unconditionally. 'And my third point: If you do not agree to Point 1, the surrender, then I will go on with the war and I will be delighted to do so. All your soldiers and civilians may be killed.'

It was agreed that this news should be delivered to Reich President Dönitz in person, von Friedeburg saying that he did not have the authority to accept Monty's terms. He wasn't to know that it was a spontaneous offer Monty had made without consulting his commanding officer or his government. In spite of that, it was abundantly clear that there was to be absolutely no negotiation. The Allies would dictate terms, and they, the defeated, would obey them. Simple. Arrangements were made, and the chastened German deputation was separated, with Wagner and Kinzel remaining at TAC HQ while von Friedeburg and Friedl returned to Flensburg. Friedl owed his position and presence to the dead Führer, and could not have been presented with a clearer indication that his sway over events had died with him. Monty's staff arranged for a break in air operations to allow the two of them to get back to Flensburg to deliver Dönitz the ultimatum. The Generaladmiral had asked for forty-eight hours. Monty had given him twenty-four. He may have put hostilities on pause – and he'd done so for the sake of his own men's lives – but he could resume them if he needed to. With the Germans went the interpreter Captain Knee, as well as a precautionary security escort. The Australian journalist Chester Wilmot accompanied them disguised as a captain, looking for the scoop.

Trumbull Warren rode with them through the recently surrendered Hamburg, where he dropped Friedl off at the German front line in a flurry of *Sieg Heil*s – if ever there was a time the Nazi 'hail victory' salute was hollow it was this. It was agreed that he would return at 2 p.m. the following day to collect von Friedeburg with the German government's answer, telling him that he would wait for only two hours, and no longer, leaving Montgomery's threat of continuing the war still hanging. At TAC HQ the two remaining Germans spent an anxious night, Kinzel being quizzed in detail about the state of the German Army, explaining to Colonel Ewart that the surrender would entail 1 million German soldiers, some 400,000 prisoners of war and 2 million civilians who had fled the Soviet advance. In the meantime, word crept out into 21st Army Group that surrender was imminent.

That evening, with the German delegation sent on its way, Monty informed his superiors of the day's events, also sending a telegram to the British Chief of Imperial General Staff, General Sir Alan Brooke. His view was that von Friedeburg knew that the writing was on the wall and that resistance could not be prolonged. He also explained to Brooke that he had sent von Friedeburg to Flensburg with the demand for the surrender of German forces in Norway. That night he wrote to his son David's guardians, the Reynoldses: 'I really do think the war in Germany is drawing to a close . . . we took one million prisoners in April, and the total since D-day is three million.' This was what the reality of winning the war was. The Germans and their leadership, so desperate to fight to the end and make sure they did not repeat the kind of defeat 1918 had dealt them, an armistice, avoiding conquest and occupation, had delivered exactly that final disastrous outcome, a generation of men lost, its cities destroyed, the country prostrate, cut up into portions by its enemies. As night fell and Monty's staff erected a marquee for the return of the German delegation, the Field Marshal went to bed at his usual time, half past nine. He liked things just so, even on a night like this.

At 09:00 the following morning, 5 May, von Friedeburg explained how Monty's demands and blunt insistence on unconditional surrender had unfolded to Dönitz and his advisors. Both Keitel, head of the OKW, and Jodl, Chief of the Operations Staff, were chiefly concerned with Germany's military honour, Jodl wondering whether surrendering the Netherlands was the right course of action even at this final hour. The deep state of delusion that had characterized the Nazi world view throughout its existence still prevailed. The old submariner was out of his depth with the disaster befalling the Reich, complaining that 'My generation is never again to see a flourishing Germany. As a nation we have been set back for a thousand years' – a bitter echo of Hitler's rhetoric. 'But we must as quickly as possible do all we can for those millions of Germans who have a chance of going on with life.'

Regardless, they knew they could not mess with Montgomery – a proposal that the Germans destroy their arms was scotched, as it sat outside the British Field Marshal's terms and conditions. The meeting concluded with a decision to scuttle naval vessels – these fell within Dönitz's old purview, after all. Von Friedeburg, once he had signed the surrender with Monty, would make his way to see Eisenhower at Reims to finalize the rest of the surrender of German forces that weren't covered by the terms agreed with Montgomery. They were already referring to the part of Germany that the Red Army had seized as 'Russia' and the rest as Germany.

Present, but not involved, at Dönitz's headquarters was Reichsführer Heinrich Himmler, his power now completely evaporated and excluded from the decision-making at Flensburg. He had offered his services as second in command of the new government to Dönitz, who had refused them – his last-minute betrayal of Hitler, offering peace feelers through his Swedish contacts, had destroyed his reputation with the new regime. Himmler may have been more realistic than his old boss, but his timing had been off – nevertheless his approach, trying to appeal to the powers of 'World Jewry' for mercy, had been just as delusional. Dönitz, now he was in charge, was ready to throw in the towel.

Come 2 p.m. the German delegation had not returned to the rendezvous. Warren decided to wait. Monty had cabled Brooke, certain that the Germans would honour their promises and that this offered him 'nice problems to solve'. At 4.30 the Germans reappeared and Warren got out of his car to greet them. With von Friedeburg and Friedl was another officer, Generalmajor Fritz Poleck, who had brought with him the German radio frequencies, code books and the locations of the German naval minefields. And there was even better news: the Germans were here to sign. At 5 p.m. the party finally arrived at TAC HQ, apart from Poleck, who had been dispatched elsewhere to hand over the intelligence he had brought with them.

With the 'victory tent' waiting, Monty had been taking time to speak to the war correspondents who were travelling with TAC HQ. It was generally agreed that he was bad at press conferences, a shortcoming of which he was keenly aware; but this one, went the consensus from the hacks, was the best he had ever given. Maybe it was the occasion and the circumstances, but Monty – whose emotions had been on display for all to see, his depression and dismay at not being allowed to run the campaign in Europe his way, as well as the recent death of John Poston – was for once on sparkling form, even if he did indulge in a little light gloating: 'No doubt that if the piece of paper [I have prepared] is signed, forces to be surrendered total over a million chaps. Not so bad, a million chaps! Good egg!'

Colonel Ewart came to inform Monty that the Germans had returned and that they were prepared to sign the document: 'Now we shall see their doings!' he exclaimed, and told the journalists to make their way to the victory tent. Outside, the sky was already black and it was pouring with rain. Aircraft thundered overhead, all portents of defeat for the Germans. Monty asked von Friedeburg to join him in his caravan for a moment, where he made sure that the Generaladmiral was going to sign. Von Friedeburg was downcast, depressed, the burden of the reality of the situation pressing him down as much as it was lifting Monty: 'He was very dejected and I told him to rejoin the others outside.' Inside the tent on the table the BBC had set up two microphones. It was time.

At 6.30 p.m. Monty entered the tent. The Germans stood to attention. One of them went to smoke – smoking was forbidden in Monty's presence in deference to his lung injury from the Great War, and only Ike and Churchill got away with it – and was stopped from doing so. Montgomery sat at the table and read out the instrument of surrender:

> INSTRUMENT OF SURRENDER OF ALL GERMAN ARMED FORCES IN HOLLAND, IN NORTHWEST GERMANY INCLUDING ALL ISLANDS, AND IN DENMARK
>
> 1. The German Command agrees to the surrender of all German armed forces in Holland, in northwest Germany including the Frisian Islands, and Heligoland and all other islands, in Schleswig-Holstein, and in Denmark, to the C.-in-C. 21 Army Group.
> This to include all naval ships in these areas.
> These forces to lay down their arms and to surrender unconditionally.
> 2. All hostilities on land, on sea, or in the air by German forces in the above areas to cease at 08:00 hrs British Double Summer Time on Saturday 5th May 1945.
> 3. The German Command to carry out at once, and without argument or comment, all further orders that will be issued by the Allied Powers on any subject.
> 4. Disobedience of orders, or failure to comply with them, will be regarded as a breach of these surrender terms and will be dealt with by the Allied Powers in accordance with the accepted laws and usages of war.
> 5. This instrument of surrender is independent of, without prejudice to, and will be superseded by any general instrument of surrender imposed by or on behalf of the Allied Powers and applicable to Germany and the German armed forces as a whole.

> 6. This instrument of surrender is written in English and in German.
> The English version is the authentic text.
> 7. The decision of the Allied Powers will be final if any doubt or dispute arises as to the meaning or interpretation of the surrender terms.

Then he repeated his threat to continue hostilities if they didn't sign. Ewart translated. The Germans nodded to indicate they understood. Monty then ordered them to sign in order of seniority. Sombrely, bitterly, silently, to the sound of cameras and the tent flapping in the wind, they signed the surrender, from von Friedeburg down to Major Friedl, whose name Monty mispronounced as 'fry-del'.

'Now I will sign on behalf of the Supreme Allied Commander, General Eisenhower.'

On signing and dating it 'B. L. Montgomery, Field Marshal', Monty wrote the wrong date and had to amend it from 5 to 4 May, initialling the correction. Perhaps the excitement, well concealed as it was, had got to him.

After months of feeling that he had been sidelined by his boss, it was Monty's moment of triumph, taking Ike's place centre-stage and with it responsibility for the war's ultimate aim – unconditional surrender. The war in Germany was over; the rest would be formalities. The Third Reich had conceded defeat, here, in the heart of the Fatherland, and to Britain's most prominent soldier.

The pen disappeared soon afterwards – someone, Monty thought, pinched it.

Among the formalities was the official cessation of hostilities at six o'clock the following morning, 5 May. Monty addressed the cameras, twinkling with satisfaction. There were prisoners to take and process, and the not so small matters of Dunkirk and the Channel Islands, which were still in German hands.

War Diaries recorded the moment, as well as how they had got wind of it: either the news came as an order or on the BBC. The 5th Battalion, King's Own Scottish Borderers in 52nd Lowland Division noted: '4 May ALL GERMAN ARMIES IN NW GERMANY, HOLLAND, DENMARK, surrender UNCONDITIONALLY to 21 ARMY GROUP (BBC announcement).' The Canadian paratroopers in Wismar wrote it up slightly differently; maybe the vodka had got to them: 'Russian–British liaison still at a high pitch, with much drinking and hand-shaking. We received word that the number of German P'sW [prisoners of war] taken by the Div. on 2 May had totalled somewhere in the vicinity of 15,000. News also came through that the German Armies in north-west Europe had surrendered unconditionally to Field-Marshal Montgomery. This was great news, but was still not what we were looking for, namely, unconditional surrender of the German nation to all the United Nations. However, it was a good start.' The War Diary entry for 1st Battalion, Royal Tank Regiment for 7 a.m. said simply: 'Consciousness with many hangovers.'

It was over. At least today's surrender was. Monty had only signed on behalf of Ike. The Americans would want their satisfaction too. Monty must have been keenly aware of it because as he drank a glass of champagne he cabled Brooke, his thoughts turning to the task for which he ruefully knew he hadn't been trained or prepared: peace in Germany.

'That concludes the surrender,' Monty said once the Germans had signed. But it was only the beginning.

It was time to pass the torch to America.

CHAPTER 5

THE CAMP

The Surrender in Southern Germany, *5 May 1945*

Of all the horrors of the place, the smell, perhaps, was the most startling of all. It was a smell made up of all kinds of odours – human excreta, foul bodily odours, smouldering trash fires, German tobacco – which is a stink in itself – all mixed together in a heavy dank atmosphere, in a thick, muddy wood, where little breeze could go. The ground was pulpy throughout the camp, churned to a consistency of warm putty by the milling of thousands of feet, mud mixed with faeces and urine. The smell of Gunskirchen nauseated many of the Americans who went there. It was a smell I'll never forget, completely different from anything I've ever encountered. It could almost be seen and hung over the camp like a fog of death.'

Captain J. D. Pletcher, 71st Division HQ

So many people were on the move as the Third Reich crumbled. Troops pushing forward or in retreat, refugees in their millions, German soldiers fleeing the Russians, Nazis on the run. A few days earlier, on 2 May, at Oberammergau, a small town in southern Bavaria that nestled in the foothills of the Alps, American troops came upon three German civilians who immediately surrendered to them. The first man explained he was Dr Herbert Wagner; the other two were Dr Wernher von Braun and General Walter Dornberger, the men who had developed the Nazi rocket programme at Peenemünde on the Baltic coast. It was their scientific knowledge, vision and direction that had led to the V-2 ballistic missile that had been terrorizing London and Antwerp. All three were quickly whisked away to Paris and then to the United States. The Americans could barely believe their luck. There would be no war crimes trials for this trio.

Yet while Nazi scientists such as these three had been able to successfully flee south from the Baltic coast, there were many people, even at this late stage in the war, still suffering from the Nazis' great project to eradicate Europe's Jews and others considered to be contaminating the Aryan master race. Since February, for example, Hugo Gryn, a Jew from Carpathian Ruthenia, had moved hundreds of miles and had been incarcerated in no fewer than three camps already and was, he supposed, on his way to a fourth – if he ever made it, that is.

The war was nearly over, that much was clear, but whether he would be alive to witness it was another matter. At the end of April 1945, Hugo was still not quite fifteen. He had a lot of life he still wanted to live.

The reduction of Hugo's childhood, of all that was familiar and safe to him, happened gradually. The first eight years or so had been wonderful, for the most part. He felt deeply loved by his father, Géza, and his mother, Bella. There had been the tragedy of losing a younger brother to illness, but that calamity aside, he and his brother, Gabi, had grown up comfortably in Berehovo in Czechoslovakia. Their father was a timber merchant and a successful and prosperous one too. Hugo's parents could afford to be generous and they were; the two brothers wanted for little. There was always enough food, and they enjoyed family holidays together. Hugo made friends at the local Jewish elementary school and existed in a peaceful and largely trouble-free society in which the Jewish community accounted for more than 50 per cent of the town. He liked the boarding school he was sent to as well, in Debrecen.

The rise of the Nazis, and with it anti-Semitism, hovered in the background, however. In November 1938, their corner of Czechoslovakia, right next to the Hungarian border, was annexed by Hungary; this had followed some terrorist activities a few weeks before. It had been unsettling to say the least. Then, following the German and Soviet invasion of Poland, the area had become flooded with refugees. There was also growing hostility towards Jewish people; even young Hugo found himself being chased and given a bloody nose a few times.

As the war progressed life became ever more difficult, especially once Hungary joined the Axis alongside Nazi Germany.

Hugo was still only young – he turned eleven just after the invasion of the Soviet Union – but he sensed the menace in the air, and that life was changing. And so it was. Following the annihilation of the Hungarian Second Army at Stalingrad, the Hungarians began looking for a way out of the war, first by opening talks with Britain and the United States, then also with the Soviet Union. Realizing that Hungary was faltering, Germany invaded in March 1944. This was a catastrophe for Hungary's Jews. Until that point they had experienced repression and anti-Semitism, but they had been protected from the Nazi plans for extermination. That now changed. Within a month of Nazi intervention in the country, Hungary's Jews were stripped of their rights and forced into ghettos. The Gryns were driven out of their large and comfortable home and moved with the rest of Berehovo's Jews to a sawmill – in which Hugo's father had previously had a business interest – and brick factory on the edge of town. The family found themselves living in a shed there.

Géza Gryn had earlier made plans to get them all to Turkey. He had arranged visas, passports and train tickets, but then, when he visited his own parents to bid them farewell, he realized he could not abandon them, nor his and his wife's sisters, brothers and families. It felt like running away. Morally, he believed it was wrong. And so they stayed.

Railway lines ran up to the sawmill and brick factory, and in early June the ghetto was dissolved and all the Jews of Berehovo were forced aboard empty wagons. Hugo found a slip of paper with the route marked: Bereza, Preuschoff, Kraków, Auschwitz. It meant nothing to him. They were told they would be resettled to the east and given agricultural work. No one was happy about it. The journey was interminable, cramped, uncomfortable. They were being treated inhumanely. Hugo was not quite fourteen, but he sensed that this was not the way to transport people to be resettled. He picked up on the growing fear of others and began to feel fearful himself.

Finally, the moment arrived when the train halted and the doors of the wagon were opened. Immediately, lean men in striped uniforms began pulling off their luggage; Hugo was very reluctant to let go of his rucksack. 'You are nineteen and you're a mechanic,' hissed the man as he tugged the bag from him. 'Don't forget, nineteen!'

'Well, perhaps you ought to say nineteen,' his father told him.

They were shoved into two lines. One male, the other female.

'I'm afraid they may separate us,' Géza said to Bella, 'but try to contact us.' They had no idea what lay in store for them, only that it did not bode well. 'Hugo will stay with me if he says he's nineteen, and if they believe him.' He asked her to look after Gabi and the money they had brought and to use it if she could. The lines were rapidly separating. Hugo kissed his mother and his brother; Bella was crying. That was how Hugo and his father left them. As they neared the soldiers, he was asked his age.

'Nineteen,' he stammered.

'And occupation?'

'Carpenter and joiner,' Hugo replied.

'All right, you will go to work.' Glancing back, he saw Gabi separated from his mother; Bella was trying to reach him but was restrained by a guard. Gabi was crying, only twelve years old and now in a line on his own along with other children and the elderly. Hugo felt an arm on his shoulders.

'Come on,' said his father, 'we are on our own now.'

They joined others from Berehovo and to begin with there

were ironic comments, even some black humour. No one knew what to expect. Most still had hope. Faith, even, that German humanity would somehow shine through. They were led to a building where they were told to strip and all their hair – on their heads and bodies – was roughly shaved by other prisoners: all of it, even around their private parts. Then a lotion was slapped on that stung viciously. Next they were showered and given new clothes, ill-fitting black trousers, a pink shirt and a cap. Hugo thought they all looked ridiculous, pathetic, like clowns at a fancy-dress ball. After this humiliation they were ushered outside, where a crowd of equally shaven women also stood gathered together in the sunshine. Men and women now began calling out names, trying to make connections. Then Hugo spotted his mother. She was waving at them, and Hugo felt his father's hand tightly on his wrist. 'Take care of yourself!' Géza called out, although whether she heard, Hugo could not tell. There was no sign of Gabi.

In the week that followed, Hugo learned much. About how to eke out food. That Géza was his best friend as well as his father and that he was doing what he could to protect his son. That people went into the two buildings with the chimneys and never came out again. That Gabi had almost certainly been murdered there on the first day. He learned to lie to survive. 'Under the present circumstances,' his father explained to him, 'we are – and we will be for some time to come – compelled to alter our moral attitude towards lots of things. I have never lied – deliberately that is – in my life before. I have always tried to do the right thing and my own conscience has governed me. But now this attitude towards "right" and "wrong" will have to change.' Once, they managed to get a message to his mother;

it was tied to a stone and thrown to her by a fellow prisoner. A small comfort. He also learned they were incarcerated in a place called Vernichtungslager-Birkenau – Extermination Camp Birkenau, a sub-camp of Auschwitz.

They had been at Birkenau for less than three weeks when they were marched out of their Camp No. 7. Any skilled workers were to step forward, but there was a warning: anyone doing so under false pretences could expect the severest consequences. Hugo and his father stepped forward; after all, Hugo had claimed he was a carpenter when they had first arrived and his father had run a sawmill. The lie seemed worth the risk. They were then marched on to rail wagons that now smelled of disinfectant; there was even a barrel to be used as a toilet which had the name 'Berehovo' on it, so the wagon had been the same one used to transport them to Auschwitz. Then, on that first trip, there had been all four of them and they had been unknowing. Now there was just him and his father, and his brother was surely dead. Fifty of them were ordered into their allotted wagon, guarded by three fully armed SS men. It was horribly cramped and they all had to sit with their knees up while the guards watched over them.

The journey lasted around twelve hours, then the train halted and at first light the doors were opened. Hugo saw a station sign that read 'Lieberose', but actually they were near the village of Jämlitz, between Frankfurt an der Oder and Cottbus, to the south-east of Berlin. They were then marched to a makeshift camp in the middle of a forest where there was also a sawmill. 'This is a good omen,' his father said to him. 'Forests and a sawmill. I am sure we will find jobs and not be entirely ignorant at them.' They had arrived at K.L. – *Konzentrationslager* – Lieberose, a forced labour camp and part of the Sachsenhausen complex. It was not large in the summer of 1944, with just several thousand inmates, and mainly carried out forest-clearing, timber-cutting and also building work. For what purpose was not explained, although they later learned that they were constructing a resort town for German officers. It made little sense; Germany was losing the war. When were these officers expecting to enjoy this still-unfinished complex?

Hugo and his father were given red triangles on their new uniforms, which indicated they were political prisoners; this was because his father had lied and claimed that was the reason for their incarceration at Birkenau and no one had seen reason to question or change it. The work was arduous, and Hugo soon realized that the meagre food they were given was not enough for the toil that was expected of him. He was still only fourteen but had the wit to work out that the only way he could survive was by expending as little energy as possible. It was not easy, but there was quite a lot of time when the guards were not watching.

Summer gave way to autumn, then winter. The camp grew with ever more prisoners arriving, including a number of Greek Jews; they struggled terribly in the cold. They were simply not used to it. The death rate rose horrendously. There were telltale signs: puffy eyes, swollen ankles and joints. Hearts and kidneys were packing up, and when that happened the damage was irreversible; death was only a matter of time. Hugo learned harsh lessons: steal food if he could, never eat the bread ration all at once, never volunteer, walk slowly, always keep well clear of the rifle butts of guards.

He was, though, party to the killing of a particularly sadistic guard who liked to swing his rifle butt at any prisoners who passed his crosshairs. Even if the blow didn't kill them, it meant death because the prisoner was unable to recover. One day, Hugo was part of a four-man work party carrying large soup containers on staves, like a litter. While they walked through the forest they momentarily paused, and the guard came over to berate them. Spontaneously they jumped on him, pinned him down and beat him to death with his rifle butt. After burying him lightly beneath leaves and twigs, they sneaked back into the work area unnoticed. His body was only found later. Hugo and the other perpetrators were never caught. They had been lucky.

Luck was with him another time but came on the back of misfortune. He was caught hiding a spanner in his shoe and given twenty-five lashes, his back ripped raw. Afterwards he was treated by one of the camp doctors. It turned out that the doctor's son had been at Debrecen, where Hugo had attended school. Taking pity on him, he told Hugo to claim he was really a medical student. The doctor would then ask for him to come and work with him in the hospital. Soon after, he was called for and asked whether he really was a medical student. Yes, Hugo replied. They had him down as a carpenter. Hugo explained that he was really a medical student. The hospital was filthy, but it was warmer than being outside. He became an anaesthetist, which involved pouring ether on to gauze and cotton wool and pressing it to a patient's nose.

Somehow, he carried on. So, too, did his father. No one had any sense of how long they'd have to keep going. Hearsay abounded: food was coming from the Red Cross; the Russians were nearing; the Allies were soon to liberate them. When the rumours proved false, morale plummeted.

Then suddenly, on 2 February 1945, they were ordered to march out of Lieberose. There had been around 3,500 prisoners in the camp at the time. Some 700 were transported away by train, while around 1,600 were told to start walking, among them Hugo and his father. 'We were marched maybe a kilometre,' said Hugo, 'and then we heard lots of firing and saw smoke. They literally killed and set on fire everybody who couldn't move.' These victims were the sick and those still in the camp hospital, which had been set on fire. That was around 1,200 prisoners. Too ill to work, they were no use to the Nazis any more. And so they were killed.

For those still standing, the march was brutal. They had no idea where they were heading. It was freezing cold, snow lay thick on the ground, and because they were marching – or rather, trudging – feeding them was difficult. They received even less food than normal, when nourishment was what they needed more than anything. At night they curled up in blankets and huddled together, tried to sleep. In the morning they were up and marching again, although the day's trudge began with gunfire as those too weak to move were shot by the guards. Hugo found that his blanket was too heavy to carry, weakened as he was, so he and his father ditched them and then picked up others as the day drew to an end; there were always plenty abandoned on the road as ahead of them were other columns of captives, mostly Allied POWs, and where there had been prisoner marches there was always detritus, including discarded blankets.

After a couple of days they reached the south-east outskirts of Berlin but were ordered on, right through this already war-torn and scarred city. Vast piles of rubble and many shells of buildings told the prisoners that Germany was losing the war, but it was not over yet and who knew when it would be. And while it continued to take its grisly course they remained prisoners, slave labourers at the mercy of their captors – men who were not merciful.

Eventually they reached Sachsenhausen, at the northern edge of Berlin in Oranienburg, one of the first and most notorious Nazi concentration camps. By this time, almost half of those who'd set out from Lieberose had died or been killed en route. But not Hugo and his father. They were still standing. Still alive. Immediately put to work, Hugo spent his first days there loading Ernst Kaltenbrunner's counterfeit money, forged on the presses at the camp. Sachsenhausen was terrible. He witnessed hangings, saw the brutality of guards and the misery of the inmates, but he and his father were not there for long. At the end of February they were ordered on to another train and sent far to the south, this time to Mauthausen in Upper Austria. Hugo could not believe it: the Germans were losing, the Third Reich was in disarray and yet they were still determined to shuffle Jews and other slave labourers about, forcing them to move vast distances. Since becoming a prisoner of the Nazis, he'd travelled by train from Berehovo to Auschwitz, by train again to Lieberose, then walked to Sachsenhausen and they were now being moved again by train – human cargo crammed into livestock wagons. It made no sense to him.

They reached Mauthausen on 28 February. Hugo was made to work in a quarry. It was awful, draining manual work at a time when he was already physically weakened; and he was still only fourteen years old. They were billeted in a Zeltlager, a tented camp, despite the freezing cold. One night, Hugo and his father were squatted in a corner of their cramped tent. Suddenly, Hugo became overwhelmed by claustrophobia and insisted they get out. 'It was an extraordinarily cold and cruel spring,' he said, 'and still snowing.' Despite this they sneaked out, found some others sheltering in the trees and, wrapping themselves in blankets, tried to sleep. A short while later, a lone plane came over and dropped a bomb which landed on the corner of the tent where they'd been earlier. Hugo could not account for it, but he'd been lucky on this occasion too.

Then, on 13 April, they were ordered to move yet again, once more with no explanation, no hint of where they were going or how far and for how long they would be expected to march. There were several thousand of them, and by this time almost everyone was already sick. And getting worse, because they were fed next to nothing. The prisoners were starving. Hundreds died. They were simply collapsing by the roadside and left there, a heap of bones covered by a thin veil of skin. Hugo and Géza knew that the war was nearly over, that this hell would soon end. The moment the Germans surrendered, they would surely be freed. But they were so weak, so frail. Time was running out for Hugo and his father, as it was for thousands more now heading to this latest camp.

Yet the end was nearing. As April 1945 turned to May, the Allied armies were making sweeping gains, not least in the southern Reich and the area of the German Heeresgruppe G, which included much of Bavaria and Austria, where Hugo and Géza were now desperately clinging on to life. Among those forging their way across the length of Bavaria, that part of Germany that kissed the northern Alps, was the US 3rd Infantry Division. This battle-hardened unit had already spent more days in combat than any other in the US Army when, on 2 May, the 7th Infantry, known as the 'Cottonbalers' and one of the 3rd's three regiments, swept into Salzburg in south-west Austria – just sixty miles from where the Gryns were now incarcerated.

The 3rd Division were part of the US Seventh Army, in turn attached to 6th Army Group under the command of General Jacob Devers. Devers's forces, which included the French First Army too, had rather played second fiddle in the European Theatre of Operations – ETO – and received noticeably less press coverage than their compatriots in 12th Army Group. Unlike General Omar Bradley's troops, the 6th Army Group boys had not landed on the beaches of Normandy on D-Day, nor was the firebrand General Patton, comfortably the most famous American combat general, part of their mob. Furthermore, General Eisenhower was not overly fond of either Devers or General Alexander Patch, the Seventh Army commander. Or perhaps more accurately, Bradley was an old and trusted friend in a way that Patch and Devers were not. At any rate, 6th Army Group had arrived in the ETO via Marseilles in southern France the previous summer more than two months after D-Day; Seventh Army had landed as part of Operation DRAGOON on 15 August, so there was a feeling they were Johnny-come-latelies too.

This, though, was to do most of the men landing there a gross injustice, and not least 3rd Infantry Division, who had disembarked in Fedala in French Morocco on 8 November 1942 as part of Operation TORCH, then fought in Sicily, later up through southern Italy and then on 22 January 1944 they had arrived at Anzio to the south of Rome as part of Operation SHINGLE. For DRAGOON, they'd carried out their fourth amphibious assault of the war – a feat in itself – disembarking at St Tropez and then advancing up the Rhône Valley and on through the Vosges Mountains, before reaching the River Rhine in November. They'd then helped clear the Colmar Pocket and finally crossed the Rhine. After this they'd captured Nuremberg, the site of the Nazi rallies of the 1930s, then Augsburg, and had liberated a major camp for forced labourers before sweeping on into Munich. In that time they'd suffered more than 25,000 casualties, two and a half times the full fighting strength of the division, of which nearly 5,000 had been killed. They'd fought in the desert, in plains, in mountains in brutal winter conditions, in the heat of high summer and again been soaked, snowed on and frozen in a third winter of combat. The division had also won more Medals of Honor, America's highest award for valour, than any other in the US Army. In other words, 3rd Infantry, the 'Rock of the Marne', had more than done its bit in this war and deserved no condescension whatsoever. Rather, it had earned the right to be showered with a bit of glory and an end-of-war accolade worthy of the current 528 days of combat it had already experienced by that Wednesday, 2 May 1945.

This was why its commander, Major-General John 'Iron Mike' O'Daniel, decided to ignore orders to the contrary and send his 7th Infantry to Berchtesgaden. After all, the 7th were already in Salzburg, and Berchtesgaden was only fifteen miles to the south. It was virtually on his doorstep and being served up to him on a plate. Eisenhower had sensibly chosen not to contest Berlin, but if there was one other prestige location within the crumbling Third Reich it was Berchtesgaden, or, more specifically, the Obersalzberg – the mountain overlooking the town which had effectively become Nazis-on-the-Hill. It was here that Hitler had his beloved Alpine retreat, the Berghof. Göring had an even bigger place just above; Bormann had a house next to Hitler's. Speer had one too, a little further down. Above this mountain conclave perched the Kehlsteinhaus – the so-called Eagle's Nest. It was hallowed ground if one was in thrall to the Nazis, but the single most prestigious part of Naziland if one was an Allied commander.

Devers had promised the capture of Berchtesgaden to the French 2ème Division Blindée under Général Philippe Leclerc. While there were political pressures on Devers to give this coveted prize to the French, Leclerc's armoured division had originally been fighting with Patton's Third Army, had already had the honour of taking Paris, and had in recent weeks been weeding out German pockets of resistance on the Atlantic coast. They'd had to be hurriedly transported across France into southern Germany and attached to Patch's Seventh Army because Leclerc refused to serve under Général Jean de Lattre de Tassigny's French First Army, whom he viewed as earlier pro-Vichy traitors. Really, it was amazing how touchy French generals could be, but Iron Mike O'Daniel felt his division were as worthy of taking the glittering prize of Hitler's lair – and the inevitable loot that went with it – as any French, and especially those who'd avoided the bitter hard yards of battling their way into Germany. He had a point.

On 4 May, with still no sign of Leclerc's division, O'Daniel had a frank conversation with Colonel John A. Heintges, commander of the Cottonbalers, who had been born in Germany before his family had emigrated to the USA. O'Daniel confessed he'd not got permission to strike for Berchtesgaden; in fact, General Patch had expressly denied it.

'Do you think you can do it?' O'Daniel then asked Heintges.

'Yes, sir,' Heintges replied.

'Then go.'

As it happened, Leclerc was issuing similar orders at the same time, as was General Maxwell Taylor, commander of the US 101st Airborne Division, who were also now in southern Bavaria. None of these troops were as well placed as 7th Infantry, however. That same afternoon, Lieutenant Sherman W. Pratt, a platoon commander in the 3rd Battalion, and his men found themselves in the vanguard of 7th Infantry's advance. Pratt was one of the very few men in the division who had miraculously survived North Africa, Sicily, Italy, France and now Germany, and so it could hardly have been more appropriate that he and his men were first to reach the town, having taken the Autobahn route from Salzburg. He thought Berchtesgaden looked as though it was from a fairy tale with its picture-box Alpine wooden houses. Yet the real prize was the Obersalzberg and the Kehlsteinhaus above. The place, however, had been bombed very heavily by RAF Bomber Command nine days earlier on 25 April. Shell craters pockmarked the hillside and the Berghof, despite being covered in camouflage netting, had been badly hit and was now entirely uninhabitable. Like almost everywhere else in the Reich, this most beautiful of places had not escaped the mighty weight of Allied air power.

It was a stunning May afternoon when Pratt and his men wound their way up the road from Berchtesgaden towards the Obersalzberg. 'We rounded a bend,' noted Pratt, 'and there before us in a broad opening lay the ruins of what had once been Hitler's house and the SS barracks.' Everyone was similarly struck by the significance of the sight before them. 'After all the years of struggle and destruction, the killing, pain and suffering,' he wrote, 'here, for sure, was the end of it.'

Of the Nazis who had lived here there was no sign. It had been to Berchtesgaden that Göring had fled, and where Bormann had hoped to continue the fight; this was the heart of the Alpine redoubt. It was where a Reichskanzlei still stood, used when Hitler had been in residence, and where many of the Führer's headquarters staff and paperwork had been sent. After the RAF had pounded the Obersalzberg on 25 April they had all fled, Göring included, who, despite being still under arrest, persuaded his captors that they would all be far better off moving in quick order to his Schloss at Mauterndorf, to the west in Austria.

Meanwhile, Général Leclerc and his leading French troops were at the edge of Berchtesgaden by 5 p.m. that day, 4 May, and he was apoplectic to discover O'Daniel's men already there; in fact, Iron Mike had held up both the French and 101st Airborne at checkpoints on the roads in until he was sure Colonel Heintges' men had secured the town and the Obersalzberg. The French eventually pulled into Berchtesgaden at around 8 p.m., the paratroopers of the 101st the following morning.

By that time, all German resistance in the southern Reich was about to cease. Following the surrender in Italy, General Friedrich Schulz, commander of Heeresgruppe G in Bavaria and southern Austria as well as latterly Heeresgruppe C in Italy, recognized that there was no point in fighting any longer; resistance in the Alpine redoubt was nothing more than any other idea emanating from the Nazi High Command at this time: a fantasy with little or no basis in reality.

And Kesselring, while he might have fretted over his oath in his arguments with Wolff, had by now accepted that the game was up and so authorized Schulz to make contact with the Allies, which he did on 2 May. Schulz's forces, however, were increasingly lacking any kind of cohesion and what remained of them were now largely contracted in small pockets or spread to the four winds; it was one thing wanting to surrender, but quite another letting all these disparate troops know it was going to happen. However, finally, the act of unconditional surrender of Heeresgruppe G – which meant all troops between the Bohemian Mountains and the Upper Inn River – took place in a large studio designed by Albert Speer in Baldham, just to the east of Munich, at a little after half past two in the afternoon.

The 3rd Infantry Division might have been first to Berchtesgaden, first to be able to crawl over the Berghof and first to reach the dizzy 6,000-foot heights of the Kehlsteinhaus, but they were not allowed to remain for long. Colonel Heintges had expected to be there for at least a week, but the following day the 506th Parachute Infantry Regiment reached the town, part of the 101st 'Screamin' Eagles' Airborne Division, and much to Heintges' disappointment the Cottonbalers were relieved, while Leclerc's men moved in on the Obersalzberg.

Yet while capturing Nazis and vast numbers of German troops was very much the Allies' ongoing mission and a key part of securing Germany's surrender, so too was liberating the astonishing number of concentration and forced labour camps. Nordhausen, a vast slave labour camp that fed workers into the Mittelbau-Dora factory where the V-2s had been manufactured, had been liberated on 11 April. The stench had been so bad that the American and British liberators had nearly all started vomiting. Buchenwald had been liberated the same day. A few days later, on 15 April, British troops had reached Bergen-Belsen, where tens of thousands of Jews had been left to starve. The arrival of Allied troops at these places of human degradation, misery and death was a watershed moment. Most found it hard to comprehend that fellow humans could be treated with such untold cruelty. Photographs and film footage of skeletal survivors, but also of piles of dead between the disease-infested huts, were quickly shown around the free world and prompted understandable feelings of shock, outrage and, of course, revulsion against the people responsible for this. It was hardly surprising that feelings towards the Germans hardened further; the enemy had continued fighting long after Germany had lost the war. Needless lives had been lost. Anger had already been rising among Allied troops, who saw no reason why they should risk their lives in this pointlessness. Now they were coming across scales of inhumanity that few could comprehend. Anger, disgust, horror and diminishing compassion for a subjugated enemy were the feelings aroused in many of the liberators.

And there were just so many camps. Every day Allied troops reached another, invariably presaged by the noticeable absence of birdsong and the rising stench that filled the air. On 4 May, the same day that Lieutenant Sherman Pratt and his men reached the Obersalzberg, it was the turn of the 71st 'Red Circle' Infantry Division. In sharp contrast to the battle-hardened 3rd Infantry Division, the 71st was one of the newest units to arrive in the ETO, landing in France only on 6 February 1945 and not heading into combat until early March. They'd seen plenty of action since then, however, and done well too, first attached to Patch's Seventh Army and then moved to join Patton's Third Army as it swept on into Austria and Czechoslovakia on the northern flank of 6th Army Group. And it was into Upper Austria, on the road to Hitler's home city of Linz, that the Red Circle Division came across the horrifying site of Gunskirchen Lager.

Among those reaching the camp that day was Staff Sergeant

Alan Moskin, an infantryman in the 66th Regiment, one of three such units in the 71st. Moskin was a few weeks short of his nineteenth birthday and a Jew from Englewood, New Jersey. A bright boy, he'd skipped a couple of grades at school and so was still only seventeen when he went to Syracuse University. Yet on turning eighteen at the end of May 1944 he was drafted into the army; even the USA was beginning to run short of manpower and every able-bodied young man was eligible for military service. Moskin was no exception.

Training was rudimentary but tough, and by early 1945 he was ready to join the conveyor belt of replacements. Over the Atlantic he went, crammed with thousands of others on to a liberty ship, landing at Liverpool in England. From there he was posted to France and to a repple depple – a replacement depot – and then sent up to join 66th Infantry, even though they were, like him, new to the ETO and yet to experience combat.

The division had first gone into action on 11 March near Ratzwiller in Alsace, having relieved positions of the 100th Infantry Division. They'd successfully broken through the Siegfried Line, the German border defences, then pushed on to the River Rhine, advancing some 180 miles in their first twenty days of action. Then, on 28 March, they were shifted to join Patton's Third Army and finally crossed the Rhine two days later.

For Alan Moskin these battles were a whir – of immense noise, violence and destruction. During his very first time in action, in Alsace, he experienced the war for real when, crouched down, something hurtled over and hit his helmet. He was a little dazed but otherwise all right, but then realized he'd been hit by a human arm – and that of one of his buddies, as he recognized the tattoo. Another time, he and his squad were scouting forward and they came up behind a disabled German tank. The panzer fired several rounds at them but Moskin and his fellows spotted one of the German troops on the tank, so he fired his rifle and saw the man fall. Approaching soon after, he looked down at the young man he'd almost certainly killed. A blond, blue-eyed youngster. A few yards away was his helmet and beside it a photograph of an older couple. Underneath the image was written '*Wir lieben dich, Mutti und Vati*.' A loving message from his parents. 'I had nightmares over the fact I saw that picture,' admitted Moskin, 'that I had killed their son.' Then his best friend in the platoon was badly wounded and was bleeding out. Moskin was holding him in his arms but orders came through to move. The officer said, 'You can't stay back with the wounded.' So he had to leave his buddy there, life draining away. He never, ever got over that: abandoning his dying friend. Moskin found combat terrifying. They all did. 'Guys were peeing their pants, worse than that from the first days in the line,' he commented. 'Nothing to be ashamed about. Everyone's scared. There's nothing abnormal about it.'

Yet by 4 May, Moskin was wondering whether he might somehow, miraculously, have made it through, even if his experiences meant that he would be damaged goods for the rest of his life. That morning they captured a lot of troops, mostly Hitler Youth. Moskin was at the head of his men when a tall youth, 'a big blonde kid', turned to him and yelled, '*Schweinhund, Schweinhund! Amerikaner Schweinhund!*', then began spitting in his face. Moskin had been awake more than twenty-four hours, was tired and also shocked by the vitriolic hate of this youth, and so raised his rifle and pointed it at the

German's temple. He flicked off the safety catch and felt his finger press against the trigger.

'College Boy! Don't be doing that,' his officer called out. Moskin lowered the rifle and kicked the boy on the backside instead. But he'd been that mad, he could have squeezed the trigger.

They pushed on towards the small town of Gunskirchen, their route taking them through a wood. It was damp but suddenly they were hit by an overpowering stench. They couldn't work out what it was. 'We just looked at each other,' Moskin recalled. 'It got into your nostrils and permeated through your body, getting worse and worse.' Then suddenly they came across a compound, a kind of makeshift camp. The gates were open so they went in, repulsed and compelled at the same time. The stench was choking. What Moskin now saw was the most horrific sight he'd ever witnessed. There were skeletal bodies everywhere – alone where they'd fallen, but also in piles. Others, still alive, stumbled towards them, skin, bones, sunken eyes and wearing outsize striped rags. Moskin and his men were not ready for this. Not ready for this vision of hell. The lieutenant knew that Moskin was Jewish, so asked him to talk to these emaciated prisoners. But Moskin, while proud of his Jewish heritage, was not religious and couldn't speak Hebrew. Instead he muttered, '*Ich bin auch ein Jude*', which was the only German he could think of.

The prisoners became very emotional at this. One man came up to him then collapsed and began kissing his feet, but Moskin's boots were covered in mud and excreta and he felt revolted. So he picked him up by his armpits and the smell was so powerful that he just wanted to push him away. 'I saw, all down his back,' said Moskin, 'he had festering sores – and lice that were crawling all over him. Man, I wanted to pull away but he was hangin' on to me . . . and I felt his tears.' Moskin began to cry too.

In disbelief, they looked around the camp. At the barracks cramped with people, some alive, others dead. Moskin was struggling to comprehend what he was seeing. How could the civilized world let this happen? How could man be so cruel to his fellow man?

Among those at Gunskirchen were Hugo Gryn and his father, Géza. They'd heard distant gunfire getting closer, then the rumbling of tanks, and suddenly, almost as one, their guards were dropping their weapons, ripping off the death's head insignia and running. Then tanks and infantrymen appeared. 'And that was, as far as I was concerned,' noted Hugo, 'the end of the war.' He watched their arrival silently, not moving, but conscious that they were now free. Hugo's father was by that time ill and weak but still conscious, and motioned to Hugo to sit beside him. Together they said the familiar blessing, praising God who had kept them alive and who had brought them, together, to that moment of liberation. Food was distributed, then medics arrived. Hugo was ill with typhoid himself but was able to move and helped the weaker ones, his father included, up into lorries. They were then taken to Hörsching near Linz, formerly a military barracks but now a makeshift hospital. Hugo shared a bed, with fresh sheets, with his father. 'And he died in my arms,' he noted, 'about three days later.'

At that moment, Hugo went berserk. Liberation had come too late for his father. It was too cruel, too unfair. He knew he could never have survived without his father being with him right until the very end. 'He was there all the time,' wrote Hugo, 'and I really believed that we had made it.'

The war was over – for Alan Moskin, for Hugo Gryn. For everyone in the southern Reich. Not all would be celebrating, however – not even the victors or the liberated.

CHAPTER 6

THE SUPREME COMMANDER WILL SEE YOU NOW

Reims, *6–7 May 1945*

Ike sighed, 'I suppose this calls for a bottle of champagne,' he said. There was no triumph in his voice, none of the elation he had shown when the photographers were there. Now he was alone with his wartime family. We drove past the chateau where he lived in Reims – there were about 10 or 12 of us – and drank champagne and discussed the events of the last few hours until dawn showed through the window. It was a sombre occasion. No one laughed. No one smiled. It was all over. We had won, but victory was not anything like what I had thought it would be. There was a dull bitterness about it. So many deaths. So much destruction. And everyone was very, very tired.

Kay Summersby, *Past Forgetting*

US ARMY GENERAL DWIGHT D. 'IKE' EISENHOWER was where the buck stopped. And it was one hell of a buck. Because the buck stopped with Ike not just for his fellow countrymen, not just for the US Army, but for all of the Allied armies in Europe. He had his masters in Washington – who in the wake of the death of President Roosevelt on 12 April were in some disarray – and in London, but he also had his subordinates, millions of them.

SHAEF HQ itself reflected the size of the task Eisenhower had undertaken, numbering 16,000 personnel, the same kind of strength as an entire division. Aided and abetted by senior officers from the Royal Navy and the Royal Air Force, Ike was at the centre of the Allied effort. These senior officers helped to carry the load, but it was Ike alone who had the ultimate responsibility.

His armies were as numerous and vast as they were diverse. Under his command were three army groups: US 12th Army Group comprising the First, Third, Ninth and Fifteenth Armies, twelve corps, containing forty-eight divisions, 1.2 million men under General Omar Bradley; US 6th Army Group with the French First Army and US Seventh Army commanded by General Jacob L. Devers, a comparatively small 700,000 men in forty-seven different armoured and infantry divisions; as well as 21st Army Group under Montgomery – the DUKEX contingent of 1,020,581 officers and men at its height – comprising the Canadian First Army and British Second Army, with additional Polish and Czech elements; First Allied Airborne Army with its seven airborne divisions, Special Air Service brigades and troop transport aircraft. He also commanded the RAF Second Tactical Air Force and US Ninth Air Force, and for the run of OVERLORD had had command of strategic air forces too. No soldier had ever commanded armies so numerous, wielded so much power, or been of so much consequence. He had the ultimate power of life and death over his men, though only one, Eddie Slovik, had faced the firing squad for desertion. Armies this large, this complex, competing among themselves for resources, priority, victory, were necessarily engines of friction, and it was Ike's task to run it all as harmoniously as possible. Eisenhower was the twentieth-century warlord supreme, the reach and scale of his power only to be eclipsed by the imminent arrival of the atomic age.

Eisenhower therefore didn't just shoulder the burden of his immediate infuriating, frustrating subordinates, the American generals and the British Field Marshal who could, in arguing so passionately when making their cases for how the war should be fought and won, drive him to distraction. By the spring of 1945 he had a million more subordinates. Of course, not all were men at arms; the Allies had a vast logistical network behind them because they were fighting every step as an expeditionary force, but Eisenhower bore the weight of this responsibility. They were all answerable to him; he was answerable to his bosses.

Death was at the core of every decision he made, for his own men, for the enemy and for the civilians in between. Every opportunity taken or ignored centred on death, slaughter, destruction. Every moment that delayed the war, every hesitation offered the prospect of more death. Ike considered Napoleon's approach to leadership as something to aspire to: 'The great leader, the genius in leadership, is the man who can do the average thing when everybody else is going crazy.' Self-control, harnessing his temperament to the task in hand, was Eisenhower's key to managing himself while he managed everyone else. He felt sure too that whatever pressure he might be under, there was someone worse off: 'The most terrible job in warfare is to be a second lieutenant leading a platoon when you are on the battlefield.' Ike shared none of the pressures of the subaltern in the foxhole or slit trench; his were of a different order. They were political rather than military.

If anyone was to take the surrender on the Western Front, it would be Ike. He was the tip of the spear: he symbolized the Allied effort, warts and all. And this was why, once Monty had got von Friedeburg's signature on the Lüneburg document, he, for all the accusations of ego and glory-hunting he faced, had passed the question of the larger surrender immediately on to his boss. It would have been impossible, and indeed out of character, for him to do otherwise.

And yet when the moment came, when Generaloberst Alfred Jodl signed the 'Instrument of Military Surrender' at 2.41 a.m. on 7 May 1945, Ike was absent. Rather than witness the German capitulation, as Monty had done, gleefully briefing reporters and dressing down the Germans sent to parlay with him, Eisenhower had instead decided that he would have nothing to do with the emissaries of the new Führer, that Dönitz's men were Nazis like Hitler's, and that was the end of it. Just as he had ignored General Hans-Jürgen von Armin when the Germans capitulated in Tunisia, so he would shun them again. As Ike saw it, this new government in Flensburg was no more legitimate than Hitler's in Berlin had been, and no more entitled to try to dictate terms in the ruins of Germany than its predecessor.

Rather than treat with the Germans, he would leave it to his staff to handle them, get them to sign, dominate them in person and dictate terms. Ike – the diplomat soldier supreme within the coalition – had no appetite for any diplomacy with the enemy. On arrival at Eisenhower's HQ, everyone on the Allied side divined that Jodl had been hoping to stall things for at least another twenty-four hours so that he could surrender not to the Soviets but the Allies, and buy more time for German formations to flee west and avoid the Red Army's righteous fury. Ike's staff were having none of it; they knew their chief believed in unconditional surrender, and they believed in their chief. If he was going to cold-shoulder the Germans at the moment of their surrender and add to their humiliation, then his staff were going to help him with it.

The months running up to the surrender had been fraught with controversy and ever-increasing pressure. Arguments about how best to proceed now that the Germans had shot their bolt and squandered their strategic reserve with the Ardennes offensive – the Battle of the Bulge – dominated every strategic conversation from that moment on. Eisenhower had had little or no time to reflect on how badly he had been caught out by the enemy, before his troublesome subordinate Montgomery offered his thoughts about how that debacle had unfolded – with a press conference Monty later openly regretted. With the German offensive thwarted, General Sir Alan Brooke set about intriguing to install the British Field Marshal Harold Alexander as Ike's new deputy, seeing an opportunity in the wake of American disarray to get British control of how the war should be run now that the Allies were poised to cross the Rhine. As the American armies grew, so British influence waned, and Brooke wanted to compensate for its demise. The gambit failed, but it was a mark of the continued intriguing which Ike faced. As Ike saw it, things would be run along these lines from now on: 'Berlin was no longer a major factor in reaching that end. Every plan, decision, and purpose of the Allied command was determined always by one inflexible rule – "Destroy the German forces, speedily and completely." . . . The war would be finished now by only one means: We must root out and destroy every remnant of military strength until no organized force remained in Germany to carry on the fight.'

Appointed Supreme Commander in December 1943, Ike had had to navigate the twists and turns of the campaign, the shifts between the military imperatives the Allies faced and the politics that came with fighting in a coalition. In the United Kingdom he had taken to protecting himself from the hurly-burly and demands of his HQ in his billet in Kingston upon Thames, Telegraph Cottage. By the beginning of September 1944, once the US forces outnumbered the DUKEX contingent and the OVERLORD campaign had actually broken out of France, Ike was given overall command of the entire Allied effort in north-west Europe, of all land forces, a move that put Montgomery's nose out of joint. Unlike the peripatetic Monty he stayed put, initially at Versailles, before settling his HQ at a technical college in Reims in mid-February, where he could keep a far lower profile. The security detail did what it could to be unobtrusive, and the building flew no standards or banners.

Once FDR had identified the world crisis for what it was

in September 1939, the US Army had had to expand rapidly, and Eisenhower's star began to rise quickly. With the backing of the Chief of Staff, General George Marshall, Ike had been elevated over many of his peers, and while he lacked the battlefield experience that they boasted and were rapidly accumulating, there was general agreement that Eisenhower's talent for organization and diplomacy marked him out as the right man for the job. But was the job right for any man? By the time the surrender came, Eisenhower had been crushed by the pressure. Friends who hadn't seen him were struck by the bags under his eyes, the exhaustion written on his face, in his posture and in his manner, his preoccupation with the tasks in hand and above all his craving for isolation. On D-Day, as the invasion got under way, after the nail-biting days of decision in the face of changeable weather, Eisenhower had welcomed the moment: there was nothing more he could do – a gigantic military mechanism had stirred into life, and until the beachhead had been established – or not, God forbid – matters were finally out of his hands. The Supreme Commander had issued his supreme command, the armada was embarked, and there were no more decisions to make. Not yet, at least.

When he was not sitting at his desk in a perpetual cloud of cigarette smoke, isolated by the solitary magnitude of the job, he would be managing his subordinates. His generals, even those he valued as his friends, were demanding. All were men of ambition and drive with their own firm ideas about how best to win the war, and often as not that meant they saw themselves as the answer to whatever questions they brought to him. The strain on his temperament began to tell: after four packs of Lucky Strikes a day, copious cups of coffee, numerous ailments, headaches and insomnia, Eisenhower would simply shut down.

On visiting him, Eisenhower's son John found him impossible. John Eisenhower had graduated on 6 June 1944 – D-Day – and at the ceremony to honour his class suddenly found himself the centre of unwanted press attention. John arrived in England on 13 June, a week after the invasion, and even though both men were delighted to be reunited after such a long time, and John was desperate to please his father and connect with him, this was not to be. Rather, John found a man who had been weighed down beneath a gigantic boulder of responsibility, who would openly laugh at him when he offered military opinions or scornfully rebuff him when he tried to make small talk. It wasn't that his father wasn't pleased to see him. It was that he couldn't express himself beyond the vast task he had bearing down upon him. He was tetchy, irritable, impossible to please. Being his father's son presented John with a trap regarding his military career: he knew that he couldn't accept any of the safer staff positions he was offered, and in turn Ike would not countenance him accepting any role on his own staff either. By the same token John couldn't go to the front in case he was captured and potentially handed the enemy a magnificent hostage or scalp. Any accusation of nepotism would damage his father's reputation even further at a time when rumours about an affair with his driver, Captain Kay Summersby, still swirled around him.

Summersby was the closest thing Ike had to a confidante. While he wrote to his wife Mamie frequently, he found it hard to convey to her the pressure or tempo of his job, and equally she found it almost impossible to reciprocate, often complaining that he missed important family occasions, in particular John's graduation, a day which, as we have seen, would have been impossible for him to attend. There was little comfort in the Eisenhowers' transatlantic relationship, and Ike's existence as a public figure left them further alienated. So it was that his personal driver, Kay Summersby, filled an emotional gap.

In later life Summersby, after Ike had died, was to claim in her ghostwritten memoir that they had had an affair, but that they had failed to consummate it. Certainly, she was the person who had spent the most time with him alone, who, whatever the war brought, had been a constant presence. Born Kathleen MacCarthy-Morrogh in Ballydehob, County Cork on 23 November 1908, she was eighteen years Ike's junior. Her father was a soldier in the British Army, and in 1939 she became a member of the British Mechanised Transport Corps, driving an ambulance in the Blitz in London. The MTC was one of the civilian organizations that sought to meet the demands of the new front line that aerial bombing had brought to Britain, driving ambulances as well as providing transport for visiting dignitaries, SOE agents and others in between. Its personnel were uniformed. Her brother James, known as Seamus, had become a commando. Before the war Kay had worked as an extra and a model and in 1936 had married Gordon Summersby, an officer in the British Army three years her junior who was a card player, boxer and accountant. By the time she met Ike they were divorced, though she kept his surname. She had briefly been engaged to an American officer, Lieutenant-Colonel Dick Arnold, but he had been killed in North Africa. Summersby was assigned to drive Ike on his arrival in the United Kingdom in 1942.

Rumours dogged their relationship wherever they went: James M. Gavin, at the time a Brigadier in US 82nd Airborne Division, who had an eye for women, wondered during the preparations for D-Day how many generals brought their drivers to tea with them. After all, Kay didn't have security clearance of any kind. Gavin's curiosity was further stimulated by the *Chicago Tribune*'s correspondent John 'Beaver' Thompson, who remarked: 'Well, I have never before seen a chauffeur get out of a car and kiss the General good morning when he comes from his office.' If only because of the amount of time they spent together they became familiar and close; as Kay drove Ike around the country, her only responsibility was his safe arrival wherever he had to be, in his hands the fate of whichever nation was in the Allies' sights.

Ike's war was one of firsts and militarily unprecedented moments. Operation TORCH, the amphibious landings in North Africa in November 1942, were on a scale which the British had not attempted before, let alone the Americans, and were, until the next set of landings in Sicily, the largest the world had ever seen. Bringing three task forces from Casablanca to Algiers, on a front that began in the Atlantic and ended deep into the Mediterranean, east of Spain, was an undertaking unparalleled in warfare. To have pulled off this assault within a year of the USA entering the war was staggering, and for the US Army to have found and backed a man to command it truly extraordinary. Even at this stage of the war, the British had chewed through generals, dropping men who failed, and swallowed their repeated defeats and false starts. In the desert they had only just succeeded in defeating the Germans and their Italian Allies at El Alamein after two torrid years of to and fro.

Eisenhower's success in North Africa, in particular his handling of the US Army's initial wobbles, most notoriously at Kasserine, had repaid his patron General George Marshall's faith in his protégé. His next task, Operation HUSKY, the invasion of Sicily – an amphibious landing more complex still, with airborne forces added to the Allied portfolio of assets – had been a success too; the Allies were developing a potent recipe for landing on enemy territory, and Eisenhower was at the centre of it all. With these accomplishments under his belt, he returned to England to prepare for OVERLORD.

As Germany fell in on itself and the Allies ran rampant in the aftermath of that campaign, Ike's disgust at the Nazis was finally cemented. On 12 April he visited the concentration camp at Ohrdruf, which the US Army had liberated eight days earlier. It was the first one the GIs had taken. At its peak Ohrdruf had contained 20,000 prisoners from all over Europe, forced to toil for long hours under horrendous conditions and with inadequate rations on obscure projects, railways lines and an underground government headquarters. As many as 7,000 people had died there, killed by disease, squalor or being worked to death. The sights that greeted 4th Armored Division's soldiers, who had found the camp – the dead stacked up like wood – are part of an all-too-familiar descriptive language now, perhaps, but the shock to the soldiers was profound. In an effort to cover up their crimes the Germans had set fire to countless bodies, not altogether successfully. Charred bones and skulls still remained in the improvised fire-pits they had built; they had also sprinkled corpses with quicklime to try to destroy them. General Patton could scarcely believe his eyes – he had vomited on arrival at the camp, and urged Ike to see the place for himself; Ike's old friend General Bradley was rendered speechless. Eisenhower's reaction similarly was one of shock, disgust and resolve – he wanted the camps publicized and seen, fearing that the horrors there were so unbelievable they would offer anyone seeking to deny Nazi crimes a fig leaf of incredulity.

On 19 April Eisenhower asked Washington to ensure that Congress sent representatives to see just who they had been fighting in Germany. 'Still having trouble hating them?' Ike said to a GI deep in his fury. His valet, Sergeant Michael McKeogh, said: 'The Boss's face was black when they came back. He said he had never seen anything to equal what he had seen that day; that no punishment was too great for a people who could do things like that. He told me a little about what he had seen, and he said that some of the things he had seen made him sick. He looked sick when he talked about them – and very angry.' The following day Ike went back for more, visiting Buchenwald where, if possible, things were even worse. These visits set Ike's mood for the surrender to come: there would be no deals to be done with the Nazis.

With the surrender signed at Monty's HQ, von Friedeburg tried to get to Reims to see Ike. The weather intervened. Rather than reach SHAEF, they were diverted to Brussels. A long drive to Reims followed. When they arrived at dead of night they were handed over to Lieutenant-General Walter Bedell Smith, Ike's Chief of Staff and point man, by SHAEF's Chief of Intelligence, Major-General Kenneth Strong. Bedell Smith, aka 'the Beetle', had been at Ike's side since Allied Forces HQ in Tunisia and had been involved in every critical phase of his boss's career. Von Friedeburg immediately laid out his intentions: they had come to surrender all troops in the west to SHAEF. Bedell Smith went through to his boss's office and relayed the news. Ike's reaction was immediate: at SHAEF they weren't going to fall for this delaying strategy either, just as Monty hadn't.

He told the Beetle to tell the Germans he demanded, perhaps predictably, 'immediate, simultaneous and unconditional surrender on all fronts'. Understandably, Eisenhower was not minded to indulge the representatives of the Wehrmacht, which had issued a communiqué on the Lüneburg surrender unlikely to impress anyone at SHAEF: 'The ceasefire after almost six years of honourable battles was agreed on the order of Grand Admiral Dönitz because fighting against the western powers no longer made sense and would only lead . . . to the loss of precious German blood. Resistance to the Soviets, however, will continue in order to protect as many German people as possible from Bolshevist terror.' This kind of talk could only alienate the Soviets, leading them to believe the Western Allies might strike their own deal with the Germans and needed to be contained. Ike's intentions made clear to Bedell Smith, he let his Chief of Staff get on with it.

Walter Bedell Smith had no qualms about facing the Germans down. He had already organized the humanitarian relief in the Netherlands the week before on 30 April, which had necessitated treating with Reichskommisar Arthur Seyss-Inquart, whom he later described as 'another of the iniquitous crew'. Seyss-Inquart was an Austrian Nazi who had laid much of the ground for the Anschluss in 1937, and who then during the war had governed the Netherlands with cruel brutality. Bedell Smith had discussed with this Nazi governor how best to meet the needs of the Dutch population, who were starving after months of being deliberately deprived of food by the Germans: the *Hongerwinter* as the Dutch knew it. Seyss-Inquart had refused Bedell Smith's suggestion that he go further and offer the Allies a surrender in the Netherlands. Seyss-Inquart had quibbled over some of the details regarding dropping food supplies and Bedell Smith found him deeply unsympathetic. 'I wonder', he said, 'if you realize I am giving you your last chance.'

Seyss-Inquart confirmed that he did. 'The consequences', Bedell Smith went on, 'to you yourself will be serious. You know what your acts have been here. You know the feeling of the Dutch people toward you. You know you will probably be shot.' Seyss-Inquart replied, 'That leaves me cold – it usually does.'

Again, as at Lüneburg, Bedell Smith and Strong, translating, had made things as plain as they could to von Friedeburg, and repeated Monty's trick of using maps to lay out the Allied position and exactly how up to their necks in it the Germans were. 'Obviously,' Bedell Smith told him, 'you do not entirely realize the hopelessness of the German situation.' A tearful von Friedeburg pleaded that he was unable to act without consulting his superiors. It was the same old story. A full surrender of the kind the Allies demanded was beyond his remit. That the Commander-in-Chief of the Kriegsmarine had been reduced to errand boy was a mark of the German collapse. He had to send his signal using the Allied cypher, as he had none himself, to Dönitz via 21st Army Group, who in turn passed it on to Flensburg, so his predicament was no secret from SHAEF. The German delegation were billeted in the nearby No. 3, Place Rodinot and waited for Flensburg's reply.

The reply came the following morning. Once more the Dönitz government was incensed by the Allied demand for total surrender. As far as they were concerned there was no way they could ask their men to surrender to the Soviets, regardless of the hopelessness of the military situation. Dönitz decided to send Generaloberst Alfred Jodl, Chief of the Operations Staff of the OKW. He flew to Reims, arriving at 5.30 p.m. His instructions from Dönitz were explicitly to attempt to string the Allies along. 'Try to explain one more time', Dönitz told him, 'the reasons why we strive for a partial capitulation to American forces. If you fail to convince Eisenhower, as Friedeburg did, ask for the following procedures for a total surrender. Two dates are to be arranged. On the first one, fighting will be suspended, but German troops will be allowed to move. That freedom of movement will end on the second date. Try to get the greatest possible span of time between the two dates.'

American patience for such stalling had worn out completely. As Ike still refused to see anyone from the German government, it was left to Bedell Smith to make this crystal-clear to Jodl. Surrender in the west alone was not an option. Jodl then echoed von Friedeburg, who 'looked pretty much the way Jodl did – tired and sick': he couldn't sign for the German Army, the Luftwaffe and the Kriegsmarine; he didn't have the authority, and it would take a day to rustle up the personnel needed to sign the surrender. From his office Ike gave this short shrift, and while his staff wore Jodl down, Ike left the technical college. Rather than wait around, he set off for a Women's Auxiliary Corps cocktail party which Kay Summersby had organized. He didn't stay long; his mood wasn't for small talk or the sight of Soviet officers drinking rye like it was vodka. In the meantime, Strong and Bedell Smith found Jodl to be out of touch with reality: he insisted on explaining to them that soon they would be fighting the Russians and that they'd be better off joining forces with the Germans instead. But his geopolitical advice was falling on deaf ears. Bedell Smith was having none of it. Jodl went further, hoping to divide the British and the Americans, saying to Strong that Germany and Britain needed to stick together as the USA and the USSR were the countries of the future and soon to be dominant. Smith told Jodl, whose posturing had run the clock down into the evening, that he had to accept the terms by midnight. They needed him to sign now, but would allow the Germans forty-eight hours to conform to the terms of the surrender. If they didn't, bombing would resume, and the Americans would refuse to accept German soldiers coming from the east to surrender. The killing would go on. Even on the brink of peace, Ike's decisions revolved around death.

Finally, at 9.45 p.m., Jodl radioed Keitel at Flensburg. Ike's threats via his frontman, Bedell Smith, had landed. Jodl knew he was out of time. His wire read: 'General Eisenhower insists that we sign today; otherwise Allied front will be closed to all those trying to surrender, and negotiations will be discontinued. I see no choice other than chaos or signing. Please send wireless confirmation that I have the authority to sign the surrender. The capitulation can then take effect. Hostilities will end at midnight on May 9, 1945, German summertime.'

Not long after 0.15 a.m., and in a state of outrage at the contents of Jodl's message ('blackmail') and its description of Eisenhower's conditions, the German government nevertheless buckled. Jodl was as loyal a soldier as there could be in the Reich, and as devoted a Nazi too, and if he was sending messages like this, time was clearly up: as noted at the time, Jodl, '[who] earlier had been very opposed to the total capitulation because it was impossible to carry through completely, must have further grim reasons if he now believes it is the only way out'.

Three-quarters of an hour later, Dönitz signalled Jodl that he had authority to sign the larger surrender. In the meantime the SHAEF staff had prepared the 'war room' for the signing of the surrender, with microphones and film cameras standing by, a rather more formal environment than Monty's tent with blankets on the tables. If anything underlined the difference between Monty, the field-based fighting general, and Ike, the coalition diplomat soldier, it was this: a bigger, grander surrender, with a grander stage to match. Twelve chairs were placed round the large table, with a further row behind them along the wall facing the Germans' seats, and plastic-covered maps lined the walls from floor to ceiling. Both Ike and Bedell Smith, nerves frayed with the tension and the late hour, complained that it looked too Hollywood.

The film cameras captured it all, Jodl arriving in a staff car, seemingly caught off guard, receiving salutes, making his way into the college past white-gloved military policemen and a hand-painted sign saying 'Visitors Temporary Passes'. Waiting for Jodl, Bedell Smith and his party smoked cigarettes, joked and posed for the cameras, showing off the pens to be used. The Soviets present looked rather more tense.

The terms were stark, though Jodl, a Hitler man through and through, would sign them in the end.

> ACT OF MILITARY SURRENDER
> 1. We the undersigned, acting by authority of the German High Command, hereby surrender unconditionally to the Supreme Commander, Allied Expeditionary Forces and simultaneously to the Soviet High Command all forces on land, sea and in the air who are at this date under German control.
> 2. The German High Command will at once issue orders to all German military, naval and air authorities and to all forces under German control to cease active operations at 2301 hours Central European time on 8 May and to remain in the positions occupied at that time. No ship, vessel, or aircraft is to be scuttled, or any damage done to their hull, machinery or equipment.

> 3. The German High Command will at once issue to the appropriate commanders, and ensure the carrying out of any further orders issued by the Supreme Commander, Allied Expeditionary Force and by the Soviet High Command.
> 4. This act of military surrender is without prejudice to, and will be superseded by any general instrument of surrender imposed by, or on behalf of the United Nations and applicable to GERMANY and the German armed forces as a whole.
> 5. In the event of the German High Command or any of the forces under their control failing to act in accordance with this Act of Surrender, the Supreme Commander, Allied Expeditionary Force and the Soviet High Command will take such punitive or other action as they deem appropriate.

At 2.30 a.m. on 7 May 1945 the press, officers and men crammed into the war room. But not Ike. He would not sign. He would not look the defeated Germans in the eye. At least not yet.

The German deputation entered, Jodl removing his gloves as he sat down, von Friedeburg sitting to Jodl's left, a solid glass ashtray between them. In the footage the Grossadmiral looks pensive, resigned to yet another admission of defeat. Jodl's countenance is impassive, cold. To Jodl's right is Major Wilhelm Oxenius, Jodl's aide-de-camp, there to translate and assist. The Nazis could say that by fighting to the end they had avoided a repeat of a 1918-style defeat – though soon after the war the generals would get started on positioning themselves as Hitler's unwilling and thwarted experts, let down by the capricious corporal. The Führer, in the last will and testament he had dictated in the bunker before his suicide, had felt otherwise – the German people had, in his view, failed the test he had put them to.

The document was signed at 2.41 a.m., Ike still not present; he paced in his office, the atmosphere one of impatience and untipped Camel smoke. Kay Summersby 'thought it rather lonely and pathetic in the Supreme Commander's office. The silence was heavy with the contrast to the bustle in the War Room.' Making a show of examining the document, and having it pointed out where he had to sign, Jodl signed for the Germans, Walter Bedell Smith witnessing it on Ike's behalf (in sharp contrast to Monty, who had not included his Chief of Staff, Freddie de Guingand, in the signing on the 5th) alongside Général François Sevez for France and General Ivan Susloparov for the Soviets, an interpreter at his side. Susloparov had signed despite there being no word from the Soviet command, the Stavka, that he was authorized to do so; nor had the Stavka replied to approve the text. Nevertheless it was official. Germany was defeated.

But German delusions lingered. Jodl leaned back in his chair and asked, in English, for permission to speak: 'I want to say a word.' He was greeted by stony silence. No one stopped him from speaking, neither did they translate his words then and there. As von Friedeburg looked down the table and Oxenius stared straight ahead, he stood and said his piece, an interpreter leaning in to listen in as he spoke, his hands shaking. He began in English:

> With this signature, the German people and armed forces are, for better or worse, delivered into the victors' hands. [He then switched back into German.] In this war, which has lasted more than five years, both have achieved and

> suffered more than perhaps any other people in the world. In this hour I can only express my hope that the victors will treat them with generosity.

No one replied, for there was nothing to say.

With the surrender signed, it was time for Jodl to meet the Supreme Commander. In the war room cigarettes were lit and champagne was poured into mess tins, but the Germans were now summoned to the headmaster in his office. Kay Summersby watched as they went in. With Ike was his deputy, Air Chief Marshal Sir Arthur Tedder, underlining the Allied effort. Their attitude, even with the surrender signed, was unyielding. They did not exchange pleasantries – Ike was in no mood for generosity. With Strong translating, Eisenhower asked Jodl if he understood the provisions of the surrender; Jodl said '*Ja*'. Ike went on to say: 'You will get details of instructions at a later date. And you will be expected to carry them out faithfully. You will, officially and personally, be held responsible if the terms of this surrender are violated, including its provisions for the German commanders to appear in Berlin at the moment set by the Russian High Command to accomplish formal surrender to that government. That is all.' Jodl, this time, did not try to make a speech and simply said '*Ja*'. With a salute the German party of three left, and as Susloparov entered, Ike allowed himself a smile and a sandwich. His valet, Sergeant Michael McKeogh, remembered saying:

'"This isn't much of a victory meal, sir. But we'll make up for it." The Boss grinned at me. "That's all right," he said. "There's nothing like a fried egg sandwich when a man's hungry."'

Ike and Tedder then went through to the war room and posed with the pens that had been issued to sign the surrender.

Ike spoke, briefly, seriously and intensely for the cameras, Tedder brooding at his side, articulating how he felt about the victory, who had won it and how. 'In January 1943,' he began,

> Late president Roosevelt and Premier Churchill met in Casablanca. There they pronounced the formula for unconditional surrender for the Axis Powers. In Europe that formula has now been fulfilled, the Allied force which invaded Europe on June sixth 1944 has with its great Russian allies and forces advancing from the south clearly defeated the Germans by land, sea and air. This unconditional surrender has been achieved by team work. Team work not only among all the Allies participating but all the services, land, sea and air. To every subordinate of this command of almost five million allies I owe a debt of gratitude that can never be repaid. The only repayment that can be made to them is a deep appreciation and lasting gratitude of all free citizens of all the United Nations.

Ike drank his champagne, drew on his ever-present cigarette and posed with the two pens; but for him the champagne reflected the occasion – it was flat. There was no pleasure in victory, no triumph in the German surrender. He felt there was little to celebrate. He even needed reminding that it was not an armistice, that the Germans were laying down their arms unconditionally. But the burden of command was something far harder to give up.

And besides, it was now time for Stalin to get what he wanted.

GUINNESS
IS GOO
TO

CHAPTER 7

VE DAY

Twenty-four Hours in London, *8 May 1945*

The unconditional surrender of our enemies was the signal for the greatest outburst of joy in the history of mankind.

Winston Churchill

On 7 May in London the British Prime Minister, Winston Churchill, was woken with the news of the surrenders earlier that morning in Reims: Jodl had signed on behalf of the Flensburg government at 2.41 a.m. Delivering the news was Captain Richard Pim, head of the map room. Churchill looked at the document and initialled it. This was the news he had been waiting so long for. He teased Pim that finally he had made up for years of bringing him bad news by delivering the best news of the war. Celebrations, though, would have to wait – a decision was made that 8 May would be 'Victory in Europe Day', rather than as the BBC had po-facedly decided 'Ceasefire Day'. Even with unfinished business in the Far East, this was bigger than any ceasefire; Churchill would have his victory.

The news was impossible to contain – the Ministry of Information told the public at 7.40 p.m. that a formal announcement of the victory would be made the next day by the Prime Minister. That said, the shooting hadn't yet stopped. The Kriegsmarine took it upon itself to sink two ships off the Firth of Forth, the Norwegian *Sneland I* and the Canadian *Avondale Park*. Nine merchant seamen were killed by U-2336, the last maritime deaths in the western theatre, drawing out the pointless killing to the very last.

Nevertheless, a national holiday was declared for 8 May. Knowing that the moment was approaching, the government made sure that the Ministry of Food had sufficient beer for the impending celebrations. Licensing hours were extended – though this conjures up the notion that they could somehow be enforced on such a day. The ministry had prepared for VE Day, instructing shops on how long they should open, reassuring people that milk would be delivered as usual and that bakers should bake enough bread for the following day. Government departments received the code words 'Mousetrap: noon tomorrow' to alert them to it being official.

For Churchill, news of the surrenders in Europe might not have marked the end, but it was certainly the beginning of the end. His government, thrown together in the turmoil of the mad summer of 1940, was approaching its finishing line, one way or another. Democratic politics had been suspended for the duration. Winning the war meant that Churchill and his coalition had achieved their aim and an election must follow; democracy could no longer be suspended. An exhausted country would face its new destiny, and moreover not wait until the war in the Far East had ended. In reality, Churchill needed the end to come. He was exhausted. Seventy years old, pummelled by the relentless round of travel, committee meetings, briefings, high-stakes decision-making and for a long time, as he had joked on the morning of 7 May, bad news, he had already been troubled by near-fatal pneumonia a couple of years previously. His lifestyle didn't exactly help either, as he drank and smoked his way through the toughest of times. Reflecting on VE Day, he said that it 'may well be there were few whose hearts were more heavily burdened with anxiety than mine'.

The Prime Minister's doctor, Lord Moran, who saw him more closely than any, considered that Churchill was done: 'the PM does not seem at all excited about the end of the war'. By the PM's own account he was 'very tired and physically so feeble that I had to be carried upstairs in a chair by the Marines from the Cabinet meetings under the Annexe'. Staying up later and later at night, not completing his paperwork, he now preferred to remain in bed and eat on his own, a sure sign that a man so convivial was out of sorts. VE Day would be another hectic day in the war for the PM, but one at least of celebration. It would be a long day, and marked out in speeches. If words had been one of Winston Churchill's most powerful weapons of war, he was going to wield them today for almost the last time.

Celebrations had begun on the evening of the 7th and went into the early morning of the 8th – at 2 a.m. ships in Southampton Docks sounded air horns and a searchlight flashed V for Victory. People made plans to go into London and join the revels. The newspaper headlines were boisterous. The *Daily Telegraph* proclaimed: 'Germany Capitulates', the *Daily Mirror* went with 'VE-DAY! It's Over in Europe', the *Daily Mail* with 'VE-DAY – It's All Over'. The *Mail* explained that the Prime Minister had 'put off the big speech until today'; though oblivious to Soviet machination around the date of the surrender, it also had the good news that 13,000 prisoners of war would be returning, flown back in Lancasters. Local papers too ran with the only story they could. The *Scarborough Evening News* opted for 'War in Europe Is Over'. The *Hull Daily Mail*'s broadsheet front page was populated with 'History Victory Announcement . . . Hull Celebrates VE-Day . . . The Nightmare Has Lost its Grip – World Wide VE Day rejoicing', with news from Sydney and Melbourne. It also offered its readers the nuts and bolts of the celebrations: 'VE-DAY + ONE: Public Holiday'.

The newspapers were also allowed, for the first time since war had been declared, to run a weather forecast. Weather forecasting had been a top-secret enterprise up to this point, something upon which the fate of nations, of invasions, of bombing raids and air defence hung. VE Day lifted such secrecy. The first forecast since September 1939 predicted rain for the afternoon. Fortunately it was wrong and a fine day followed, with sunshine – the 'King's weather'.

On the train on their way into London were Land Army friends Cynthia Covello and Joyce Digney. On the 7th, inspired by pictures of Armistice Day celebrations from the end of the Great War, they had decided to come up to town from Surrey and join the crowds. Places of worship, understandably, became a focus as the day progressed. People had started to make their way to St Paul's Cathedral and Westminster Abbey to informal thanksgiving services. Cynthia and Joyce made St Paul's their first stop – there they said prayers for the friends and family they had lost during the war. The cathedral was turning over the crowds in quick order, getting through twenty services in succession. A major service was held at noon, with the Lord Mayor of London in attendance, and broadcast live on the BBC. HMV later offered souvenir recordings for purchase.

If anywhere symbolized London's defiance and survival it was St Paul's, standing as it did in a sea of ruin, the bombs of the Blitz having fallen all around it yet somehow miraculously spared it. With peace in Europe the cathedral would be threatened from the skies no more. None the less, the Dean made sure he didn't forget people still fighting in the Far East, reading intercessions for them too. Canon Alexander, reading the lesson, took on the tone of victory, the Song of Moses offering the kind of rhetoric that suited the success the Allies had achieved in the west: 'The enemy said, I will pursue, I will overtake, I will divide the spoil; my lust shall be satisfied upon them; I will draw my sword, my hand shall destroy them. Thou didst blow with thy wind, the sea covered them: they sank as lead in the mighty waters.' After their service, Cynthia and Joyce went up west to go on the razz and celebrate. Joyce later wrote to Cynthia's family depicting the scene: 'We walked all over London, and unless you were there, you could not believe the euphoria; hugs, kisses, smiles and laughter. It was like a gigantic family coming together.'

Outside London, the pattern was similar. Canterbury Cathedral was packed with 5,000 people at 10 a.m., standing shoulder to shoulder for a service of thanksgiving and prayers. With the Archbishop and the Dean away in London, the Bishop of Dover gave the blessing; at St Albans Cathedral a service in the evening at seven o'clock was crammed with children. But it was to be London and Churchill that became the focus of the day.

Absent from London and unable to join Churchill in the celebrations was his wife Clementine, who was in Moscow with the British Red Cross. As chair of the Aid to Russia Fund she was on a tour of the Soviet Union. She sent a telegram to her husband which reached Downing Street at 10.45 a.m., congratulating him on 'this supreme day' and saying that it could not have happened without him.

A quarter of an hour later the cast of *Brief Encounter* were told they had the day off – the cameras were leaving Denham Studios to capture the extraordinary events in London. At Buckingham Palace a semblance of business as usual remained: the Guard, known as the Westminster Garrison Battalion and made up of men from the different Foot Guard regiments who had medical reasons not to be posted overseas, changed at 11.00 a.m. (though in khaki rather than their parade uniforms), with the Irish Guards taking their place. Of all the days to be in uniform and on duty! Inside the palace, in the ballroom, the King was holding an investiture, awarding medals to over 270 recipients. The Prime Minister was expected for lunch.

At the Savoy Hotel, ever a bastion of luxury despite the strictures of war, they did not wait until lunchtime to start serving a VE Day-themed lunch. From 11.30 a.m. patrons could sit down to enjoy a menu which featured La Coupe Glacée des Alliés and La Citronette Joyeuse Déliverances. Noël Coward, the playwright and film star, lived at the Savoy, having been bombed out earlier in the war. He did what pretty much everyone else did that day. He joined the throng, listened to the speeches and found himself deeply moved by public feeling.

Meanwhile Joyce and Cynthia had found their way through the crowds to the Chandos pub at the end of St Martin's Lane, where demand was so high the staff were not bothering to wash up the glasses. The girls had to scrounge glasses off people who had finished their drinks.

Among the communication traffic at Downing Street was a message at noon from Harry S. Truman, the new US President. He had inherited the special relationship from his predecessor, and in the torrid weeks since FDR's death had been on a crash course in international and Allied relations. 'With warm affection, we hail our comrades-in-arms across the Atlantic.' Such a message was hard to get wrong, even for a novice. Churchill would reply the following day with boilerplate Churchillese: 'Your message is cherished by the British nation, and will be regarded as if it were a battle honour by all his Majesty's Armed Forces, of all the races in all the lands . . . All were together heart and soul. I express to you our admiration for the firm, far-sighted and illuminating character and qualities of General of the US Army Eisenhower.'

Over lunchtime the crowds had continued to grow in the city centre. Mass Observation was there to keep tabs on them, its observers compiling their impressions of events and what they had heard around them, eavesdropping in places like pubs or simply keeping their ears open to nearby voices. It had been put together before the war by a trio of like-minded left-wing activists: Tom Harrisson from Bolton, an anthropologist, the South African-born but Winchester College- and Magdalene College, Cambridge-educated surrealist poet Charles Madge, who had been a Communist between the wars, and the film-maker Humphrey Jennings, who went on to make *London Can Take It*, the Blitz-resisting propaganda film that had played so well in the USA in 1940. Mass Observation was unique; it was pioneering work, predating and predicting the kind of public opinion polling or market research we take for granted now. The idea was to offer a window into people's feelings, and thanks to MO events like the Abdication Crisis of 1936 can be seen from the bottom up. The contributors remained anonymous and the results they published were paid for out of their own pockets. By the end of the war MO had become one of the Ministry of Information's barometers of public mood, regarded by some as offering a better reading than government sources.

One of the MO observers, doubtless present with a sense of watchful detachment, reported: 'Moved towards Trafalgar Sq. The fountains are playing, and music is being relayed over the loudspeaker. The Sq. is littered with paper and wood and Inv. Counts 10 bottles. 9 land girls, arm in arm, 4 wearing paper hats skip by St. Martin in the Field singing. There is the sound of bells.' Another noted: 'There were crowds of people and everybody seemed to be on good terms with one another. People were walking along the streets arm in arm, singing and shouting at the top of their voices. Soldiers were shaking hands and talking to people they had apparently never seen before. It was a good feeling to be in a crowd again.' And at Piccadilly Circus: 'Crowds round bonfire, much shouting and singing. It is impossible to see much of the fire because of the denseness of the crowd, but flags move in a circular way indicating that people immediately nearest must be dancing around fast.'

MO contributors were also prone to offering their own opinions. Diarist 5331, Kathleen Hay, a shop assistant from Dewsbury, wrote: 'Listened to the King and everything. Struck by stress on ourselves and America and lack of praise of Russia. Margaret said again and Zillah agreed that we were celebrating too soon. Walked home at 10 and watched the bonfires – it was now dry – and amazed by the beautiful fireworks . . . Home with mixed feelings. Relief, yes, but also foreboding in my heart. Margaret said she wouldn't be surprised if the fighting flared up again.'

At Trafalgar Square there was a cacophony of noise: music relayed over loudspeakers, church bells ringing out and groups of women bursting into song. The square became littered with wood, paper and bottles. Those celebrating were making the most of it. A conga line snaked round the base of Nelson's Column. The threatened rain had not come, and it was warm, so once they'd left the Chandos, Cynthia and Joyce decided to cool off in the fountain, taking off their shoes and rolling up their trousers. Two sailors joined them – one of them dived into the fountain and dragged Joyce into the water – she was furious, shouting at the matelot and then dunking him. They were captured on film, Joyce's yellow jumper as bright as her smile. They dried off at a bonfire near Waterloo Station and caught the train back to Surrey.

Churchill's speech was yet to come. At 1 p.m. he had been to the palace for lunch, where the King and the Prime Minister had congratulated each other on the end of the war in Europe; meanwhile at the Cabinet Room the BBC crew were putting equipment in place for his broadcast. At 2.30 Churchill berated the engineer and seems to have blown his nose by way of a soundcheck. The BBC had got into the mood properly, with Allied flags at Broadcasting House, and like much of the capital the Corporation had made the most of the end of the blackout – the building was floodlit too. To follow the PM's speech the BBC had prepared a sequence of celebratory programmes. But this was Churchill's moment alone – his chance to define the victory on his own rhetorical terms.

At 3 p.m., after a fanfare, he began with the formalities:

> Yesterday morning, at 2.41 a.m., at Headquarters, General Jodl, the representative of the German High Command, and Grand Admiral Doenitz, the designated head of the German State, signed the act of unconditional surrender of all German land, sea, and air forces in Europe to the Allied Expeditionary Force, and simultaneously to the Soviet High Command. General Bedell Smith, Chief of Staff of the Allied Expeditionary Force, and General François Sevez signed the document on behalf of the Supreme Commander of the Allied Expeditionary Force,

> and General Susloparov signed on behalf of the Russian High Command.

That he omitted Alexander's and Montgomery's surrenders in Italy and Germany suggests that Churchill, even when addressing the British public, had his eye to his international partners rather than to national prestige. This broadcast was for global consumption, and he had already had a bellyful of Stalin's complaining. He went on:

> To-day this agreement will be ratified and confirmed at Berlin, where Air Chief Marshal Tedder, Deputy Supreme Commander of the Allied Expeditionary Force, and General de Lattre de Tassigny will sign on behalf of General Eisenhower. Marshal Zhukov will sign on behalf of the Soviet High Command. The German representatives will be Field Marshal Keitel, Chief of the High Command, and the Commanders-in-Chief of the German Army, Navy, and Air Forces.
>
> Hostilities will end officially at one minute after midnight to-night (Tuesday, the 8th of May), but in the interests of saving lives the 'Cease fire' began yesterday to be sounded all along the front, and our dear Channel Islands are also to be freed to-day. [A huge cheer greeted this.]
>
> The Germans are still in places resisting the Russian troops, but should they continue to do so after midnight they will, of course, deprive themselves of the protection of the laws of war, and will be attacked from all quarters by the Allied troops.

> It is not surprising that on such long fronts and in the existing disorder of the enemy the commands of the German High Command should not in every case be obeyed immediately. This does not, in our opinion, with the best military advice at our disposal, constitute any reason for withholding from the nation the facts communicated to us by General Eisenhower of the unconditional surrender already signed at Rheims, nor should it prevent us from celebrating to-day and to-morrow (Wednesday) as Victory in Europe days.

At this stage, with so many lives spent needlessly as the Germans had prevaricated and failed to face reality, Churchill's position made perfect sense. There was celebrating to be done, but more work too.

> Today, perhaps, we shall think mostly of ourselves. Tomorrow we shall pay a particular tribute to the . . . our heroic Russian comrades, whose prowess in the field has been one of the grand contributions to the general victory. The German war is therefore at an end.
>
> After years of intense preparation, Germany hurled herself on Poland at the beginning of September, 1939; and, in pursuance of our guarantee to Poland and in common with the French Republic, Great Britain, the British Empire and Commonwealth of Nations, declared war upon this foul aggression.

The guarantee to Poland, like Banquo's ghost, was a tawdry reminder of how Poland had already been sold out to the

Soviets. Churchill then, revealingly, as the old imperial strategist he was, resisted the urge to say that Britain had fought alone; that was a narrative for later and for others. This victory had been a British, imperial and Allied effort. The 'we' was imperial:

> After gallant France had been struck down, we, from this Island and from our united Empire, maintained the struggle single-handed for a whole year until we were joined by the military might of Soviet Russia, and later by the overwhelming power and resources of the United States of America.
>
> Finally almost the whole world was combined against the evil-doers, who are now prostrate before us. Our gratitude to all our splendid Allies goes forth from all our hearts in this Island and throughout the British Empire. We may allow ourselves a brief period of rejoicing; but let us not forget for a moment the toils and efforts that lie ahead. Japan, with all her treachery and greed, remains unsubdued. The injury she has inflicted on Great Britain, the United States, and other countries, and her detestable cruelties, call for justice and retribution.
>
> We must now devote all our strength and resources to the completion of our task, both at home and abroad. Advance, Britannia! [His voice broke as he declared this.] Long live the cause of freedom! God save the King!

God Save the King! With the broadcast out of the way, Churchill set off for the Commons in an open-top car, standing on the front seat, shaking hands, as the car trickled forward through the hordes of people, pushed not by its engine but by the crowd.

Above: (**left**) One of the last photos of Hitler, taken on 19 April 1945; (**right**) The sofa in the Führerbunker on which Hitler killed himself on the afternoon of 30 April 1945.

Above: The charred remains of Hitler and his new wife, Eva, were discovered lightly buried at the bottom of this shell crater on 4 May, although it was not until a day later that it dawned on SMERSH agents that one of bodies was that of the former Führer.

Left: The Goebbels family. At the back is Harald Quandt, Magda Goebbels' son from her first marriage. He survived the war, but the six children she bore with Josef were all murdered by her and her husband in the Führerbunker.

Above: (**left**) Karl Wolff, left, with Himmler, right, a photo taken before the war when the SS still wore black; (**right**) The first unconditional surrender of German forces was in Italy at Allied HQ in Caserta on the afternoon of 29 April 1945. Victor von Schweinitz signs as Eugen Werner watches on.

Right: It's all smiles after the war in Italy was over. Karl Wolff (far right) invited one of the negotiators, the German-American businessman Gero von Schulze-Gaevernitz (centre left), to visit him and he duly arrived in Bolzano on 9 May 1945. Centre right is Heinrich von Vietinghoff.

Karl Wolff's insurance: Italy's art treasures being safely recovered from the police station in the tiny Alpine village of San Leonardo.

Above: Montgomery signing the surrender on the Lüneburg Heath, 4 May 1945.

Right: The link-up of British and Soviet forces near Wismar on the Baltic coast, 3 May 1945.

Below right: Montgomery (left) with his patron and shield, the Chief of the Imperial General Staff, Sir Alan Brooke.

Below: John Poston (left) with Carol Mather (right) and friend in Brussels early in 1945. Monty's liaison officers were his eyes and ears on the battlefield and served as a substitute family.

Left: An American Sherman tank picks its way through the ruins of Nuremberg, the scene of the Nazi rallies of the 1930s.

Below: American troops of the 71st Infantry Division reaching the Gunskirchen concentration camp. It was here that Hugo Gryn and his father were finally liberated.

Below: (**left**) Troops of the 7th Infantry, part of the 3rd Infantry Division, pass through the heart of Berchtesgaden; (**right**) 'We fight for the future of our children.' An American soldier gazes up at this utterly delusional graffiti.

Right: Alfred Jodl signs the unconditional surrender of all German forces at Reims on the morning of 7 May 1945, ending the war in Europe. Jodl had done all he could to delay the inevitable and avoid facing the reality of Germany's situation.

Below: Kay Summersby, Eisenhower's personal chauffeur.

Above and below: Celebrations in Trafalgar Square and crowds at Piccadilly Circus.

Above: **(left)** Truman is sworn in as President, 12 April 1945; **(right)** President Truman's muted VE Day address, 8 May 1945 – his sixty-first birthday.

Left: Berlin civilians confronting the reality of a shattered city now swarming with Red Army troops.

Below left: The Soviet flag was first raised over the Reichstag at 10 p.m. on 30 April. This famous photo, however, was taken on 2 May.

Below right: Wilhelm Keitel signs the final surrender documents to the Soviets at Karlshorst, a suburb of south Berlin, in the early hours of 9 May 1945. It was the moment when the war in Europe was irrefutably at an end.

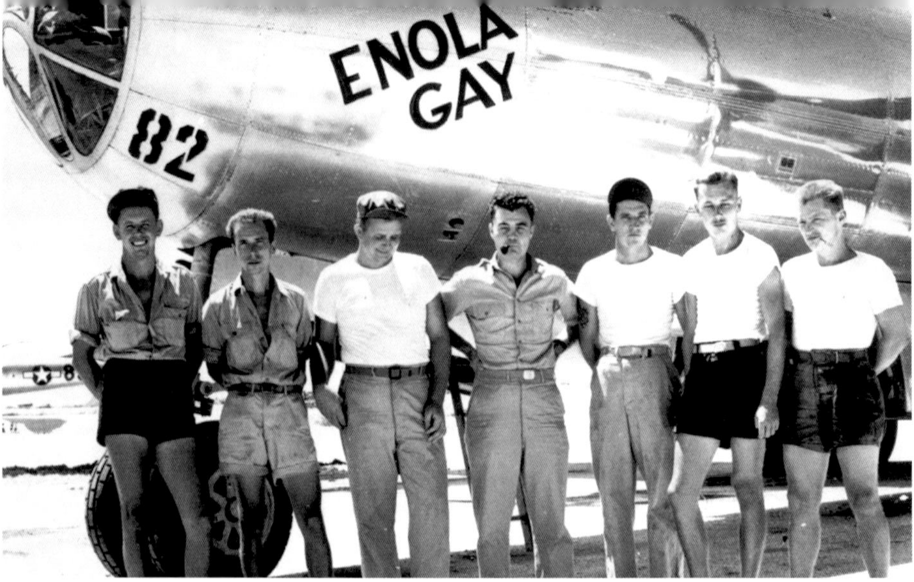

Above: The crew of the *Enola Gay*, who dropped the atomic bomb on Hiroshima on 6 August 1945. The captain and pilot, Colonel Paul Tibbets, is in the centre with pipe.

Below: The flattened remains of Hiroshima after the bomb. A new age had dawned. Even so, the Japanese government was in a state of denial.

Far left: Japanese coup leader Kenji Hatanaka.

Left: Japanese War Minister Korechika Anami.

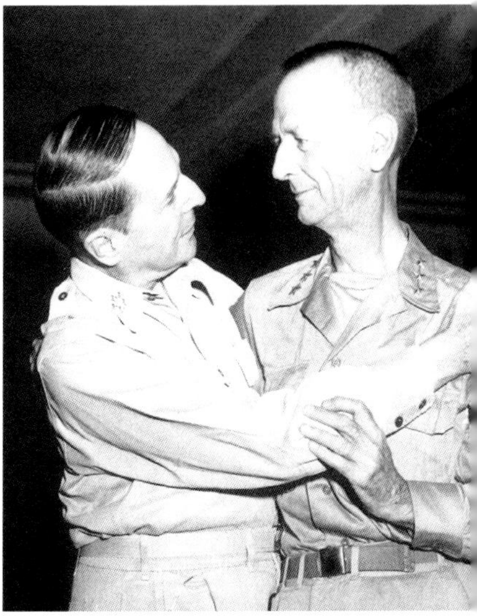

Above: (left) MacArthur with the Emperor-god, Hirohito, diminutive and diminished but still ruling – the condition of an unconditional surrender. The Emperor had submitted to the profane and in doing so saved his skin. **(right)** MacArthur reunited with an emaciated Jonathan Wainwright, 30 August 1945.

Above: Japanese representatives on USS *Missouri*.

Left: Fly-past over Tokyo Bay, 2 September 1945.

Listening was former diplomat, author and National Labour MP Harold Nicolson. A Churchill devotee, Nicolson may have been an MP since 1935, and living a louche life in his notoriously open marriage with Bloomsbury Set muse and author Vita Sackville-West, but he was the youngest son of the 1st Baron Carnock, had been to Wellington College and Balliol College, Oxford ('the best of both the plutocratic and the bohemian', as he put it) and knew what was U and what was non-U. Appalled at the sight of three Guardsmen wearing paper hats with their uniforms, he had eaten lunch at the Beefsteak Club in Irving Street, round the corner from Trafalgar Square. Big Ben struck three and then Churchill's voice cut through the sudden hush from the speakers in the Square. The atmosphere was electric as Churchill cried, 'Advance, Britannia!' The crowd broke into cheers when the broadcast ended and Nicolson headed to the Commons to hear Churchill speak again.

At the same time Lord Moran, Churchill's doctor, was listening; he had gone to the House of Lords Library to hear the broadcast. He liked the rhetoric, coming as it did from a man of letters, though he found the 'Advance, Britannia!' a little tinny for his liking. 'The peer next to me, I could not put a name to him, for all sorts of unfamiliar faces turned up for the occasion, thought it strange there was no allusion in the speech to God.' Moran, knowing the patient well, felt there was no doubt in Churchill's mind 'to whom the credit was due'.

Clementine Churchill immediately sent a telegram from Moscow congratulating him on the speech. With her was the former French Prime Minister Édouard Herriot, who had been liberated by the Soviets a few days earlier after years of internment. He confessed that he had wept at the sound of her husband's voice, which he had last heard during the climax of the Battle of France in the summer of 1940. The end of the war was tying up loose ends even as it birthed a new world.

Churchill entered the Chamber to a hullabaloo, MPs rising as one to welcome him, waving their order papers. The Commons had been the scene of some of Churchill's toughest and most exposed political moments. When he had first become Prime Minister on 10 May 1940 he had refused to be Leader of the Conservative Party, alienated as he was from the Tory rank and file after years of politicking against the leadership in the 1930s. In the darkest days of the war, the debates had been as intense as the suspended state of democracy could allow and he had still had to see off motions of no confidence. Indeed, the debate of 1–2 July which followed the fall of Tobruk and the end of the disastrous Gazala lines battles in the desert saw some of the bitterest criticism of Churchill's government. Arguments had been raised about the conduct of the war, and the War Office's failure to deliver the equipment the country needed to win was all aired. His predecessor had fallen over far less: the failure of the campaign in Norway in April 1940 was small beer compared to the repeated disasters – Greece, Crete, Singapore, Tobruk – that had befallen the British and imperial war effort by mid-1942. The Tory Party could, and would, turn on prime ministers, even ones who had won a general election, something Churchill had never done. But all of this was behind him now as he rose to speak at the dispatch box.

At some pace he repeated the speech he had made in his broadcast, but added extra paragraphs for the Commons. He sought to flatter the House, telling the assembled MPs that it was the 'strongest foundation for waging war that has ever been seen in the whole of our long history'. He even affected rare modesty: 'We have all of us made our mistakes, but the strength of the Parliamentary institutions has been maintained under the fire of the enemy.' This was Parliament's victory, and he, somewhat self-consciously as the great Parliamentarian, was claiming it for the House and for himself. He then recalled how, at the end of the previous war, the Commons, rather than debating, had gone to give thanks. As Harold Nicolson wrote that night: 'Winston then proposed that the House attend St Margaret's Church to give thanks for the country's deliverance. The Serjeant at Arms put the mace on his shoulder and, following the Speaker, we all strode out . . . into the sunshine of Parliament Square.'

The Lords had assembled at Westminster Abbey at around 3.30 p.m., Black Rod leading the procession, with Lord Addison representing the Labour peers and Lord Samuel the Liberals. The Archbishop of Canterbury led 200 peers into the abbey and the Dean read an adapted version of Lincoln's 1865 inauguration address, asking God to bind up the nation's wounds. But it was the MPs of the Commons who drew the crowds.

As they started arriving at St Margaret's on foot the crowd went wild, thousands cheering and hollering, blowing whistles and ringing bells. The Speaker led them into the church, following the mace held by the Serjeant at Arms. A war of modernity that had seen the leap from biplanes to jet planes, radar and electronic warfare and the invention of the computer, and soon the delivery of the atomic bomb, was having its final stages acted out in ancient pomp and tradition. Churchill and Arthur Greenwood, Leader of the Opposition, followed the Speaker and sat at the front. The Cabinet came next. Many of the MPs were in uniform. They sang the national anthem and Psalm 124:7. The Dean then read out the names of the twenty-one MPs who had been killed during the war, from Allen Apsley, a Lieutenant-Colonel in the Glosters, killed in Malta in 1942, to Arnold Wilson, an air gunner in the RAF Volunteer Reserve who had died in 1940. MPs had perished in all the theatres of war, at sea and in combat. One, Flight Lieutenant John Rathbone, who had been an air gunner, had been killed on a bombing raid. Two others, Robert Bernays and John Campbell, had died together in a plane crash over the Adriatic. If this was a people's war, then they were, in this sense, true representatives of the people. Harold Nicolson wept as the names were read out. They are commemorated now in the Palace of Westminster with coats of arms. The MPs sang heartily and meaningfully 'Oh God Our Help in Ages Past' and, with a blessing, retired back to the Commons, the Speaker again leading them. Churchill gave the V for Victory signs as he went, ruffling the hair of boys in the crowd before he headed for the Smoking Room.

Once parliamentary business was finally done, Churchill made for Buckingham Palace again. The Royal Family had been putting the balcony to good use, appearing eight times over ten hours, waving to the assembled crowds. Churchill took a bow with the King, Queen and Princesses Elizabeth and Margaret, the former in her uniform. In the rush to get there Churchill had forgotten to bring a cigar – he sent his bodyguard back, knowing that the crowd expected him to have one.

Almost whack-a-mole style, Churchill started to pop up all over Whitehall, moving from location to location. At 5.40 p.m. he spoke from the balcony of what was then the Ministry of Health, accompanied by the Cabinet, telling the crowds that the victory did not belong to a party or a class: 'it's a victory of the Great British nation as a whole'. To his claim that it was their victory they shouted back, 'No, it's yours!' In this speech, which was not being broadcast, Churchill referred to Britain as being 'all alone for a whole year'; this was not an imperial or Allied framing of the war. This was England. He went on, playing the crowd, playing the hits:

> There we stood, alone. Did anyone want to give in? [Shouts of 'No!'] Were we down-hearted? ['No!'] The lights went out and the bombs came down. But every man, woman and child in the country had no thought of quitting the struggle. London can take it. So we came back after long months from the jaws of death, out of the mouth of hell, while all the world wondered. When shall the reputation and faith of this generation of English men and women fail?

Churchill's rhetoric, which for much of his life had been concerned with grand historic themes, with the path of destiny, could not but feast on the moment presented to him. Whether he was improvising or had been percolating these phrases for years, he went with the mood.

> I say that in the long years to come not only will the people of this island but of the world, wherever the bird of freedom chirps in human hearts, look back to what we've done, and they will say 'Do not despair, do not yield to violence and tyranny, march straight forward and die if need be – unconquered.' Now we have emerged from one deadly struggle – a terrible foe has been cast on the ground and awaits our judgment and our mercy.

But Japan remained.

> But there is another foe who occupies large portions of the British Empire, a foe stained with cruelty and greed – the Japanese. I rejoice we can all take a night off today and another day tomorrow. Tomorrow our great Russian allies will also be celebrating victory and after that we must begin the task of rebuilding our health and homes, doing our utmost to make this country a land in which all have a chance, in which all have a duty, and we must turn ourselves to fulfil our duty to our own countrymen, and to our gallant allies of the United States who were so foully and treacherously attacked by Japan. We will go hand and hand with them. Even if it is a hard struggle we will not be the ones who will fail.

Mention of the Japanese drew booing. They were, after all, spoiling the party. Ernest Bevin, the Minister of Labour, called for three cheers. An acknowledgement, maybe, that soon normal politics would resume and the Labour Party would be centre-stage.

At 6 p.m. the King addressed the country on the radio, the speech also being relayed on speakers. He had asked Churchill to look over it when Winston had come to the palace earlier; when it came to public speaking, both had to overcome a stammer. Millions listened as the King thanked 'Almighty God for a great deliverance. Speaking from our Empire's oldest capital city, war-battered but never for one moment daunted or dismayed.' He acknowledged that the Japanese were yet to be dealt with, but for now, 'when the dreadful shadow of war has passed from our hearths and homes in these islands, we may at last make one pause for thanksgiving and then turn our thoughts to the tasks all over the world which peace in Europe brings with it.' The King remembered those the country had lost:

> Let us remember those who will not come back, their constancy and courage in battle, their sacrifice and endurance in the face of a merciless enemy: let us remember the men in all the Services and the women in all the Services who have laid down their lives. We have come to the end of our tribulation, and they are not with us at the moment of our rejoicing.

The King spoke of Empire and Commonwealth, reflecting the difference in his role from that of the Prime Minister, how he was above diplomacy and could be little concerned with keeping Stalin onside. God and faith, our strength and shield, Empire and Commonwealth, just triumph and proud sorrow – these were the King's expressions of the day.

With the speech completed, the Royal Family took to the balcony again, the crowds roaring their approval amid a sea of waving Union Jacks. Churchill's duties, however, continued with him drafting a telegram to his wife that she would read on Radio Moscow passing on his best wishes to the Soviet people. It is unclear whether it ever went out, but it looked optimistically to a future of cooperation between the British and Russian peoples, upon which the world depended. He then went for dinner with his daughters Sarah and Diana, as well as the latter's husband, Duncan Sandys, Minister of Works, and the press baron Lord Camrose. Sandys had been intimately involved in tank design development as secretary to the chief engineer of tank design, and would have understood some of the bruising Churchill had taken in the Commons regarding the inadequacy of British tank production. They could forget about that now.

Noël Coward mingled with the crowds. He walked down the Mall and stood among countless others outside Buckingham Palace. The 'crowd was stupendous. The King and Queen came out on the balcony, looking enchanting. We all roared ourselves hoarse. After that I went to Chips Channon's "open house" party which wasn't up to much.' Harold Nicolson was also at Channon's party. The American-born Conservative MP Henry 'Chips' Channon had been a more than enthusiastic appeaser – his attitude before the war towards Germany and the direction the Nazi Party was taking it in could best be described as sympatico. When he got home, Nicolson wrote bitterly: 'I wish I had not gone to that party. The Amalienburg room is lit by candles and all the Nürembergers and Munichois were there. I sit with Sibyl and Ivor Novello and get away fairly soon.' Noël Coward walked home to the Savoy with Ivor Novello: 'I suppose this is the greatest day in our history.'

The revelry continued into the night. Couples had sex in Green Park and a bonfire made up of deckchairs and park benches, passed along by the crowd in a human chain, burned into the night as people enjoyed the end of the blackout. There were other famous faces in the crowd: the Royal Princesses had been allowed out into the capital by the King and Queen in a group of sixteen trusted household members – including Group Captain Peter Townsend, with whom Margaret would later have a scandalous affair.

Terrified of being recognized, Elizabeth pulled her cap down over her eyes. She told the BBC decades later: 'A Grenadier officer among our party said he refused to be seen in the company of another officer improperly dressed. So I had to put my cap on normally.' The Princesses joined a conga outside the Ritz, then returned to the palace and watched their parents on the balcony from below, though they had cheated 'slightly by sending a message into the house, saying we were there'. Lady-in-waiting Jean Woodroffe was stunned by her encounter with the British people in full-flow revelry:

> There were places like Green Park and St James's which one would never have walked through at night in the war – and there we were. There was the usual thing of people kissing and hugging – and even making love. I was shocked by it – I hadn't experienced that sort of thing happening before in public.

The Princesses and their many chaperones eventually made their way back to the palace, just another few faces in the massive crowd. The parties went on into the night. Reports came from Edinburgh that the city had run out of beer.

At Downing Street people were perhaps already a little jaded – a telegram to the British chargé d'affaires in Moscow read: 'We are utterly indifferent to anything the Soviets say by way of propaganda. No one here believes a single word.'

The 8th of May had been the British people's and Winston Churchill's day. The next, the 9th, would be Stalin's.

CHAPTER 8

HAPPY BIRTHDAY, MR PRESIDENT

VE Day in America,
8 May 1945

We can repay the debt which we owe to our God, to our dead, and to our children, only by work, by ceaseless devotion to the responsibilities which lie ahead of us. If I could give you a single watchword for the coming months, that word is work, work, and more work. We must work to finish the war. Our victory is only half over.

President Harry S. Truman, 8 May 1945

It was around 3 a.m. on the morning of 7 May that General Sir Hastings Ismay, Churchill's chief staff officer and military advisor, was woken by the telephone beside his bed. The Supreme Allied Commander, came a crackled voice, was on the line. Ismay had experienced a number of such nocturnal calls during the war and they never brought good news, so he wondered what possible further setback had now taken place.

'Is that you, Pug?' came Eisenhower's voice.

'Yes, Ike. What has happened?'

'They have signed on the dotted line. It's all over.'

Ismay's wife had heard Eisenhower's words and her eyes filled with tears. Ismay felt a lump in his throat too. But having passed on his congratulations, he then thought he should tell Churchill; in the excitement of the moment he'd forgotten to ask Eisenhower whether he intended to call the Prime Minister. Unfortunately his line was already dead, so he had to collect a few coins, put on his dressing gown and slippers and walk 100 yards down the road to the nearest call box. He swiftly got through, to be told that Churchill had just been informed. Ismay returned to bed, but sleep eluded him. 'It was impossible to be completely happy about the future,' he noted. 'Japan was still unconquered; and apart from that, there was no certainty that we would not again have to fight for our lives in Europe before many years had passed.'

Ismay did eventually get back to sleep, dreaming of grappling an enormous bear, but none the less presented himself later that morning at No. 10 Downing Street. Ismay had arrived expecting the announcement to be made almost at once, although he then learned that Eisenhower had suggested telling the world at 6 p.m. London time, which would allow it to be made at a decent hour in the Soviet Union, across Europe and throughout the United States. It would also give the Germans time to order all further hostilities to cease. Churchill saw no reason why either Truman or Stalin would disagree, and so told the British Chiefs of Staff and War Cabinet to be ready to appear on the balcony of Buckingham Palace at 6.30 that evening. He also began preparing a victory speech.

Not for the first time, however, Stalin then began throwing his weight around and insisting that the Soviet Union maintain the narrative of surrender. The Germans might have capitulated to the Allies in Reims but they hadn't done so to the Red Army. There could be no announcement, Stalin insisted, until the Germans had formally capitulated to Marshal Zhukov in Berlin. Telegrams sped back and forth. Stalin maintained that there was no sign of the Germans slackening the fight on the Red Army's front – which was not really true – and so proposed delaying the official instrument of surrender until it was signed in Berlin at one minute after midnight on 9 May. It would then be announced to the world at 7 a.m. the same day.

Churchill was outraged. It was ridiculous, after five and a half long years, to keep this moment of victory from people. He immediately cabled Truman and asked the President to ring him as soon as possible on the open line, asking for 'Colonel Warden Whitehall 4433'. 'I will address you as Admiral,' Churchill wrote on the telegram. 'We can then both tell UJ what we are going to do.' 'UJ' was Uncle Joe – Stalin.

Events were moving fast, however, and beyond the control of even Stalin, let alone Churchill or Truman. At 2.27 p.m. on the afternoon of 7 May, Count Schwerin von Krosigk, the newly appointed Foreign Minister in the Dönitz regime, announced in a radio broadcast from Flensburg that Germany had surrendered twelve hours earlier. For Ed Kennedy, a highly regarded American war reporter for the Associated Press news agency, it provided the scoop of a lifetime. He'd been in Reims the previous night, had witnessed the surrender, but, like the other few pressmen there, had promised to agree to the media embargo until authorized to the contrary. Now, though, the news was out, albeit via the lips of the Germans, not the Allies. Kennedy considered the ban now null and void. The wider public deserved to know. And so, less than an hour after von Krosigk's broadcast, Kennedy rang the London bureau from Paris and was connected to Lewis Hawkins in the Associated Press's London newsroom.

'This is Ed Kennedy, Lew,' Kennedy told him. 'Germany has surrendered unconditionally. That's surrendered unconditionally. That's official. Make the date Reims, France, and get it out.' Kennedy had sent about 300 words including a quote from General Alfred Jodl, then the line went dead. It was enough, however. In no time, AP had wired the news all around the free world. In Britain and in the USA, radio stations broke into programmes to broadcast this stunning announcement. That afternoon, the edition of the London *Evening Standard* led with the headline 'GERMANY SURRENDERS'. Stalin might have been demanding that the end of the war could only be announced when he said so, but in the West the democratic governments had none of the hold over people that he had in the Soviet Union. Supreme Allied HQ was incensed by this betrayal of trust by Kennedy and suspended him immediately from any further access. The damage was done, however, and in the United States and throughout Britain the celebrating began. Huge crowds quickly formed in London, New York and other major cities.

Yet while the partying had spontaneously already started, the lack of any official confirmation by the Allies was both stark and baffling. Jonathan Daniels, the Presidential Press Secretary at the White House, was inundated but that morning remained tight-lipped. 'There is nothing official to announce here at this time,' he told waiting reporters. 'We do not know when there will be an announcement.'

This was clearly a ridiculous situation. At 4.10 p.m. London time, Churchill spoke by telephone to Admiral William Leahy, the President's Chief of Staff, and urged the Americans to ignore Stalin and announce Victory in Europe immediately that evening, as Eisenhower had originally planned. Leahy, however, replied that President Truman did not feel he could act without the approval of Uncle Joe. The announcement must wait until 9 May. Churchill called off, then tried again an hour later. Crowds were out celebrating in the streets, he told Leahy, and were beyond any kind of control. They really should make the announcement at noon Eastern War Time and 6 p.m. London time. But again Truman insisted on deferring to Stalin. Then Churchill appealed directly to Stalin. 'As the whole world has now been informed of the surrender,' he signalled to the Kremlin, 'I propose that I should make the announcement at 6pm our time this evening corresponding to noon Washington time and 7pm Moscow time. Otherwise it will seem that it is only the Governments who do not know.'

The Prime Minister now had to wait and see how not only

Stalin but the still-new American President would respond to this latest appeal. And really, it was Truman's opinion that mattered most. Over the past year, the United States had emphatically eclipsed Britain as the leading nation of the free world, and while the Soviet Union might have been the enemy of their enemy and have been fighting on the same side, it was all too clear that ideologically, politically and culturally, Stalin was looking – and acting – increasingly like a future enemy, not a long-lasting ally. If the special relationship between Britain and the United States that had been so successfully forged in this war was to continue, it was obviously imperative that Truman was treated with the utmost respect and courtesy and that his opinion, when sought, was given the very greatest consideration. A month earlier, Harry S. Truman had been a nobody outside the USA. But he most certainly was not any more. No matter how much Churchill might have been chomping at the bit over the timing of VE Day, it was Truman's verdict that now counted and would dictate the outcome.

On 7 May 1945, Truman had only been President for a little over three weeks. Silver-haired, bespectacled, but with a healthy, affable face that matched his character, he was the polar opposite of Roosevelt. While FDR had been an aristocratic, patrician, highly educated member of the East Coast elites, Truman hailed from rather more humble beginnings and had experienced none of the privilege Roosevelt had enjoyed. Truman was also the only President so far this century not to hold a college degree. And while Roosevelt had been a man who kept his cards close to his chest and played his politics with Machiavellian cunning, Truman was a straightforward, plain-speaking, Midwesterner from Independence,

Missouri. Even militarily there was a difference, for while Roosevelt was a naval man through and through, Truman's heart was with the army. He'd had a fine record as an artillery officer in the last war and had continued in the National Guard on returning home, rising to the rank of colonel.

Truman's father had been a farmer and livestock dealer. The family had moved several times before settling in Independence, and although Truman developed a love of music, history and reading, he was not an outstanding student and instead of university headed to Spalding's Commercial College, a business school in Kansas City, which he attended for a year only and where he learned book-keeping, shorthand and how to type. He began his working life in the mailroom of the *Kansas City Star* before taking on a job as a timekeeper for rail construction crews on the Atchison, Topeka and Santa Fe Railway. Later he returned to the family farm, where he courted a local girl, Bess Wallace, who turned down his marriage proposal. Then the war and army life intervened, but on his safe return and with his improved prospects, she finally agreed to marry him. His war service and his time in the army had a deep effect on him; he had been commissioned as an artillery officer, proved a natural leader of men and taken part in much of the major fighting in which the American Expeditionary Force was involved. In the Meuse-Argonne offensive, for example, his artillery regiment had provided fire support for the future General George S. Patton's tank brigade. His unit had also fired some of the very last shots of the war, on 11 November 1918.

Back in Missouri and newly married, he co-owned a small department store, although this soon went bankrupt. He then ran to become a county judge in Kansas, despite having no law degree, and won, although only with the strong backing of

Thomas J. Pendergast, the political boss in Kansas. A Democrat, Pendergast used an increasingly large network of family, friends and business associates to effectively rig local elections in and around Kansas City, and there is no doubt that Truman won as Judge of Jackson County because of 'TJ' Pendergast's backing. He also helped Truman then get elected to the US Senate for Missouri in 1934.

Pendergast was eventually brought down by tax evasion – as was the mobster Al Capone – in 1939, but actually his fall was the making of Truman, who was then able to emerge from his shadow and became widely regarded for his honesty, decency, straightforwardness and ability to cut to the chase and act with both clarity and purpose. And as the United States began to rapidly rearm, towards the end of 1940, Truman took charge of the Committee on Military Affairs, set up to ensure that there was a clampdown on waste and profiteering. In the years that followed, it was reckoned that the Truman Committee, as it became known, saved the public purse some $15 billion, and its work led to Truman being on the cover of *Time* magazine, arguably the most influential publication in America. There was something of the coming man about him.

Even so, being a senator was really the limit of his ambition. He had evolved into a very good one, with a reputation as a safe pair of hands and all-round good man: approachable, collegiate, a dab poker player and the archetypal Midwesterner with a slightly folksy, uncomplicated air about him. And he was genuine, honest and open. Unsurprisingly, though, he was also a home politician to his core; and this did not make him an obvious choice as running mate for President Roosevelt, who in November 1944 would be attempting to win the vote to be President for an historic fourth term. FDR was utterly convinced it was essential he remain in office until the war was won, and with good reason. No one else in US politics had the depth of knowledge or the relationship with the Chiefs of Staff or coalition partners that Roosevelt had so skilfully built up. The vision for the United States' involvement in the war had been largely his; it had also been Roosevelt who, before the war had begun in 1939, had carefully and cunningly prepared the ground for massive rearmament. And it had also been Roosevelt who had provided the vision and ambition for this to get under way following the defeat of France in June 1940. At the time, it had been one of the most astonishing volte-faces in American political history, for Roosevelt had first been elected in 1932 on an isolationist ticket. Now he was turning that on its head, transforming the US economy in the process, leading America to becoming the arsenal of democracy, and winning a third term in November 1940. What followed was unprecedented in history and transformed the American armed forces into the most technically proficient in the world, with a navy and air force larger than that of any other nation. He was truly a colossus of the Allied war effort.

Roosevelt's health, however, had been declining rapidly by the time of the 1944 election; he'd never been well since a crippling bout of polio as a young man, but he'd been determined to continue to lead his country for as long as he could. Recognizing that there was a real possibility he might not be alive for a further four years rather changed matters, because it meant the Vice-President might well end up taking over. To ensure he won again, he therefore needed a VP who would not upset a potentially large proportion of the voting public. His current VP was Henry A. Wallace, but he was now considered too left-wing. Most assumed that James F. 'Jimmy' Byrnes, a highly competent and hugely experienced politician as well as a close friend of FDR's, would be the pick. But Roosevelt was concerned that Byrnes would try to throw his weight around too much and also that his Southern connections might disaffect voters, particularly black Americans. However, having revealed little beforehand, the President decided to go with Truman as his running mate, a man he knew little, but who he thought would alienate no one and who, as VP, would play the part well. Truman was liked; he had no obvious enemies. People thought him a decent fellow, and so he was. VPs needed to keep the Senate on board and focus on the home fires. That was just the man FDR wanted.

Truman had had no ambition whatsoever to be Vice-President and had been rather dumbfounded to learn that Roosevelt wanted him on the ticket. 'I was floored,' he admitted. 'I was sunk.' But he didn't feel he could say no; he did, though, agree only with considerable reservations. Being nominated for VP was a big enough deal as it was. But on the ticket with Roosevelt, one of the greatest American politicians to have ever lived, in wartime, and with the Great Man in poor health, was an altogether more daunting proposition.

At the Democratic Convention in July 1944, as American forces were about to break through in Normandy and storm Tinian in the Pacific, and were continuing to bomb Nazi Germany, Truman duly beat Henry Wallace for the nomination. It was quickly termed 'the Missouri Compromise' by his detractors. A few months later, in November, Roosevelt secured a fourth term with 432 of 531 Electoral College votes. It was a landslide. On 20 January 1945, on a rather solemn, sombre occasion, Harry S. Truman, from Independence, Missouri, was sworn in as Vice-President. The brevity of the ceremony – just fifteen minutes – was in no way commensurate with the enormity of its significance.

In the months that followed, Truman was as busy as ever, presiding over the Senate, attending endless receptions, pressing the flesh and performing a domestic role for which Roosevelt had not the time, inclination or energy. In February, FDR had flown to Yalta on the Black Sea, a huge distance from Washington, for the latest conference of the 'Big Three' – him, Churchill and Stalin. He was only sixty-three but looked at least a decade older; the President was fading. On his return he gave a speech to a joint session of Congress, reporting on the conference at Yalta, but sitting, not standing, to spare his legs, and reading slowly from a prepared script. 'Never before have the major Allies been more closely united,' he told them, 'not only in their war aims but also in their peace aims.' But he also gave a grave warning. 'Twenty-five years ago,' he added, 'American fighting men looked to the statesmen of the world to finish the work of peace for which they fought and suffered. We failed – we failed them then. We cannot fail them again and expect the world to survive again.' Most in the House Chamber that day were deeply moved, in part by the President's words, but as much by Roosevelt's appearance and his obvious profound physical decline. Afterwards, Truman briefly met with him. 'I saw the President immediately after his speech,' he noted. 'Plainly, he was a very weary man.' Roosevelt then headed to Warm Springs, Georgia, to recuperate. Truman's meeting with the President, was, however, only the second time he had seen him since 20 January. Nor had he even once met the Secretary of State, Edward Stettinius, or half the rest of the Cabinet. There had been no briefing on international affairs, no attempt to involve him in matters of war, no opportunity for him to meet key players. Nor had there been any introduction to or correspondence with Allied heads of state or senior commanders. The President was clearly ill, but the possibility of an early demise remained an elephant in the room that few, if any, were willing to confront. And as a consequence, Truman, while fulfilling the traditional role of Vice-President to the letter, was woefully underprepared for taking on the job of Commander-in-Chief should the worst occur.

Shortly before 5 p.m. on Thursday, 12 April, after the Senate had adjourned, Truman went to the office of the House Speaker, Sam Rayburn, to discuss a particular piece of legislation. He'd no sooner entered Rayburn's office, however, than he was told that the President's Press Secretary, Steve Early, wanted to speak to him urgently. Truman immediately returned the call and was told to hurry over to the White House as quickly as possible. No explanation was given, nor did Truman ask for one, but assumed that the President must have returned from Warm Springs or that something significant was brewing in the war.

It was 5.25 p.m. when he reached the White House. He was straight away taken in an elevator to the second floor and then ushered into Eleanor Roosevelt's study. The President's wife was there with her daughter and son-in-law. Also present was Steve Early. Mrs Roosevelt rose, stepped towards him and gently placed an arm on his shoulder.

'Harry,' she said gently, 'the President is dead.'

Truman felt utterly dumbfounded and for a moment could not speak. Then, after collecting himself, he said, 'Is there anything I can do for you?'

'Is there anything *we* can do for *you*?' she replied. 'For you are the one in trouble now.'

Roosevelt had died of a cerebral haemorrhage while still at Warm Springs, having earlier complained of a terrible headache. That day he'd dictated a number of missives, not least to Stalin over the negotiations in Italy; they had proved his last act as President. The news was released in the United States and around the world at 5.47 p.m. Eastern War Time. At the White House most were still in a state of shock, not least Truman. Secretary of State Stettinius arrived with tears running down his face. Other Cabinet members also appeared, as well as the Chief Justice. By 7 p.m. most of the Cabinet had assembled in the Cabinet Room, including Henry Wallace, the former Vice-President, who had since his demotion remained an impressively staunch and loyal supporter. Truman's wife, Bess, also arrived and silently took her husband's hand. Truman looked absolutely dazed. A Bible was needed to swear him in, but the only one that could be found was a Gideon edition; it would have to do. With this, Chief Justice Harlan Stone swore in the new President at 7.09 p.m. 'So help me God,' Truman said as he ended his Presidential oath. He would need God's help in the weeks to come.

It would be some time before he moved into the White House, but it was his office from the outset. Roosevelt tended not to see anyone before late morning but it was a 9 a.m. start for Truman on 13 April in the Oval Office, which remained exactly as FDR had left it. The new President had already told the Cabinet that he intended to keep them all in post and pursue the same foreign and domestic policies as FDR. 'I made it clear, however,' he noted, 'that I would be President in my own right and that

I would assume full responsibility for such decisions as had to be made.' But, he added, he would always listen to advice. They could differ with him, but the final decision would always be his and once a decision was made he expected them to support him. 'Their experience with President Roosevelt', he noted, 'and their knowledge were necessary to me in this crisis.'

And a leadership crisis it most certainly was. No one was more keenly aware of the huge chasm Roosevelt had left with his death. It needed to be filled not only by swearing in Truman, but by him very rapidly absorbing an enormous amount of information – information that then had to be effectively processed and analysed. Among the first tasks of the day was for him to be brought urgently up to speed on the military situation. That morning he was joined at various times by General Marshall, the Chief of Staff and most senior military figure, Admiral William Leahy, who had been Roosevelt's Chief of Staff and most valued and trusted military advisor, Admiral Ernest J. King, the Commander-in-Chief of the Navy, and Henry Stimson, the most experienced politician in Washington, who had first served under President Teddy Roosevelt. Although now in his seventies, Stimson was Secretary of War. Later in the afternoon Jimmy Byrnes arrived, who had been Roosevelt's special advisor at Yalta.

That came after a brief lunch at Capitol Hill with some friends, arranged some time before and which he preferred not to cancel, largely because he wanted to let them all know that he would be needing them in the days and weeks to come. Afterwards, as he left the Senate Office, a number of office boys and reporters were waiting for him, wanting to shake his hand. Truman's eyes filled with tears. 'Boys,' he said, 'if you ever pray, pray for me now. I don't know whether you fellows ever had a load of hay fall on you, but when they told me yesterday what had happened, I felt like the moon, the stars, and all the planets had fallen on me. I've got the most terribly responsible job a man ever had.'

'Good luck, Mr President,' one of the reporters called out.

'I wish you didn't have to call me that,' Truman replied.

Despite this heart-warming show of support, the jury was still out on Truman. Roosevelt had been such a towering figure and the parallels with that other great President, Abraham Lincoln, were all too obvious. Both men had died almost at the moment of victory. And both had been replaced by comparative nobodies. Andrew Johnson, who had succeeded Lincoln, had not been up to the giant task and there were many who suspected Truman might equally fall short at an arguably even more critical hour.

The following Monday, 16 April, the day after Roosevelt's hastily arranged funeral and with the final Red Army Battle for Berlin now under way, Truman gave an address to Congress. 'Today,' he told them, 'the entire world is looking to America for enlightened leadership to peace and progress. Such a leadership requires vision, courage and tolerance. It can be provided only by a united nation deeply devoted to the highest ideals.' He would defend those ideals with all his heart and strength. 'That is my duty,' he added, 'and I shall not shirk it.' There was still hard fighting ahead to ensure there was lasting peace, he told them. 'So that there can be no possible misunderstanding,' he continued, 'both Germany and Japan can be certain, beyond any shadow of a doubt, that America will continue the fight for freedom until no vestige of resistance remains.' Only unconditional surrender, as put forward by Roosevelt at Casablanca more than two years earlier, would be sufficient.

He also skilfully acknowledged both Roosevelt and the current war leaders. 'The grand strategy of the United Nations' war has been determined due in no small measure to the vision of our departed Commander-in-Chief. We are now carrying out our part of that strategy under the able direction of Admiral Leahy, General Marshall, Admiral King, General Eisenhower, Admiral Nimitz and General MacArthur. I want the entire world to know that this direction must and will remain unchanged and unhampered.' The debt to those who had already sacrificed so much was immense, but it was America's duty to lead the world towards peace and prosperity. 'I ask only', he finished, 'to be a good and faithful servant of my Lord and my people.'

Truman had nailed it. The speech was pitch-perfect. Repeatedly, he had to pause as Congress applauded, and he received a standing ovation at its end. He was the Midwesterner who had suddenly stepped up and shown remarkable statesmanship. Truman was not like Roosevelt in any way except for his determination to continue the late President's strategy. There was a palpable sense of relief that they would get through this crisis, that Truman had indeed been a shrewd choice by FDR; and that sense of collective reassurance brought with it a feeling of unity too. They were all in it together. Truman's energy, his innate decency, his obvious sincerity and determination all counted in this moment. Great though Roosevelt had unquestionably been, these characteristics of Truman's, laid bare in his address to Congress that Monday, suddenly felt like a breath of fresh air. He had, at the very least, bought himself a huge amount of goodwill – and some time.

And yet events were moving at a rush. The war in Germany was coming to a close, but how soon was not clear. Then there was Japan and the rapidly fracturing relations with the Soviet Union. These were considerable issues to confront, especially considering the rising casualties. Although the US armed forces were now a staggering 16 million-strong and the States had the world's largest navy and air forces, nearly 200,000 American service personnel had so far been killed in the war; April 1945 would be one of the bloodiest months for the US Army in Europe, while at the same time the US Army and Navy were fighting the most brutal battle to date in the Pacific on Okinawa. In all, by 17 April the USA had suffered 900,000 casualties in the war. War fatigue was starting to bite, but despite continued advances in Europe the latest threat on the horizon was clearly now coming from the Soviet Union. Edward Stettinius had provided Truman with a detailed foreign policy report on 13 April. 'Since the Yalta Conference,' ran the brief, 'the Soviet Government has taken a firm and uncompromising position on nearly every major question that has arisen in our relations.' An OSS report for FDR sent at the beginning of the month was even clearer. 'Russia will emerge from the present conflict as by far the strongest nation in Europe and Asia,' it ran, 'strong enough, if the United States should stand aside, to dominate Europe and at the same time to establish her hegemony over Asia. Russia's natural resources and manpower are so great that within relatively few years she can be much more powerful than either Germany or Japan has ever been.'

On 22 April, Truman was due to be meeting the Soviet Foreign Minister, Vyacheslav Molotov, but a day ahead of him came W. Averell Harriman, the ambassador to the Soviet Union. One of the wealthiest men in America, tall, handsome, urbane and ferociously intelligent, he knew more about Stalin and the Soviet Union than any other living American. Truman had never met him before, and he arrived looking exhausted and with a fatigue-induced tick in his right eye; as well he might after the machinations of the Russians and having flown in from Moscow, a huge journey in 1945. Harriman told him that Stalin wanted to dominate as much of Europe as possible, including Poland, but would not want to risk a break with the United States. He was still too much in need of American financial and material aid to risk it. Britain, especially, being part of Europe, was very concerned about encroaching Soviet ambitions. The bullying tone of Stalin over the surrender negotiations in Italy had been a case in point. They were also trying to muscle in on much of eastern Europe and the Balkans. Harriman had written to the State Department earlier in the month warning about the severe threat from Russia. 'We must clearly recognize that the Soviet program is the establishment of totalitarianism,' he wrote, 'ending personal liberty and democracy as we know and respect it.' Liberty and democracy were precisely the values for which so much American blood had already been spilled. Now, at their first ever meeting face to face, Harriman told Truman bluntly that Soviet control of Poland and Romania meant political control, with the ghastly apparatus that came with that: secret police, an end to the freedom of speech, puppet governments. The Soviet Union did not remotely share the Western Allies' principles.

On that Sunday, 22 April, the conversation with Molotov was a typical first round: a few exploratory jabs but not much more. The following day, however, by which time Truman was now fully up to speed and had got the cut of Molotov's jib, he was considerably more forthright, living up to his promise of plain speaking. Much of the discussions concerned the fate of Poland. The country bordered the Soviet Union, Molotov pointed out, but was far from the United States. The Poles, he added, had been working against the Red Army. Truman cut in, telling him he was not interested in propaganda; rather, he was concerned that the Soviet Union was not living up to the agreements thrashed out at Yalta, in which it had agreed to allow free elections in Poland and to accept pro-Western elements in a coalition government. He told Molotov sharply that an agreement had already been reached on Poland; he expected Stalin to keep to his word and then there would be no further sticking point on the matter. Truman wished it to be clearly understood that while he wanted friendship with the Soviet Union, that could only be on the basis of the mutual agreements signed at Yalta. It was not a one-way street.

'I have never been talked to like that in my life,' Molotov told him.

'Carry out your agreements,' Truman replied, 'and you won't get talked to like that.'

Three days later, on 25 April, Truman was visited at the White House by Henry Stimson, who wanted to talk to him on a highly secret but urgent matter. Alone in Truman's office, Stimson produced a brief memorandum he had only finished writing that morning, which he passed to the President. 'Within four months,' Truman read, 'we shall in all probability have completed the most terrible weapon ever known in human history, one bomb of which could destroy a whole city.' This weapon had been developed together with British scientists, but only the United States had the capability of producing it. This was not a monopoly that could last, however, and it was likely that within a matter of years the Soviet Union would be capable of making such a weapon too. This was the Manhattan Project, or 'S-1' as it was code-named. Although some 200,000 people were involved in its creation, very few had any notion about what was the end result of their work, and despite it costing billions from the public purse, almost no one outside the programme knew of it either. The project had been undertaken because back in 1941 it had been believed that the Germans were also creating an atomic bomb. In fact, the Germans had decided as early as July 1942 not to prioritize that kind of weapon and had never had the remotest chance of achieving it.

Now, in April 1945, it was only the United States that could conceivably use such a world-changing weapon. Its immense destructive power was due to the sudden release of energy caused by the splitting, or 'fission', of the nuclei of a heavy element such as plutonium or uranium. The process of this splitting caused a huge amount of thermal energy as well as gamma rays. When multiplied, a chain reaction could be caused that would result in a massive explosion, the destructive power of which was out of all proportion to any conventional bomb. The significance of this scientific breakthrough was obviously world-changing. The science was incredibly complicated, and harnessing such power into a single bomb enormously difficult. For obvious reasons, secrecy around the project was paramount.

Certainly, Truman, despite having chaired the Truman Committee, had been completely in the dark. Secrecy had been paramount and, it seemed, had been safeguarded very successfully. Roosevelt had backed it from the outset, Leahy knew and so too did Marshall. General Leslie R. Groves was the military head of the project, Stimson told him.

After taking a moment to digest this earth-shattering news, Truman expressed as much concern about the future role an atomic bomb might have on the world as he did about its potential to shorten the war. Stimson and Groves, who later joined them, stressed that the bomb was still not ready, but it now looked as though it might be possible to carry out a first test sometime in July. It meant that before long, Truman would have yet another gargantuan responsibility on his shoulders. Both Leahy and the Chiefs of Staff reckoned that, as things stood, it might take another eighteen months or more to subdue Japan by conventional warfare. Although economically and materially the Japanese were broken, there was no escaping the terrible truth: that the closer Allied troops got to the Japanese home islands, the harder the enemy hit back. Peleliu, Iwo Jima and now Okinawa had become bywords for brutality in which no quarter was given. The Japanese fought until they died. It meant the prospect of an invasion of Japan was a truly terrible one. Already, air forces and troops were being sent from Europe to the Pacific. Now, though, there was potentially a bomb that might end it all. The President could receive the advice of his military chiefs and his closest political advisors, but ultimately, using the bomb and all its consequences would have to be his decision and his alone. This humble man from Independence, Missouri who had never wanted to be President.

Such considerations and enormous responsibilities weighed on his mind on Monday, 7 May 1945 as he considered Churchill's wish to announce VE Day ahead of the Soviet Union. It had been felt he had gone in perhaps too hard on Molotov, so he was now anxious to play a slightly more placatory hand.

This was why he was not minded to go with Churchill's suggestion of a separate announcement over the end of the war in Europe. Delaying the declaration to keep in line with the Soviet Union was frustrating, but a small concession in the big scheme of things. However, he now accepted that, thanks to Ed Kennedy's unauthorized release of the news, the Western Allies should celebrate Victory in Europe Day together on 8 May. The ceasefire had already begun; the sop to Stalin was to agree that, officially, hostilities would end on the morning of 9 May. It was the kind of pragmatic compromise full of good sense that had already marked these first weeks of his presidency.

It was at 8.15 a.m. on Tuesday, 8 May 1945 that President Truman greeted reporters at the White House. He had a little statement for them, he said, but wanted to be absolutely clear that what he was about to say was strictly embargoed for a further forty-five minutes, that is 9 a.m. Eastern War Time. Then, breaking into a half-grin, he told them he would only be speaking for seven minutes, if that. 'You have plenty of time,' he told them. The pressmen laughed. Truman had now been President for just twenty-six days, not quite four weeks.

'This is a solemn but glorious hour,' he began. 'General Eisenhower informs me that the forces of Germany have surrendered to the United Nations. The flags of freedom fly all over Europe.' Then he deviated a moment from his script. 'It's celebrating my birthday, too,' he added. 'Today.'

'Happy birthday, Mr President!' said a number of the pressmen.

Truman smiled, but only fleetingly, then looked grave. 'For this victory, we join in offering our thanks to the Providence which has guided and sustained us through the dark days of adversity. Our rejoicing is sobered and subdued by a supreme consciousness of the terrible price we have paid to rid the world of Hitler and his evil hand. Let us not forget, my fellow Americans, the sorrow and the heartache which today abide in the homes of so many of our neighbours – neighbours whose most priceless possession has been rendered as a sacrifice to redeem our liberty.' And he warned them that there was still plenty of work to come. They must all contribute, ceaselessly. 'We must work to finish the war,' he told them. 'Our victory is only half over.' He then immediately went on to talk about the war against Japan, with a warning as to what the Japanese people could expect until such time as they surrendered outright. 'The West is free,' he continued, 'but the East is still in bondage to the treacherous tyranny of the Japanese. When the last Japanese division has surrendered unconditionally, then only will our fighting job be done.'

It was his sixty-first birthday and he looked fit and well enough; but there was little joy in this VE Day speech, nor much time to celebrate the day. Great events were taking place, events that would shape the future world for generations to come. What astonishing responsibilities lay on those shoulders. So far, this humble man had more than risen to the occasion, had surprised many and appeared to be capable of bearing up under the demands made of him. Yet, while for those now celebrating the war seemed to be at the end, Truman's time upon the biggest stage of all was just beginning. Enormous problems lay ahead: dealing with the ambitions of the Soviet Union, possibly more dangerous than those of Nazi Germany; vanquishing Imperial Japan; potentially unleashing a weapon of untold power; ensuring that war-torn Europe rose again in a new age of peace and freedom; and overseeing the continued rise and prosperity of the United States of America. Had one man ever faced such a challenge? If his tone was a little sombre on this momentous day, it was hardly surprising.

Happy Birthday, Mr President.

CHAPTER 9

AMID THE RUINS PART 1

The Surrender in Berlin, *9 May 1945*

A huge, unfamiliar city. The smoke from burning buildings shrouded its outlines, whole districts of ruins gave it the appearance of fantasy. Just under six years before, an invasion of Europe, criminal and unprecedented in its brutality, was launched from here, and now to here it had returned.

Yelena Kagan, interpreter, Third Shock Army

On the early afternoon of Tuesday, 8 May, Feldmarschall Wilhelm Keitel was back in Berlin. He'd flown to Tempelhof in a British C-47 Dakota from Flensburg, accompanied by von Friedeburg, the new head of the Kriegsmarine, Generaloberst Hans-Jürgen Stumpff of the Luftwaffe, and two staff officers. They flew to Stendal first, where they joined a number of other British transport aircraft. These were also heading to Berlin with Eisenhower's representatives on board: Air Chief Marshal Sir Arthur Tedder of the RAF and the Deputy Supreme Allied Commander; General Carl 'Tooey' Spaatz, the head of US Strategic Air Forces; and Général de Lattre de Tassigny of France, as well as a number of staff and other officers. From here they flew on to Berlin. The city was still burning, the ruined capital of the Reich shrouded in a yellow fog of smoke. A Red Army guard of honour was waiting for them – or rather, was there for the Russians' victorious Allied comrades. The Germans' aircraft parked up a little way away, but Keitel had been able to watch the ceremony from afar. Once this was over, the German contingency, in Berlin to formally sign the instrument of surrender, were hustled into waiting cars. Keitel was separated, with just one Russian officer to accompany him; this, he learned, was Marshal Zhukov's quartermaster.

They drove across Belle-Alliance-Platz and on through the shattered city. Barely a single building had been left untouched. Keitel was shocked by what he saw: in these streets the total, complete collapse of the Third Reich had been laid bare. They reached Karlshorst, a former German Army engineer school to the south of the city, and were then led into an anteroom. It was a little after 1 p.m. and they were early; the surrender ceremony was not due to take place until a minute after midnight.

'When we were riding through the streets of Berlin,' Keitel told the Red Army translator, 'I was appalled at the extent of the destruction.'

'Herr Field Marshal,' the Russian replied, 'were you not appalled when the Germans, on your orders, wiped off the face of the earth thousands of Soviet towns and villages leaving millions of our people, including many thousands of children, buried under the ruins?'

Keitel shrugged nervously but said nothing.

Ten days earlier, another person passing through Berlin had been equally struck by the scale of devastation. Yelena Kagan was a twenty-five-year-old interpreter attached to the Third Shock Army. Originally from Gomel in Belorussia, her family had moved to Moscow, where she studied philosophy at Moscow State University. She had wanted to go straight to the front but had been initially drafted as a munitions worker and then trained as a nurse before her knowledge of languages – and especially of German – saw her posted to a school for interpreters, and from there, at last, in February 1942, to the front. She'd been an army interpreter ever since, mainly interrogating prisoners but also poring over captured documents. She found it fascinating and was keenly aware that she was now about to play a part in a significant moment in Soviet and world history.

She had crossed into Germany at a checkpoint with a large,

roughly constructed archway and sign that said: 'This was the German border'. A second sign had been erected just beyond on which had been daubed: 'Take a good look: this is fucking Germany'. She and her companions had reached Berlin that same night, 29 April. The city seemed to be on fire, huge tongues of flame rising high above the silhouetted and jagged remains of buildings. Searchlights swept the sky while there was an ever-present rumble of artillery that filled the ears and made the ground tremble. The city in ruins. Sharp on the air was the stench of charred timber, of explosive, of decay. They paused for the night, waiting for orders, still in the outskirts, and Yelena sat on an abandoned oil drum beside an equally abandoned bakery with boarded-up windows above which was gilded writing: 'Franz Schulz Feinbäckerei'.

It was a dismal scene, and even more so by morning. Every so often there would be a rumble of falling masonry as another building collapsed. Slowly, Berliners emerged from their subterranean existence to look for food and water; mains supplies had been cut off and both commodities were in pitifully short supply. Closer to the centre, non-stop gunfire could be heard – small-arms hammering away, artillery rounds exploding, smoke, fumes swirling and rising into the air and sneaking down wrecked streets. Yelena found the air utterly suffocating. She was struck by how cruelly pointless was the German High Command's insistence on continuing to fight. Berlin was surrounded. It was all over; it had been for months. It had been years, in fact, since Nazi Germany had had any slight hope of turning the war round and winning.

The closer she and her team got to the centre, the more suffocating became the air. Yelena felt grit in her teeth and smoke on the back of her throat. Female soldiers were directing traffic, which came to a halt as a bunch of weary Frenchmen, forced labourers for the Reich, trudged down the road, one with a French flag draped over his case. There were fires, some small, some larger, in every street; no one was putting them out. 'Unsere Mauern brachen, unsere Herzen nicht!' someone had written on a broken wall. 'Our walls have broken but not our hearts.' 'It was very difficult to find your way through the city by map-reading,' noted Yelena. 'We had run out of Russian signs and the German ones had mostly disappeared along with the walls.' They only made progress by asking civilians they came across. They pushed on, the streets becoming increasingly deserted as they neared the government district but the sound of battle getting closer. An occasional bullet zipped and hissed by. Tinny-sounding machine-gun fire up ahead. The crash of a wall or an entire building collapsing. They reached Potsdamer Platz, just a few hundred yards south of the Reichskanzlei, set themselves up in the basement of a house owned by a tailor and his family and began the process of interrogating 'squealers' – captured prisoners, many of whom were just boys in outsize uniforms. 'We were interested in just one thing,' wrote Yelena. 'Where was Hitler?'

Not everyone in Berlin had been in thrall to Hitler, not even when, in those distant days before the war, he had won back the lands lost in 1919 and so many believed he was truly Germany's saviour. Ruth Andreas-Friedrich and her partner, the German-Russian conductor Leo Borchard, had always thought Nazi anti-Semitism abhorrent and throughout the war, at great personal risk, they had led an underground resistance movement called 'Uncle Emil' from their home in Steglitz, an area of Berlin south of Tempelhof. Before the war they helped Jews escape; during it they supported a number who, incredibly, were still living underground in the city, providing food, false papers and organizing accommodation. They'd also distributed leaflets written and printed by the White Rose resistance group in Munich. More recently they'd produced leaflets of their own, an act of even more courage since the July plot of the previous summer. Nazi paranoia had led to greater clampdowns on any who dared speak out against the regime, and perpetrators were dealt with mercilessly.

Somehow, they'd survived. They'd been hiding in a cellar while the Battle for Berlin raged: Ruth, Leo – who had adopted a false identity, Andrik Krassnow, since the start of the war – along with four illegals plus a Mongolian soldier who'd been endlessly eyeing up the women. Andrik could speak Russian, however, and had managed to keep the Mongolian from assaulting the women by drinking with him most nights. On 1 May, with the battle having passed them, they headed back to their home in Steglitz, picking their way through the destruction. 'We clamber over bomb craters,' noted Ruth in her diary. 'We squeeze through tangled barbed wire and hastily constructed barricades of furniture.' She struggled to comprehend the insanity of trying to defend the city with sofas. A tank riddled with holes blocked their way, the air heavy and oppressive with the stench of sweat and death. Burnt-out buildings. She spotted an old man sitting by a piece of broken wall, a pipe in one hand, a lighter in the other. But completely motionless. Only when she saw a fly crawl across his face did she realize he was dead.

Eventually they reached their home. Relief – it was still standing. Once inside they hurried upstairs, assailed by an overwhelming stench. The place had been ransacked and excreta left on the bathroom floor. 'Buffaloes must have done this,' stammered Andrik. There was no water, no electricity, no telephone. 'Only chaos,' noted Ruth. 'Total and impenetrable chaos.'

The following day, 2 May, having done their best to clean up the house, they learned that Hitler was dead; they hadn't realized he was even in Berlin. 'Suddenly,' she wrote, 'we become aware of the absurdity of this moment. Hitler is dead! And we act as if it didn't concern us. Events have overtaken him. The Third Reich has vanished like a ghost.'

The battle was over, but not for all German soldiers in Berlin. Some still fought on. Or rather, a number were still trying to flee westwards, to join up with General Wenck's forces or even reach the Americans. So desperate had the German Army been for troops in these dying months of the Third Reich that they had become increasingly dependent on men usually considered far too old for fighting or boys way too young. It was why, back on 29 March, Helmut Altner, aged only seventeen, had been conscripted into the Grenadier-Ausbildungs-und-Ersatz Bataillon 30 – a training and replacement battalion – part of the 309. 'Berlin' Infanterie-Division. So had begun a bewildering and frequently terrifying few weeks in which he'd found himself repeatedly facing untold cruelty and violence and forced to abandon the last vestiges of childhood in very quick order. Altner had even been on the Seelow Heights when Zhukov's offensive had been launched but had managed to be among the few remnants of 9. Armee that had fallen back to Berlin; of his original company, only a handful had made it to the city.

It was in the early hours of Tuesday, 1 May that Altner

learned that Hitler was dead, when his friend, Hermann Windhorst, passed him an armed services report just printed. Windhorst was fifty-eight and from Hamburg, one of those recruited at the same time as him. At first Altner felt as though someone had hit him over the head. 'But then,' he wrote, 'it is all the same to me, it hardly bothers me, for the time is over when I once thought that the heavens would collapse if that man no longer lived.' Altner, Windhorst, his friend Wegner and a handful of other stragglers that now included SS girls, Waffen-SS and Volkssturm were sheltering in the cellars of an old army barracks in Spandau, to the west of the city. A few hundred yards to their east was the Olympic Park, built for the 1936 Games, a time when much of the world seemed in awe of Hitler and the new Nazi Germany. It had been the site of vicious fighting over the last couple of days – fighting which had involved Altner and his comrades.

With this bombshell news, however, everyone was now wondering whether that meant the end of the war. They were still discussing this when Leutnant Stichler, the one officer in the original company still with them, ordered them out of the cellars to the barracks canteen where, incredibly, pay was being issued. A long line of maybe 1,000 troops of varying units, ages and equipment lined up. When it was Altner's turn he handed over his paybook, watched it get stamped with the familiar Nazi swastika and eagle motif, and was then handed sixty Reichsmarks.

Through that surreal day of uncertainty, more and more people reached the barracks: civilian refugees, Volkssturm, a handful of Waffen-SS – the latter always sticking out like a sore thumb with their better uniforms, superior weapons and distinct appearance. Then news arrived from Dönitz: that night they were all to break out and try and make it west to join General Wenck. Berlin had been surrounded for a week and the city was sure to fall at any moment. All supplies in the barracks were to be distributed to prevent them from falling into enemy hands. That meant bottles of schnapps, packets of long-life bread, even sweets and tinned meat. Everyone grabbed what they could then gorged themselves. Perhaps predictably, very soon a number of soldiers became drunk and were throwing their arms round each other. 'All the dams of discipline have been burst open,' noted Altner. 'Who knows what tomorrow will bring? We are only living for today!' Yet later that afternoon a further order of the day arrived from Dönitz talking about the ongoing fight against Bolshevism. He was demanding unconditional commitment, discipline and obedience. What a word 'unconditional' had become. Anyone holding back was a coward. 'The oath of loyalty sworn to the Führer applies without repetition to me as the Führer's appointed Head of State and successor as Commander-in-Chief of the Armed forces. German soldiers, do your duty!' Obergruppenführer Wolff would have flatly disagreed about the oath, but young Helmut Altner was hardly in a position to dispute the matter; he had read this with both astonishment and despair. Hitler was dead but the language was just the same, and as if to prove the point, soon afterwards a major came round and assured them that within a few days there would be peace with the Western Powers, and then they'd only have the Soviets to deal with. 'Whoever wants to desert', he told them casually, 'will be shot. The war goes on!'

Meanwhile, the German High Command clutched to the last threads of power. Feldmarschall Keitel had been on the move almost constantly, but on 1 May was at Wismar on the Baltic coast, the latest headquarters of the Kriegsministerium and OKW. Keitel was fifty-six, tall, patrician and a lifelong soldier. He'd been severely wounded in the last war but, having recovered, began to work his way up the career ladder as a staff officer, remaining in the army after the armistice and on into the era of the Third Reich. By 1938 he'd become chief of the OKW, which in fact had been, at the time, the world's first tri-service General Staff. This, on paper, had been a very good idea, but in reality was little more than Hitler's mouthpiece and Keitel had been only too willing to allow this. Most senior commanders and Nazis loathed one another, and while he got on well with his deputy, Jodl, Keitel had gained little more than contempt from his peers, who referred to him as 'Lackeitel', a play on *Lakai* – lackey. In truth, that was exactly what he had always been ever since 1938. Göring complained that Keitel had a sergeant's mind in a field marshal's body; even Hitler once said that Keitel had been made the highest-ranking officer in the Wehrmacht only because he was as loyal as a dog.

Keitel liked to pretend that he questioned Hitler's decisions and offered a counterweight, but in reality the Führer had always done exactly what he wanted and brooked little disagreement; the only person tricked into thinking otherwise had been Keitel himself, who had spent the war smothered by a combination of self-delusion and extreme arrogance. Even once the Battle for Berlin had got under way and it became clear that the city would be lost, Keitel was unable to influence Hitler's mind about leaving, despite daily efforts to get him to evacuate to Berchtesgaden. But it had ever been thus with Keitel and Hitler. He'd last seen the Führer on 23 April and heard his voice for the final time on the 29th, after listening in on a conversation between Hitler and Jodl; before the call had finished there had been a loud bang and the line had gone dead. From then on, plain-language communications with the Führerbunker had been lost.

Now he was on the Baltic coast in one of the last enclaves of Nazi power. The journey there had been traumatic. Several times they'd had to jump out of their car to avoid marauding Allied planes, while all along the roads had been terrible scenes of refugees and chaos – columns which they 'ruthlessly' drove through. Chaos, panic, desperation; these were the watchwords for Keitel. The situation was hopeless, Berlin was clearly finished, communications with the Führerbunker and, frankly, anyone, were challenging. It was not until the night of 1 May, however, that he was called by Dönitz, now in Plön, who asked for an interview with him at 8 a.m. the following morning.

There he finally learned that his master was dead and that Dönitz was Hitler's successor. If Keitel was distraught at this news, he never said or wrote anything to that effect; seven years of devoted service were instead swept under the carpet. Rather, he and Dönitz discussed who should take what roles in his new ministry. Himmler arrived, offering his services, but Keitel told Dönitz that the head of the SS was insufferable and advised that he cast him aside. What they were not doing on 2 May, however, was discussing how to urgently bring about the end of hostilities.

That same day, Red Army troops from the Third Shock Army, part of Zhukov's 1st Belorussian Front, broke through the final defensive ring and into the Reichskanzlei. The massive building had survived remarkably well, with most of the damage caused by artillery and small-arms rather than Allied bombs.

After a vicious firefight in the main hall, military and civilian staff emerged with their hands up as Soviet troops swarmed through the rooms and long corridors and down into the underground complex of cellars. Yelena Kagan was among the first in behind the assault troops. There were a number of wounded still in the building; she hurried past men groaning in pain. Intermittently, shooting suddenly broke out again, but her job was to find Hitler and quickly get her bearings in this huge complex. General Krebs had reported to Chuikov that Hitler had killed himself, but the Soviet Union was run on paranoia, suspicion and doubt and even the main state newspaper, *Pravda*, had that day questioned whether rumours of the Führer's death were just another Nazi trick to cover up his escape. So the sooner Yelena and her colleagues could prove what had happened to him either way, the better; but identifying who among the prisoners was best placed to enlighten them was not straightforward.

Eventually they found one of the mechanics, Karl Schneider, who confessed he'd been ordered to bring cans of fuel to the Führerbunker in the Reichskanzlei garden. He claimed to have brought eight jerry cans, each of twenty litres. Schneider had not seen Hitler but reported that the Führer's chauffeur, Erich Kempka, had told him their leader was dead. He was then asked to find more fuel the previous day, 1 May; by siphoning it from the fleet of cars in the Reichskanzlei garages he had managed to produce another four cans. Colonel Klimenko thought this seemed suspicious. Klimenko was head of the SMERSH unit, attached to the Third Shock Army. Yelena Kagan had, in turn, been seconded to him for the operation to find Hitler. Together with Schneider the mechanic, a cook called Wilhelm Lange and Major Bystrov of the Third Shock Army, they picked their way across the blackened rubble and glass-strewn, shell-cratered garden of the Reichskanzlei to the entrance of the Führerbunker. It was dank, dark and fetid down there. The place was a mess – papers strewn everywhere, the sign of a complex left in a hurry. Yelena began gathering them by the light of a hurricane lamp. It didn't take her long to discover a mass of documents left by Bormann and the diary of Goebbels.

In the early hours of Tuesday, 2 May, Helmut Altner and the 2,000 or so stragglers at Spandau had broken out of the barracks – a motley lot including women and children as well as troops. Out into the streets, past the S-Bahn station and to another barricade, which Altner nimbly jumped over before diving down the street. It was still dark but the air was alive with the tinny crackle of small-arms fire. A German four-barrelled cannon was providing cover, pumping shells towards Spandau town hall, from where enemy machine guns were firing. Dead littered the streets. Somehow they had to get across the road bridge, which was still intact, and over the Havel. Altner was stuck at the underpass of the bridge's ramp. A truck suddenly sped towards it, the windscreen splintered, running over the dead and wounded as it surged forward. Machine-gun salvoes burst out, grenades exploded, but it provided brief cover for Altner and his comrades to quickly scamper from the underpass to the other side of the road, ready to run across the bridge. Occasionally, people were jumping out of the shadows of the wrecked buildings by the embankment and making a dash for it. Shots rang out. Altner glanced around and saw that amid the troops there were also women with babies in their arms – all trying to get across the bridge and head west.

A deep breath, and then he jumped up and ran, bullets pinging all around him and the surface of the bridge slick with blood. Bodies strewn on the road and over the railings. Vehicles also desperately trying to cross, some straight over the dead. A smashed truck had hit the bridge superstructure and was across half the roadway, a woman and a soldier taking cover between its wheels. Altner paused by a pillar and a dead man as more shells hit the bridge. 'I jump up again,' he wrote. 'I can see figures ahead of me running and stumbling as though through a fog. I am without feeling and run, jumping over the dead and trampling on the wounded. Everyone is for himself.' Then he was on the far side, crouching by the barricade, lungs gasping for air. He'd made it but glanced back at the carnage: more tanks trying to cross, crushing people as they went, others riddled with bullets, Hitler Youth, young girls, old men, women with babies. 'Death plays his dance,' he noted, 'mowing his bloody path.'

He pushed on, leaving the mayhem on the bridge, part of a raggle-taggle force. A factory up ahead and a Waffen-SS half-track at a crossroads; a machine-gun team, dead – killed while trying to set up the weapon. Part of the crowd from the barracks crouching by the factory gate. Mortars started up, the shells crashing nearby. They hurried on, through the gate and the factory, past abandoned lathes and milling machines and out into a half-smashed shed. They clattered over collapsed planks, past more dead strewn around several craters. Ahead was a railway embankment and housing, as well as summer houses with gardens and allotments. They had reached Gartenstadt Staaken.

Artillery rounds seemed to be following them, one hitting the shed and sending timber swirling into the air. They spotted a small air raid shelter in one of the gardens ahead, crowded with people. Altner hurried past and into the nearest house and then down to the cellar – shelter until the shelling stopped. The cellar was full too and smelled of sweat and blood. More explosions. The house shook. The windows in the basement rattled. Altner couldn't bear it there, packed into the cellar, so went back up into the house. Traces of blood streaked the hall floor. All the windows were broken, with glass everywhere. Altner headed upstairs and looked out over the garden; the small air raid shelter had now gone – nothing more than a big hole in the ground and bodies strewn and scattered around. A man was brought into the house with a wound to the abdomen and his scrotum torn off. Altner knew he would die without help – and there was none.

At last the shelling stopped and Altner and the others moved off, climbing over fences, along culverts and across paths. They stopped at another house, hurried down into the cellar and there Leutnant Stichler pulled out his map. Incredibly, about twenty of them from the barracks were still together and in one piece. They had to get to the Döberlitz training area, Stichler told them; the Wenck army was behind that village. Once they were there, they would be safe. They could get some rest for several weeks in the Wenck camp while the relief army retook Potsdam and Nauen. It was, of course, fantasy, but they had to hold out for something – some glimmer of hope. Altner looked around. There was no sign of Wegner or his other friends. Of the 150 men with whom he had joined and headed to the front, only he and his friend Blaczeck were in the cellar now with Stichler.

It had quietened down so Stichler led his small posse back out, where they found a number of trucks, tanks and several assault guns parked up under the trees. A Luftwaffe general was talking with some Waffen-SS officers. Soon after, they were ordered to get going and move off. The last exodus from Berlin. A roar of engines, thunderous in the morning air, and they were away, but then came renewed firing – the enemy opening up from the buildings as the tanks rumbled past. Only the wounded were to be taken on vehicles; the fit and able were to walk, but now there was a sudden rush as troops hurriedly clambered on to any vehicle they could, aware that these could save them. Altner clung to the front wing of a truck, fingers gripping the slits in the bonnet. A young girl was on the other side, others clutching the cab for dear life. As it raced off and swung round a corner, Altner very nearly fell off. Up ahead was a wounded man in the street – a look of shock then the truck thundered straight over him. A moment later there was a scream and the girl on the right wing had gone too.

They were clear of the suburb and now heading towards the heathland of Döberitz. Several vehicles ahead were stuck in the sand of a track, while eight horses were straining to clear a gun that had slipped into a ditch. Civilians, soldiers, a mass of people trundled past. Altner wondered how they'd got there. Then another hold-up as a truck up ahead got stuck on a bend. They paused, then moments later shells screamed in and the truck was hit and burst into flames. People jumping off, running into the fields, clothes on fire. The car in front couldn't move either because a mangled body had become caught in the wheels. Altner headed towards a ditch to take cover when something hit him and knocked him to the ground. 'I look at it in horror,' he wrote in his diary. 'It is a bloody something without either head, hands or feet, just a bloody smashed torso.' Scrambling to his feet, he ran along the ditch as if possessed, his uniform covered in blood, then up and out into the open field. Red Army aircraft were thundering over, dropping bombs and strafing. The track became a column of burning, twisted vehicles. Dead and wounded strewn everywhere and a herd of cattle, gone demented, stampeding crazily. Altner paused then ran forward again when suddenly a fountain of earth, stone and grit erupted in front of him and he was flung to the ground. Stabbing pain in his foot. He wondered whether this was the end but pulled himself up, despite the searing agony, only to be nearly knocked over again by a riderless horse careering past. 'But I hurry on,' he wrote, 'not looking. I just want to live, only to live.'

It was still not quite midday on 2 May.

CHAPTER 10

AMID THE RUINS PART 2

The German Surrender to the Soviet Union in Berlin, *9 May 1945*

All of a sudden rockets shot into the air, one after the other. Fountains of coloured light dissolved into the sky, leaving dense trails of smoke. Cheerful little sparks danced around, promising a long-awaited peaceful life. I didn't know where the fireworks were coming from. Perhaps someone was celebrating the end of the war, as we had prematurely done the day before? It was the eve of the great day of celebration, Victory Day.

Ilya Krichevsky, Red Army soldier

MEANWHILE, YELENA KAGAN AND THE SMERSH TEAM had been finding a number of dead in and around the Führerbunker, but not Hitler. They did, though, discover the bodies of Josef and Magda Goebbels around 5 p.m. that day, 2 May. Two blackened corpses had been discovered in the garden, placed on an unhinged wooden door and brought out into Vossstrasse in front of the Reichskanzlei. Smoke still filled the street. Smashed vehicles had crashed into the walls of this enormous building, which was now pitted by war damage. Goebbels was blackened and charred but still recognizable; there had not been enough fuel left to incinerate him and his wife. There even remained ragged remnants of his uniform and a yellow tie that somehow had survived the flames. The metal prosthesis on his leg, however, worn to correct the club foot with which he'd been born, clinched it.

Curiously, it was not until the following day, 3 May, that the Goebbels children were discovered by Lieutenant Leonid Ilyin. All were lying in their bunk beds, the smell of bitter almonds quite sharp still in the dank bunker air, the girls all in nightgowns, the boy in pyjamas. Their faces were pink, a consequence of the potassium cyanide they'd each been given. 'The children seemed alive,' noted Yelena Kagan, who saw them, 'and only sleeping.' They only learned their identity, however, after bringing Vizeadmiral Hans-Erich Voss back to the scene of the crime. Voss had been the Kriegsmarine liaison officer to Hitler and had attempted to break out of the Führerbunker the previous evening. He'd been captured soon after and also confirmed the death of Hitler and his new wife. They now had half a dozen men who had served in the bunker in their hands and all said the same thing: that Hitler had shot himself and that his body had been burnt.

'Did you know these children?' Major Bystrov asked him as they brought him into the room where the dead children were still in their bunks.

Voss nodded. 'I saw them only yesterday.' He pointed out Heide, the youngest, then named them all.

There was too much smoke, too many fumes, to remain in the government district all night so Yelena and her team headed back to the outskirts, and while they were walking down a street looking for a house to sleep in they suddenly heard the distinct call of a nightingale. 'It had seemed that here in Berlin not only all living things, but even the stones of the city had been drawn into the war and were subject to its laws,' she wrote. 'But then, all of a sudden – a nightingale, in complete disregard of everything, was irrepressibly getting on with what nightingales get on with.' It was, she thought, an extraordinary reminder that life would continue, despite all that had happened.

Helmut Altner had also witnessed something of the beauty of the natural world among the carnage that same day, Thursday, 3 May. Earlier, as dawn had been breaking, he'd felt utterly exhausted; the remaining strength in his body was rapidly seeping away. Despite having a shard of shrapnel in his foot and still sticking out from the top of his boot, he'd walked all through the previous afternoon, across the entire

Döberitz training area. Of course, on the far side there had been no sign of Wenck's army, nor had there been any chance to rest. Instead, their ever-dwindling band had tramped on west, towards the town of Brandenburg. Now, early on the 3rd, they had paused in a wood, some 500 of them that were left from the thousands who had broken out from Spandau. Altner was soaking from the morning dew and shivering with cold. He leaned against a tree and rummaged in his haversack with numbed fingers, pulled out his last tin, then took out the pocket knife his mother had given him the day before he headed to the front, but the blade broke. A major watching this then silently handed him his knife. Finally prising open the tin, Altner spread sausage over a couple of pieces of long-life bread he'd saved, and ate. 'Strength returns to my body,' he noted, 'with renewed courage to face life.'

They pushed on. A Waffen-SS officer reckoned there might be a gap in the Russian lines between Päwesin and Weseram; if they could just get through there then they could maybe reach the Elbe and the Americans. On they went, across open fields in the sunshine, as though the war was a thousand miles away. Butterflies flitted by; the ground was steaming as the sun now burned off the dew. A village in the distance, then figures and vehicles up ahead. They thought they were German and so kept moving towards a wood. Then suddenly the whine and scream of shells once more and everyone began running. Altner hurried on, then found himself wading through a marshy area, heading for the wood. He was now with older Volkssturm men as they kept going, the trees – which seemed to offer sanctuary – getting closer. Then suddenly shouts from behind and Altner turned to see they were Russians. He kept running but shots rang out and he realized with sudden clarity that it was all over. Throwing away his pistol then pausing to catch his breath, he trudged slowly towards the enemy. 'Somewhere a lark rises singing,' he wrote, 'but I do not see it. I am dead beat and empty. We have been through hell. And the sun shines over the spring countryside as we go across the fields with pounding hearts, an aircraft engine in the distance sounding like a big bumble-bee. Everything was so pointless, the dead, the flowing blood, the horror.' Altner assumed that they would all be shot. A Russian soldier stood waiting for him, then offered his arm, supporting him and guiding him. Then he took out two cigarettes, lit both and gave one to Altner. 'War over!' he said. 'All go home!'

And at that moment, Altner felt quite overcome: the release of tension, the relief that it was over, that the enemy was human after all – it consumed him and he broke down and wept.

The same day, 3 May, Feldmarschall Keitel and Grossadmiral Dönitz began discussing how to end the war, albeit not before heading further north into Holstein to Flensburg, the latest government headquarters in the ever-shrinking Reich. Dönitz realized there was nothing left to fight for except to save as many as possible from falling into the clutches of the Red Army; he was every bit as aware as Keitel of the savagery with which the Germans had treated prisoners and civilians of the Soviet Union and it was clear they were now reaping what they had sowed. 'It was obvious to us', noted Keitel, 'that when the time came we would be asked to capitulate on the spot and without further ado; so it was a matter of expediting the transfer of what was still over three million troops from the Eastern Front to the American occupation zone, to prevent them falling into Russian hands.'

There was something in this, yet it was now inconceivable that any more than a trickle of these troops would be able to flee to the west. Across the Elbe, the boundary of what had become east and west, there was now only one bridge, at Tangermünde, and that was collapsed, allowing only a handful at a time to cross. The fate of the majority of those millions of German troops was already sealed, whereas with every hour the war continued, more people would die. In any case, the German High Command had already passed the point when they could influence anything. As the Russian soldier had told Helmut Altner, the war was over. Dönitz and men like Keitel had just one task: to surrender as soon as possible. Unconditionally. It was entirely typical of the warped, twisted, arrogant thought processes of these corrupted commanders that they should think there was still any hope, or any point to continuing the war a moment longer.

Meanwhile, Berliners were already confronting the Russian hordes and experiencing what it was like to be vanquished. Ruth Andreas-Friedrich, her partner Andrik Krassnow and the four refugees they were looking after were spending the days trying to clean up their home. All amenities were still down. 'Hauling water from the well takes hours every day,' noted Ruth in her diary. 'We work like slaves. Kindle the fire, gather wood, chop wood, sweep up the rubble. Cleaning up, constantly cleaning up.' Russian troops appeared from time to time, neither unfriendly nor friendly, but taking whatever they wanted. 'They look right through us as if we don't exist,' she jotted. '"Clock, clock," they say sometimes. '"Schnapps" and "Velocipede".'

While many of the victors were still roaming the streets looking for loot, Yelena Kagan, on the other hand, had been working flat out at the Reichskanzlei. On 4 May she briefly managed to escape, however. She had been interrogating a German stoker who had been called in to fix a faulty ventilator in the Führerbunker and who had inadvertently become a witness to Hitler's wedding. The interrogation had gone on and on, and combined with the vast mass of papers she was having to pore through, she was relieved to be able to get out for a brief tour of the ruined city. In the company of their driver, Sergey, she walked up towards the Brandenburg Gate and then to the still-smoking Reichstag. Above the skeleton of its dome the red Soviet flag fluttered. The lower windows were now boarded up and already covered in graffiti. With a stubby pencil Sergey wrote, 'Hello to all Siberians!' Yelena felt too emotional to speak, but silently added her own greetings to all Muscovites.

Outside, the streets were mostly deserted of civilians but Soviet vehicles rumbled through cleared mounds of rubble, directed by Red Army girls with white gloves. They crossed a bridge over the Spree, inching past a German truck that was upside down. Someone had written on the side, 'All our wheels are turning for the war'. Yelena spotted a German woman sitting on the bridge, legs outstretched, her head thrown back and laughing hysterically. Yelena Kagan greeted her but the woman looked at her with dazed, unfocused eyes, then shouted, 'Alles kaputt!'

That same day, 4 May, Hitler's body was finally unearthed, not that his discoverers knew it then. His remains were found by chance by a Red Army private, Ivan Chourakov of the LXXIX Corps, part of the Third Shock Army. Under the instructions of Colonel Klimenko, they had decided to give the Reichskanzlei garden one last search. Now, though, Chourakov's attention was drawn to the loose soil in a shell crater just beyond the bunker exit and then, on closer inspection, he spotted the remains of human legs. He and Klimenko began digging and discovered not one but two bodies. Klimenko didn't think either of them could be Hitler because he'd heard reports that two bodies discovered the previous day were likely to be those of the Führer and his wife. Unbeknown to him, this had already been discounted, but Klimenko only learned of it that night and so early the next day he sent four of his men, under Captain Deryabin, to dig up the remains in the shell hole – remains that had been unwittingly discovered once already but then reburied. They uncovered a male and female and two dead dogs. One of these was Hitler's Alsatian, Blondi.

Yelena Kagan was witness to the recovery of the bodies and then, early the following morning, 6 May, to their abduction. That day, the Fifth Shock Army was taking over the command of Berlin and ordered the Reichskanzlei and bunker complex to be cleared. Colonel Klimenko was determined not to lose his precious bodies now he'd found them, and certainly not before they had been forensically examined, so having wrapped them in sheets, and behind the backs of the new sentries, his men passed them over a wall of the Reichskanzlei garden to where trucks were waiting. And then they were whisked away to SMERSH headquarters, now at Buch, just to the north of Berlin.

On 6 May, Ruth Andreas-Friedrich dared to venture out into the suburbs. Thousands of civilians were clearing the streets and she was struck by the look of fear and even panic in many of the faces. 'Dismay and terror,' she wrote in her diary. 'Wherever we go there is pillaging, looting, violence. With unrestrained sexual lust our conqueror's army has flung itself upon the women of Berlin.' She and Frank, one of the refugees at her house, visited a friend, Hannelore Thiele. She could not stop crying and told them she thought she probably ought to kill herself.

'Was it really that bad?' Ruth asked her.

'Seven,' her friend replied. 'Seven in a row. Like animals.'

They also visited another girl, Inge Zaun. 'She is eighteen years old and didn't know anything about love,' wrote Ruth. 'Now she knows everything. Over and over again, sixty times.' Inge seemed impassive, almost indifferent. It was impossible to defend oneself, she pointed out. The Russians had pounded on the door and senselessly fired their weapons. The first time they came, they made her father watch; she thought she would die. Then they came the next night too. Now an officer had taken her as his mistress, so it was only one she had to deal with. Ruth and Frank spoke to another man whose daughter had been raped twelve times already. It seemed no one could talk of anything else; rape and suicide.

Later they walked back through the streets, the *Trümmerfrauen* – the rubble women – clearing the debris. For many, this was the only way to earn any money or secure any food: seventy-two Reichspfennige and a single ration card was the daily wage. They worked in columns of twenty or so, picking out bricks but also beams, fireplaces, toilets and anything salvageable and clearing away the rest. Evening was drawing on, but as Ruth and Frank walked back to the house the diggers were still working, stooped figures amid the rubble. One man, seeing them go past, looked at them with hate. 'Commissars,' he hissed. 'Bloody stool pigeons.'

Meanwhile, that same day, 6 May, Dönitz decided he wanted nothing more to do with Himmler, who was hanging around the new headquarters in Flensburg like a bad smell. At 5 p.m. he summoned the Reichsführer and told him that all ties between him and the government were now dissolved. Keitel then informed Himmler that he was no longer to visit Dönitz's headquarters in any capacity. Meanwhile, Jodl, still Chief of Staff of the OKW, was sent to Reims to negotiate the surrender with Eisenhower. The new Nazi High Command, soaked in delusion, was continuing to try and buy time.

In Berlin, however, the war had now been over for several days. Yelena Kagan continued to work tirelessly. If she wasn't helping to interrogate the stream of German prisoners who had been witness to Hitler's last days she was poring over vast numbers of documents. Yelena was also struck by the many nationalities now trapped in Berlin. On her way back to SMERSH headquarters in Buch she and her team came across a cart and lone cow to which was attached an Italian flag. Music was blaring from the nearest house, and, curious, they went inside to find a number of Italians gathered round an old piano while one of them played with gusto. These were all former Italian troops who'd been disarmed by the Germans at the time of the armistice back in September 1943 and then deported to Germany as forced labour. On seeing the Russians suddenly in their midst the pianist stopped playing, and after the Italians had hastily gathered a number of boxes and hurried back out to the waiting cow and cart one of them shouted, 'Hitler kaputt!' as they left. He was certainly that, Yelena thought to herself. There was no two ways about it; and she knew, as she'd seen what remained of him.

They still needed firm proof; publicly there seemed to be some doubt over whether he was alive or dead. Yelena couldn't understand why her own side weren't making a statement. If anything, an even greater shroud of secrecy had been imposed on the entire operation to find and identify Hitler's remains, so that only a team of three were now involved. This no longer included Colonel Klimenko, for example. Rather, it was headed by Colonel Vassily Gorbushin of SMERSH, one other more junior officer and also Yelena, who was to continue as interpreter. Their task was to prove that the charred mass they had, with its revolting stench of burnt flesh, was indisputably that of Hitler. A commission of army doctors was established at Surgical Mobile Field Hospital No. 4961, and under the watchful eye of Medical Service Colonel Faust Shkaravsky, the principal forensic medical expert on the 1st Belorussian Front, Major Anna Marants carried out the autopsy, not that either knew who the body was suspected to be. It was 8 May; the Führer's remains were carefully dissected and examined while VE Day was being celebrated by the Western Allies.

Their examination confirmed that the body was a male of fifty to sixty years old and approximately 165cm in height. They also discovered that the corpse's teeth were remarkably undamaged by the flames, and while a section of the skull was missing the jaw and upper teeth were extracted. Afterwards Colonel Gorbushin handed Yelena a red jewellery box. It contained Hitler's teeth, he told her. She was now answerable for its safekeeping. This was because their actual safe was still with the rear echelon and hadn't yet caught up and he thought that Yelena, as a female, was less likely to get drunk and lose the box. 'It was decidedly tiresome to be carrying a box about,' she noted, and found herself turning cold whenever she thought about its contents. 'It burdened and oppressed me,' she added.

*

Like most other Germans, Ruth Andreas-Friedrich heard the news of the surrender soon after some Russians appeared at her home and stole the two bicycles she and her companions had made from salvaged parts. The announcement more than made up for the loss, however. 'Liberated from bombs!' she wrote. 'Liberated from blackouts! Liberated from the Gestapo, liberated from the Nazis!' That night they celebrated with all the drink they had left in the house.

Yet it was not officially over until the German High Command signed the surrender formally here, in the wrecked capital of the Third Reich. And that, Stalin had dictated, should take place just after midnight on 9 May. While Dönitz had remained in Flensburg, Keitel now found himself pacing up and down in an anteroom at the Karlshorst barracks for much of the afternoon of 8 May, increasingly riled at being kept waiting. Ruth Andreas-Friedrich and her friends in the Uncle Emil resistance group might have been celebrating, and most of the free world similarly drinking the cup of victory, but Keitel spent long hours along with von Friedeburg and Stumpff contemplating the humiliation to come, albeit one that had included a sumptuous lunch at around 3 p.m. that afternoon. 'Our patience was being sorely tried,' noted Keitel. 'At five o'clock we were taken into another building and served afternoon tea, but nothing happened.' At 10 p.m., all patience exhausted, he demanded to know what on earth was going on and when the signing would take place. It was astonishing that the man about to sign an unconditional surrender, who had earlier witnessed the devastation of Berlin – for which he had a direct responsibility with his abject and servile fawning to Hitler – should now be getting hot under the collar about being made to wait by his victors.

His wait finally came to an end just after midnight, as Stalin had ordered, when they were led into a hall in which covered tables had been laid out. On the right-hand side of the room, under the Allied flags, was the top table and there sat Marshal Zhukov, flanked by Air Chief Marshal Tedder and General Spaatz. Three other tables led from this and it was to the third, closest to the entrance doors, that the German delegation was brought. 'Every corner of the hall was packed,' noted Keitel, 'and brilliantly lit by spotlights.' Keitel came in, raised his field marshal's baton in salute then unsteadily approached the table at the edge of the room, near the door. His monocle, that strange appendage so loved by the Prussian military elite, fell out of his eye. As he sat down, his face red and blotchy, he took off his gloves and carefully rearranged his monocle, then did his best to sit ramrod-straight and stare down his conquerors, occasionally stroking his chin. The entire ceremony was filmed, of course, and the cameras caught a brief moment when Keitel's mask slipped. A sudden glance behind him, and in that couple of seconds the cameraman captured the fear on his face. He then signed nine copies of the instrument of surrender – three each in English, Russian and German. Then Stumpff and von Friedeburg – who must have been getting used to signing surrenders by now – followed suit. After them it was the turn of Spaatz, Zhukov and Tedder.

And then it was done. The time: 12.43 a.m. Toasts followed, then more toasts and more again, but the Germans had been whisked away by then; they were prisoners of the Western Allies, after all, not the Soviets.

The following morning all three German commanders were taken back to Tempelhof, having been driven once more through the wrecked city. 'We flew straight back to Flensburg,' noted Keitel, 'relieved to be in a British aircraft and in the air.' They touched back down again at around 10 a.m.

The war against Nazi Germany was over. Officially. But what of Hitler's teeth? Yelena Kagan had been about to go to bed late on the 8th when she was called to listen to the live broadcast of the surrender ceremony. She was still clutching her red jewellery box but put it down on the floor as she and Major Bystrov and a further officer called Major Pichko clinked glasses and drank to the end of the Great Patriotic War. Soon after, she headed back down the wooden stairs then suddenly stopped, as though electrified by the enormity of the moment. 'God almighty,' she thought, 'is this happening to me? Is this me standing here at the moment Germany surrenders, with a box in my hands containing the indisputable remnants of Adolf Hitler?!'

But they were not the indisputable remnants yet. That could only be proved by locating copies of Hitler's dental records. How, though, in a ruined city of millions, amid the chaos, were they ever going to find the Führer's dentist? Somehow luck was with them, however, as they set off through the shattered city, Sergey driving his captured Ford 8 saloon over barricades crushed by tanks and along channels through cleared mounds of rubble. At the first German hospital they came to they were told they should try and find a renowned laryngologist, Carl von Eicken, who headed the Charité Clinic and who had definitely treated Hitler in the past. He would know the Führer's dentist. It took them some time to find the Charité Clinic in a ruined city of few street signs, but they did successfully locate it and also von Eicken, who admitted to having treated Hitler twice, once in 1935 and again in 1944 after the July assassination attempt. He didn't know who Hitler's dentist had been but called a student from the dentistry department at the clinic. Incredibly, this student dentist was not only able to confirm that Dr Hugo Blaschke had personally attended to the Führer's teeth, but also agreed to take them to him. Back into the Ford 8 they clambered and drove to the Kurfürstendamm, formerly one of the most desirable districts of Berlin. Once more luck was with them, because Blaschke's private clinic was at No. 213 and was still, miraculously, largely intact. Blaschke, it turned out, had been flown to Berchtesgaden in anticipation of Hitler's evacuation there but his dental assistant, Käthe Heusermann, had remained in Berlin.

The ever-helpful student, who, it turned out, was from Bulgaria, volunteered to go and fetch her; she lived at No. 39–40 Pariserstrasse, Apartment 1. When Fräulein Heusermann duly arrived and saw Colonel Gorbushin and Sergey she burst into tears; she had already been raped by Russian soldiers. After they had assured that they meant no harm she calmed down and admitted that they did hold Hitler's dental records, then produced a box of patients' cards, which, with bated breath, they watched her methodically go through. At last she extracted Hitler's medical card but, frustratingly, there were no X-rays. Fräulein Heusermann suggested they might be at Blaschke's other office in the Reichskanzlei itself, so off they went again, back to the place where Hitler had breathed his last.

It was now empty and quiet and guarded by a sentry who refused to let them in. Gorbushin produced a pistol and a stream of invective and in they went. The Reichskanzlei was dark and even more cavernous, and they had only one torch between them. None the less, after descending to the depths down two flights of stairs, their steps echoing ominously, they found Blaschke's room. It was boxy and small, complete with a dentist's chair and a small desk. And there they at last retrieved Hitler's dental records as well as a set of X-rays of his teeth.

Now armed with what they had been hunting, it was time to return to Buch, but at the Brandenburg Gate the Ford 8 conked out. Suddenly guns boomed out and for a moment Yelena thought the worst until realizing that it was, in fact, a victory salute. Eventually Sergey got the car going again and they continued on their way to Buch, taking Käthe Heusermann with them. The city suddenly seemed quiet; Yelena saw no lights on in the streets of shattered houses; Berlin was a dark, forbidding place. There were hardly any Red Army troops about either; having celebrated all day, they seemed to have quietened down. Berlin was eerily still. Nor was there any victory drinking for her on this day the war officially ended. She was exhausted and so went straight to bed.

The following day, 10 May, Käthe Heusermann was able to match the teeth Yelena had been safeguarding in the red jewellery box with the X-rays. They were one and the same. So that clinched it. They had found Hitler. He was not alive; all that bile, all that hatred, all the devastation and destruction and mass murder had been reduced to a mass of charred remains, broken bone and a set of remarkably well preserved teeth. He was as dead as the Third Reich.

'The world goes wild celebrating victory,' noted Ruth Andreas-Friedrich. 'Meanwhile Berliners ponder where to find something to eat.' The end triggered many different emotions. For the victors, for the vanquished. For the victims of this terrible catastrophe of a war. Helmut Altner had been shown mercy and simply told to go home. Ruth and her friends, meanwhile, would somehow have to try and rebuild their lives amid the ruins. Keitel now faced long weeks and months of interrogation – and would eventually end up on the end of the hangman's rope. Perhaps that would shake off some of the entitlement and appalling arrogance. And these days of victory prompted many emotions in Yelena Kagan too. Her heart sang with joy at the thought that she was still alive, that she really might return home, stare up at a peaceful sky. The war was over. War was no more. But at the same time she was close to tears: 'at the afflictions of the past,' she wrote, 'and from bewilderment over the future you now face'.

In many ways, there were no victors at all.

CHAPTER 11

LOST IN TRANSLATION

The Surrender of Japan, *15 August 1945*

3) The result of the futile and senseless German resistance to the might of the aroused free peoples of the world stands forth in awful clarity as an example to the people of Japan. The might that now converges on Japan is immeasurably greater than that which, when applied to the resisting Nazis, necessarily laid waste to the lands, the industry and the method of life of the whole German people. The full application of our military power, backed by our resolve, will mean the inevitable and complete destruction of the Japanese armed forces and just as inevitably the utter devastation of the Japanese homeland.

The Potsdam Declaration

WITH THE WAR IN EUROPE OVER, UNFINISHED business had been the order of the day at the Potsdam Conference. The Allied leaders were no longer the fabled Big Three of Yalta: Roosevelt was dead, his successor, Harry Truman, with destiny thrust upon him, taking his place; Churchill, having lost the 'khaki election', was on his way out and replaced, during the conference, by the man who had been his deputy, the Labour Prime Minister Clement Attlee; and Stalin, the immovable object at the head of the irresistible force that was the Soviet Union.

At Potsdam the Allies turned their gaze from the smouldering ruins of Germany to the Far East. Their deliberations, along with their Chinese co-belligerent, Chiang Kai-shek, about this next stage of the war were straightforward, and the conclusions realized in the form of the declaration issued there. In plain enough language, or so it seemed, the Allies laid out their terms for an end to the fighting with Japan – again demanding unconditional surrender. The declaration's tone was suitably strident: 'We will not deviate from them. There are no alternatives. We shall brook no delay.'

The declaration also offered the Japanese 'prompt and utter destruction', something the Allies knew they could now deliver. During the conference President Truman received news that the Manhattan Project's Trinity Test of 16 July had been a success – he took the opportunity to hint to Stalin that things were going to go up a gear. Stalin was all too aware: the

Manhattan Project had long been penetrated by Soviet spies. Stalin had not put the Soviet Union's name to the declaration; rather Generalissimo Chiang Kai-shek had signed it, underlining China's role as a belligerent. The USSR was not at war with Imperial Japan. At least not yet.

But communication between the Allies and Japan was not a simple thing. Nuance could go missing, plain speaking could be obfuscated. Getting the Japanese to understand that they too were finished was difficult. And as far as the Allies were concerned, they *were* finished. Prompt and utter destruction was a reality.

The terms of the declaration were boilerplate Allied stuff, from freedom of religion to prosecution of war criminals, 'including those who have visited cruelties upon our prisoners', guarantees that while reparations would be exacted eventually the Japanese would be allowed to rejoin world trade, reassurances that there was no Allied intention to enslave the Japanese people or destroy the nation. But it had a message for the people in charge: 'There must be eliminated for all time the authority and influence of those who have deceived and misled the people of Japan into embarking on world conquest, for we insist that a new order of peace, security and justice will be impossible until irresponsible militarism is driven from the world.'

It was, to be sure, a classic Allied document in that it clearly stated plenty of intention but beyond that was vague on the details. There was no mention of the Emperor, who was the cornerstone of the Japanese polity, the *kokutai*. But the Allies were on a roll and in a hurry; they'd put one war to bed, now it was time for the other, and these questions were for the Japanese to answer – they had, after all, wanted war.

It is safe to say that the Japanese government had not got the war it had wanted. The strike on Pearl Harbor in December 1941, intended as a show of force to bring a humbled United States of America to the negotiating table, had led, after a year of conquest in 1942, to Japan slowly and surely being crushed by the emerging superpower. Time and again the Japanese, whose grand strategy could best be described as overreach, were defeated bloodily and mercilessly by the American and Allied effort. Nearly every island and territory the Japanese had captured and overpowered at the start of the war in the Far East, when they had caught the world on the hop, had been ripped from their hands. Those that hadn't were left to dangle.

In Burma too, where the forces of the British Empire had at first been so discombobulated by Japanese aggression and tactical resourcefulness that they had lost the entire country, the relentless pressure exerted by the British-led Indian Army had resulted in the Imperial Army's greatest single defeat. By any measure, Japan, which by the end of the war was to have lost 3,365,900 dead, was on its knees and the economy had completely collapsed – steel production, which had exceeded 8 million tons in 1943, had shrunk to the thousands. The war, which had been about extending Japan's reach and its Imperial frontiers and pushing the outside world and its empires further away, had rebounded back on to the Japanese.

And now the home islands were in the noose. Okinawa, 340 miles from the Japanese mainland, had finally fallen on 22 June after six weeks of savage fighting, a typhoon of steel that overlapped the end of the war in Europe. The Americans had sent a vast fleet to deliver an eventual quarter of a million men to Okinawa. The Japanese lost 110,000 soldiers, killed in the fighting. Kamikaze planes, bitter symbols of the spirit of Japanese resistance, screamed futilely down on to the vast Allied naval fleet off the islands. The aircraft carrier USS *Bunker Hill* was hit by two of them within thirty seconds and was not sunk. At Okinawa Japanese dedication to not surrendering, to fighting to the end or committing suicide, horrified the Americans, who had suffered 12,500 dead and lost thirteen destroyers, with kamikaze attacks costing the US Navy many of its 8,000 or so casualties (about half of whom were killed) as well as hundreds of ships damaged and 763 aircraft lost. And there was more hideous bloodshed. Civilians were encouraged to kill themselves rather than join the surrender – at least 145,000 died. If ever a battle was a bloodbath, it was Okinawa. It struck dread in American hearts, and resolve in Japanese assessment of how the war might end.

Okinawa showed the way: whatever unachievable grand strategy had led to the disaster now facing Japan, in the knowledge that its people could and would go down fighting the government had one simple objective: to extract the most favourable peace from the vengeful Americans that they could, by making the price of the Americans' ultimate victory as bloody and costly as possible. The Americans had in place a naval blockade designed to force the Japanese economy into autarky. They had also switched their policy of aerial bombing away from their earlier somewhat ideological efforts of precision bombing to low-level fire bombing, with apocalyptic effect. The B-29 bomber, the Superfortress, had been designed, developed and built at huge expense to drop bombs on industrial targets from vast altitude, though on arrival in the skies over Japan the unanticipated high winds of the stratosphere rendered it almost impossible to hit targets with any degree of certainty. Raids in 1944 were perceived as not delivering the desired results. Frustrated with the lack of progress, at the turn of the year the USAAF had replaced Brigadier-General Haywood Hansell, the dedicated precision bombing advocate, with General Curtis LeMay, who switched to fire bombing. On the night of 9–10 March 1945, for Operation MEETINGHOUSE, 334 B-29s abandoned all pretence of precision and, eschewing their stratospheric capability, swooped low over Tokyo, dropping incendiary bombs which resulted in the death of at least 100,000 civilians. In terms of sheer destruction it was incredibly effective. The firestorm that followed destroyed a quarter of the city, 267,171 buildings, some sixteen square miles, displacing a million people and crippling its industrial output, but still didn't dispel the Japanese will to resist. Alongside this LeMay ran a campaign mining Japanese home waters, the uneuphemistically named Operation STARVATION. But for as long as they remained unconquered, the home islands of Kyushu, Honshu, Shikoku and Hokkaido would have to be fought for.

This was the price the Japanese were going to make the Americans pay for peace, with both governments locked into a suicide pact. The Japanese relied upon a murderous cynicism about the value of their own citizens' lives which was in turn bolstered by a culture that scorned the very notion of surrender, while the Americans were committed to a spiral of escalatory vengeance. For the Japanese the key to peace was more bloodshed.

Japan had mobilized its population unlike any other power – 6 million men had gone into uniform – and the Japanese war of expansion had been very personnel-hungry over a vast area. There were Japanese soldiers as far flung as China, Burma, the Philippines and New Guinea. As Japan lost its grip on its conquests, so it expanded its mobilization radically. The deployment of kids and the elderly in March 1945 made the German Volkssturm look decidedly half-hearted. Every man between fifteen and sixty was conscripted, along with all unmarried women between seventeen and forty, some 18–20 million, over a quarter of the population. Through extensive public information, the Japanese government made sure that its people knew the horrors which would be visited on them by the Americans when the time came, so if and when the Allies arrived on the home islands they would be met by a population determined to fight to the last round. And, with the cataclysmic destruction of Japanese cities from the air by the USAAF – run by airmen entirely set on winning the war from the skies alone – there was plenty of evidence to hand as to what the enemy had in mind for the Japanese. The carnage at Okinawa offered proof of concept. But there was, they believed, a lifeline: the Soviets.

Even as the Western Allies had been making sure that they honoured their commitments to the Soviet Union in dividing up Europe into various spheres of influence, so the Japanese were imagining the possibility that Stalin might be able to offer them a helping hand in dealing with their war with the West. This amounted to wanton wishful thinking – while the Soviets and Japanese had concluded a neutrality pact in April 1941 that put the seal on the border conflicts they had fought two years previously, the Soviets had decisively defeated the Japanese in the Battles of Khalkhin Gol, at a time when the Red Army was still reeling from Stalin's purges.

By 1945 the Red Army was a different beast altogether, one that had shattered German armies at will. Despite that neutrality pact, Stalin had assured the Allies at Tehran in 1943 that once he was done with Germany he would turn east, a 'Germany First' policy of the Soviet Union's very own. Plucking a number out of the air, he said that ninety days after Germany fell he would be able to intervene against the Japanese. None of this was known to the Japanese government, and crucially the Americans in turn knew that the Japanese didn't know. The Americans, having broken the Japanese 'Purple' cipher, were reading all the Japanese diplomatic service's traffic, and therefore were aware of the state of the Japanese position, such as it existed beyond fighting on. Any negotiation aimed at enticing the Soviets into offering an olive branch could only fail.

Nevertheless, even as it considered the politics of surrender, the Japanese government was certain it could rely on its people's resolve. Political calculations rested on top of a cultural certainty: the distaste for surrender itself. Unlike in Germany, where the question of surrender without honour preoccupied many, a direct legacy of the 1918 armistice which the Nazis had been able to use to propel their country into the abyss, in Japan surrender itself was dishonourable. After all, Germany had been defeated before while Japan had not. It sat outside the national experience. *Bushidō* – or at least conceptions based on interpretations of the idealized code, going back to the 1600s – dominated Japanese military culture, and after fifteen years of war and militarization, this same military culture dominated the civilian sphere totally. *Bushidō*, the 'way of the warrior', at a glance looks not unlike European medieval concepts of chivalry, but its emphasis on the dishonour of surrender offered the Japanese government both an opportunity – in that its soldiers would fight on when others, even the most fanatical Germans, might quit – and an impediment: how, if this was the way things were done in

Japan, could the government, and therefore the Emperor, surrender with honour?

The blood-soaked casualty figures from the fighting in the Far Eastern theatre show the reality of the commitment to *bushidō* culture in Japan and in the Japanese military in a way that is far harder to deny or dispel than the degree to which Germany was committed to Nazism. The death toll and how it manifested itself, through suicide, makes this clear. While, in Europe, some of the Nazi Party faithful, from the man at the top down through gauleiters, governors and judges and officials, did kill themselves when the end arrived, in as far as it is possible to divine their motivations it was as much to do with fear of what would happen to them if and when their enemies sought justice. For Japanese commanders, surrender was in itself unacceptable and suicide preferable – death, however it came, either fighting on to the finish or taking one's own life, was the way battle should end. In the combat on Iwo Jima from 19 February to 26 March, the Americans took a total of 216 prisoners from a Japanese Army and Navy force of 20,000, at which the Americans had had to throw 110,000 troops in total, costing them 6,821 dead as well as 19,217 wounded. On Okinawa civilians hurled themselves from the cliffs rather than be taken prisoner – this can be seen to be believed in American footage.

Only one Japanese unit broke the taboo and surrendered in the entire war: the 1st Battalion of the 329th Infantry on New Guinea, also known as the Takenaga Unit, who had been chased into the interior by the Australians. They numbered only fifty men. In April 1945 their officers decided that enough was enough – Japanese troops tended to travel light, hoping that their victories came quickly and they could scavenge supplies from their enemies or the local inhabitants wherever they were fighting. Prolonged campaigns being hunted down didn't sit well with this tactical style. The Australians were astonished to discover one of their own leaflets, which suggested the Japanese surrender, with a scrawled offer to do just that, left on a pole in the jungle. Contact was made on 2 May, and Lieutenant-Colonel Masaharu Takenaga parlayed terms; the next day five officers, four warrant officers, thirty-three NCOs and other ranks went into the bag. It was a unique triumph for the Australian forces, and one they made much of – new propaganda leaflets dropped on the enemy spread the word, causing the commander of the Eighteenth Army, General Hatazō Adachi, to break down and cry at the dishonour they had shown the Emperor.

As Emperor, Hirohito was where the *bushidō* buck stopped. At least, within the *kokutai*, that was the rule the highest echelons of Japanese politics claimed to observe. Following Okinawa, though, the Emperor found himself strangely out of step with the recently created Supreme Council for the Direction of the War, the Gunji Sangiin. This core council, known as the Big Six, was running the war and advising the Emperor. The Big Six consisted of the Prime Minister, retired Admiral Kantarō Suzuki, seventy-seven – he had been Commander-in-Chief of the Grand Fleet in the 1920s; Minister of Foreign Affairs Shigenori Tōgō, sixty-two, Minister of the Army General Korechika Anami, fifty-eight; Minister of the Navy Admiral Mitsumasa Yonai, sixty-five; Chief of the Army General Staff General Yoshijirō Umezu, sixty-three, and Chief of the Navy General Staff Admiral Soemu Toyoda, sixty. These men had been part of the Japanese higher echelons throughout the war and intransigence sat at the heart of their thinking – their resolve remained intact in spite of their attempts to marshal a Plan B with the Soviets.

By 30 July, four days after the Potsdam Declaration, the Japanese ambassador to Moscow, Naotake Satō, wrote to Tokyo to say that he thought the only thing that would be on offer from the Allies was unconditional surrender. He was being strung along. The Soviets had also indicated that they would not be expecting the neutrality pact to last beyond its five-year limit. This was as much as the Big Six knew of Allied intentions beyond the Potsdam Declaration. With their country being destroyed by blockade and air raid, and facing a threat of prompt and utter destruction, unable to see outside their situation, the Big Six voted to reject the Potsdam Declaration by four votes to two.

Rather than address its points in detail – and there had been argument about this within the Cabinet – the Big Six had decided to release a bowdlerized version of the declaration for public consumption, issued on 28 July, which left out mention of the threat of prompt and utter destruction. With this release, Prime Minister Suzuki said to reporters that in light of the content of the declaration, which was in his view nothing new, the government's response would be *mokusatsu* – a word that could be interpreted in a number of different ways. Literally, the characters meant 'silent kill', but it could also be read as 'no comment'. At any rate, the Japanese Imperial news agency, Domei, translated *mokusatsu* as 'the Japanese government ignores this, and we are determined to continue our bitter fight to the end'. Or rather, that is how American translators read Domei News's interpretation; and this left little room for nuance, whatever Suzuki's intentions might have been. Furthermore, Suzuki wasn't alone – there is no record of the Emperor disagreeing with his position, and Navy Minister Yonai, when asked why the Prime Minster had made the statement, had replied: 'If one is first to issue a statement, he is always at a disadvantage. Churchill has fallen, America is beginning to be isolated. The government therefore will ignore it. There is no need to rush.' Quite the response to the declaration's 'brook no delay'. The Big Six, contemplating the defence of Japan, had decided to ignore an ultimatum and continue a war that they calculated might cost them 20 million lives. They had correctly assessed that the likely battle, a mainland invasion by the Allies, would not come until the autumn. But there was something even the hard-hearted Big Six could not ignore.

Preceded by a weather scout, the single Superfortress named *Enola Gay* appeared over the city of Hiroshima a little after 8 a.m. on 6 August 1945, and at 8.15, following a six-minute bomb run, dropped the four-and-a-half-ton weapon. Its altimeter fuse ensured that it detonated by firing its fissile materials at one another 580 metres above the Shima Surgical Clinic. The B-29's captain, Colonel Paul W. Tibbets, had been selected because of his undeniable skill and expertise at precision bombing and had led the USAAF's first such raid in 1942 over France. However, like so many of the bombs dropped during the Second World War, the one christened Little Boy still missed its intended target. Not that it mattered much. Its contents did what they were designed to do – not unremarkable given that this was only the second atomic bomb ever detonated, and because Little Boy employed a different mechanism to the Trinity bomb it was in and of itself a test firing also – and in an instant the explosive power of 15,000 tons of TNT was detonated over the city of Hiroshima. According to the US Bombing Survey: 'Its duration was probably less than one tenth of a second and its intensity sufficient to cause nearby flammable objects . . . to burst into flame and to char poles as far as 4,000 yards away from the hypocenter . . . At 600–700 yards it was sufficient to chip and roughen granite . . . the heat also produced bubbling of tile to about 1,300 yards.' The British Mission report stated: 'Witnesses say that people who were directly under the explosion in the open had their exposed skin burnt so severely that it was immediately charred brown or black: these people died within minutes or at most hours. Both in Hiroshima and Nagasaki, burns on exposed skin were very severe up to about 1,500 yards from the centre of the damage. At this distance, some escaped with less severe burns, although very severe burns were occasionally reported at nearly 1½ miles from the centre of damage. Mild burns extended to distances of 2½ miles and more. Stories that white people were unharmed in Hiroshima where the darker skinned Japanese received fatal burns were not substantiated.' Either way, the survey concluded that the dead 'were killed as it were several times over, by each lethal agent separately'.

Eyewitnesses – sufficiently far from the bomb's detonation to survive – spoke of the single plane, the sudden light, clothes simply igniting. Although shelter would have done little, one of the ironies of the Hiroshima bomb is that the all-clear had been sounded before it was dropped – sirens had wailed for the plane *Straight Flush*, flying ahead of *Enola Gay*, to take meteorological readings. If there wasn't a suitable gap in the weather, Tibbets had been ordered to return to base.

Estimates regarding the casualties have been the subject of debate ever since. After all, with so many people simply vaporized, how could the dead be counted? Between 66,000 and 100,000 citizens were killed by the explosion in a city with a population of 320,000, along with a similar number injured. It was intended as a clear signal to the Japanese, and as such represented the pinnacle of Allied efforts to fight the war using technology rather than manpower: 'steel not flesh'. Though, critically and vividly illustrated by the atomic bombing of Hiroshima, the flesh in that formulation was Allied flesh – enemy lives were still there for the taking. The USAAF's film about the Hiroshima bomb laid out the air force's assessment of the damage done: '4 square miles in the centre of the city contained ¾ of the total inhabitants, here the population density per square mile was slightly greater than Brooklyn, New York . . . there were numerous one to five man workshops in the commercial and residential districts. These provided a fourth of the city's total industrial production.' The whole place, like every other Japanese conurbation, counted as a target. Area bombing's logical conclusion, as pitched its advocates since the 1920s, was reached on the morning of 6 August 1945; the core aim was to make it impossible for the enemy to carry its population with it further into war. Despite the devastation, the Americans expected that they would have to do it twice, with targets already drawn up and the prospect of a third bomb later in the month.

Hiroshima was one of the sixty-six cities that the USAAF had not yet destroyed, but for the purposes of the atomic bomb it had been chosen as a military target. It was the base of the headquarters of the Second General Army and at its centre was Hiroshima Castle. For all Truman's distaste about attacking civilians, the President was able to satisfy himself that Hiroshima did fit the bill as a legitimate military target. In his diary on 25 July 1945, while he was in Potsdam, the President had noted:

> The target will be a purely military one . . . The weapon is to be used against Japan between now and August 10th. I have told the secretary of war, Mr Stimson, to use it so that military objectives and soldiers and sailors are the target and not women and children; even if the chaps are savage ruthless merciless and fanatic we as the leader of the world for the common welfare cannot drop this terrible bomb on the old capital or the new.

Kyoto and Tokyo had been spared from atomic destruction. Was this cant on Truman's part, or an expression of his intuition that the atomic bomb was ushering in a new kind of warfare that would put all previous assumptions and calculations aside? The Tokyo fire bombing somehow didn't count compared to the power and potential of the atomic bomb. This was a new kind of war: shock as much as anything else mattered, shock and the reaction it might prompt.

The Japanese reaction to Hiroshima was mixed. The initial report from Kure Naval Station wasn't able, quite, to figure out what had happened: 'Today 3 B-29s flew over Hiroshima at a high altitude at about 08:25 and dropped several bombs. A terrific explosion accompanied by flame and smoke occurred at an altitude of 500 to 600 meters. The concussion was beyond imagination and demolished practically every house in the city. Present estimate of damage: about 80 per cent of the city was wiped out, destroyed, or burnt, and casualties have been estimated at 100,000 persons.'

On the technical side there was disbelief that the Americans could have devised such a weapon, an estimation based on their own difficulties in building one. Japanese scientists were as in touch with the scientific possibilities of atomic weapons as anyone else in the world. Yoshio Nishina, Japan's leading atomic scientist, had before the war studied under Ernest Rutherford in Cambridge and Niels Bohr in Copenhagen. Nishina joined the army's atomic weapon programme at the end of 1942, and so central was he to the project that in 1943 it was named Ni-Go after him. But neither time nor resources were on Japan's side; American dominance of the seas and skies was throttling every single aspect of the Japanese war effort. On 13 April 1945 Ni-Go's 'Building 49' was destroyed in an air raid. On 28 June Nishina reported to the army that he was giving up on researching nuclear weapons; it was too difficult to acquire the materials he needed and, more than that, he thought the Americans would be facing the same difficulties and would be unable to build an atomic weapon. By the time the Manhattan Project successfully conducted the Trinity Test, the Japanese had talked themselves out of the possibility.

The most reliable source the Japanese had regarding what had happened was the American President, Harry S. Truman, who took to the radio on 6 August to explain. The atomic blast at Hiroshima could only achieve its true political effect if what it could do was made public. That which had been most secret was now public knowledge.

Truman stated bluntly: 'Sixteen hours ago an American airplane dropped one bomb on Hiroshima, an important Japanese Army base. That bomb had more power than 20,000 tons of T.N.T. . . . The Japanese began the war from the air at Pearl

Harbor. They have been repaid manyfold. And the end is not yet. With this bomb we have now added a new and revolutionary increase in destruction to supplement the growing power of our armed forces. In their present form these bombs are now in production and even more powerful forms are in development.'

Truman went on to explain that the 'force from which the sun draws its power has been loosed against those who brought war to the Far East'. In his 1,100-word broadcast he ran through a brief history of British and American cooperation on the atomic bomb, the 2 billion dollars it had cost, and sang the praises of the scientists and industrialists who had made the bomb possible: 'What has been done is the greatest achievement of organized science in history.' And then, in a broadcast intercepted by the Domei News company at 1.00 a.m. on 7 August, he restated the threat at the heart of the Potsdam Declaration and his dissatisfaction with Suzuki's *mokusatsu*: 'We are now prepared to obliterate more rapidly and completely every productive enterprise the Japanese have above ground in any city . . . Let there be no mistake; we shall completely destroy Japan's power to make war. It was to spare the Japanese people from utter destruction that the ultimatum of July 26 was issued at Potsdam. Their leaders promptly rejected that ultimatum. If they do not now accept our terms they may expect a rain of ruin from the air, the like of which has never been seen on this earth.'

The Americans also took measures to circumvent the Japanese government's tight control of information, and let the Japanese population know about the escalation of war. For once the USAAF wasn't dropping bombs on Japan, they were dropping 16 million leaflets with photographs that outlined the destruction in Hiroshima on forty-seven Japanese cities, potentially covering 40 per cent of the population. Radio broadcasts – every fifteen minutes – detailed the disaster that had befallen Hiroshima. Given the lack of detail the Japanese government had allowed its people so far, this perhaps amounted to a deluge, and from a source they might not be familiar with; nevertheless the Allies were doing what they could to get their message through. The message being: utter destruction.

Rumours swirled around the centres of power – the army, keen to downplay Hiroshima, denied that the bomb was atomic. The day after it had been dropped, Nishina wrote to a colleague saying that if Truman was telling the truth, the Americans had achieved a 'great victory over us'.

That morning he was ordered to join an army survey team, led by the head of the General Staff Headquarters Second Division, General Seizō Arisue, one of several teams dispatched to the benighted city to investigate whether the weapon could have been an atomic bomb. Arisue was a true believer in the Japanese strategy to fight the Americans to a standstill, having said: 'If we could defeat the enemy in Kyushu or inflict tremendous losses, forcing him to realize the strong fighting spirit of the Japanese Army and people, it would be possible, we hoped, to bring about the termination of hostilities on comparatively favourable terms.'

He and the army were hoping to discover that Truman's broadcast had merely been propaganda. On the flight to Hiroshima Nishina was told by one of the officers with him, Lieutenant-Colonel Seiichi Niizuma – who had been involved with the Army Minister in the decision to shut down the Ni-Go project – that the weapon couldn't be atomic as they were too difficult to make. When Arisue did land, he was greeted by an officer half of whose face had been badly burnt. Nishina had been delayed by a faulty aircraft and took the time to write to a friend, saying: 'If Truman's broadcast turns out to be true then I think the time for all of us related to Ni-Go to literally cut our stomachs has come.' Nevertheless there was still a concerted effort to deny that the bomb was atomic – claims that the Americans had dropped more than one weapon or seeded the sky with magnesium to deliver the flash began to be circulated. But Nishina quickly ascertained the truth when he took radiation readings in the hypocentre of the explosion.

And there was other, somewhat confusing and contradictory information. Flight Lieutenant Marcus McDilda was shot down in his P-51 Mustang over Osaka on 8 August and passed on to the Kempeitai, the Imperial Japanese Army's secret police. The Kempeitai handled the 350,000 prisoners of war who had been brought to Japan. Torture methods were part of their standard training; they were also, in China, connected to weapons research at the notorious biological weapon research facility Unit 731. McDilda, who had been beaten up by civilians as he was paraded through the streets of Osaka, very quickly found himself being pumped for information regarding the explosion at Hiroshima – how many of these bombs did the Americans have and where were they going to be deployed next? Needless to say, a fighter jock like McDilda knew nothing about the world's hitherto most secret weapon. However, under torture he quickly realized the Kempeitai were desperate for information, as desperate as he was to survive – they had told him that he would be beheaded if he didn't tell them what he knew. A sword was held to his lips to make the point. So McDilda sang like an ill-informed canary. He told his torturers that the Americans had 100 of these bombs and that the next targets were Tokyo and Kyoto – later claiming that these were the only cities he had heard of in Japan. Warming to his subject, and the Kempeitai's response to it, McDilda elaborated, leaning hard on what chemistry he could remember from his schooldays:

> As you know, when atoms are split, there are a lot of pluses and minuses released. Well, we've taken these and put them in a huge container and separated them from each other with a lead shield. When the box is dropped out of a plane, we melt the lead shield, and the pluses and minuses come together. When that happens, it causes a tremendous bolt of lightning and all the atmosphere over a city is pushed back! Then when the atmosphere rolls back, it brings about a tremendous thunderclap, which knocks down everything beneath it.

It was nonsense, but it was good enough. McDilda was flown to Tokyo as a result, and was handed over to a civilian scientist who immediately realized that the Flight Lieutenant was bullshitting. It saved his life, as fifty prisoners of war in Osaka were murdered shortly thereafter.

But McDilda's fictions added to the information confusing the Japanese and those who still refused to believe in the atomic bomb. On 9 August, Chief of the Navy Staff Toyoda said that he doubted whether the Americans had any more of these 'atomic' bombs, again drawing on what he knew about Japanese efforts to build a bomb. He also expressed a belief that the USA would not convince anyone that using the bomb could shorten the war and save thousands of lives.

He was, of course, wrong. At 11.01 a.m. on 9 August the USAAF dropped its second weapon, killing a further 60,000 people. The Americans were having to repeat themselves for emphasis. Ultimately this was the bomb that changed the world – because it showed that the Americans could and would deploy another atomic bomb. Again, it missed its target, and again to the people on the ground this barely mattered. Fat Man, the bomb dropped on Nagasaki, was a different device to Little Boy, and because of the geography of the city – chosen because of poor weather over the main target, Kokura – fewer people were killed. But for all its relative human inefficiency compared to Hiroshima, the destruction at Nagasaki was total.

Eyewitnesses did what they could to describe the aftermath of a device so powerful it had melted the Mitsubishi steelworks in the centre of the city and tossed railway locomotives hundreds of yards. Among those witnesses were British prisoners of war; the Petty Officer of HMS *Exeter* was four miles from the centre of the explosion in Fukuoka Camp No 11. The flash was so intense it 'would have lit up the whole of England'. The blast wave took twenty-two seconds to reach them. Then:

> About four minutes after the explosion a dense white cloud appeared over the target, a man-made cloud of terrific density, so dense that smoke from thousands of fires created by the bomb could not penetrate it but arose in huge columns in outer extremities of this pure white cloud.
>
> A little later, looking through a pair of common sunglasses at the cloud, colours appeared that I have never seen before; it looked like a giant catherine wheel, only

> very slowly revolving and milling, green merging into purple and reappearing as blue as Arctic ice pack, only to disappear and reappear as blood-red.

People near the hypocentre were simply vaporized, some leaving traces of shadows on the buildings that somehow withstood the blast and fire. On board the B-29, called *Bockscar*, the reporter William L. Laurence, who had witnessed the Trinity Test, talked to the radio operator, Sergeant Ralph D. Curry, twenty, of Hoopeston, Illinois. The small talk on the plane was about what dropping the bomb might achieve.

> He is a typical American youth, looking even younger than his 20 years. It takes no mind reader to read his thoughts.
>
> 'It' a long way from Hoopeston, Illinois,' I find myself remarking.
>
> 'Yep,' he replies, as he busies himself decoding a message from outer space. 'Think this atomic bomb will end the war?' he asks hopefully.
>
> 'There is a very good chance that this one may do the trick,' I assure him, 'but if not then the next one or two surely will. Its power is such that no nation can stand up against it very long.'
>
> This was not my own view. I had heard it expressed all around a few hours earlier before we took off. To anyone who had seen this man-made fireball in action, as I had less than a month ago in the desert of New Mexico, this view did not sound over-optimistic . . .
>
> Does one feel any pity or compassion for the poor devils about to die? Not when one thinks of Pearl Harbor and of the death march on Bataan.

News reached the Big Six, who were deep in deliberation and continued as planned. They were now deadlocked in two blocs. Prime Minister Suzuki, with Foreign Minister Togo and Minister of the Navy Yonai, favoured accepting the terms of the Potsdam Declaration but on the sole condition that the Emperor remain in place. Opposed were Minister of the Army Anami, Chief of the Army General Staff Umezu and Toyoda, who wanted conditions added, notably those that left them in place in government, safe from the possibility of being tried for war crimes, and Japan remaining armed, in effect blocking the possibility of surrender altogether.

The army were content that preparations for the land battle on the home islands were in place, and that the atomic bombs were nothing to worry about. Fighting the Americans in one last gigantic bloodbath would deliver the peace Japan needed – and mobilization and the army's *Ketsu-Go* strategy would dictate the terms of the end of the war. As part of *Ketsu-Go*, the air force was going to be used in a kamikaze rather than a ground support role, with 3,000 planes earmarked for this purpose. Civilian morale, which certainly didn't dictate policy in Japan in any sense, was noted to be declining, but not enough to change anyone's mind. Except perhaps their fate was stirring the conscience of the Emperor.

The meetings ground on to the 9th, and at midnight the Emperor, who'd been lobbied intensively during the afternoon, was requested by Suzuki to be asked his opinion and make a decision, an unprecedented step in a political tradition of divine nods and winks. And besides, there was more than the bomb to consider: the Soviets had come to the party, invading 'Manchuko' – the Japanese name for its satrap in Manchuria – that same day, catching the Japanese Kwantung

Army off guard. The Red Army burst through its lines – armed to the gills with Lend-Lease equipment and supplies – and it quickly became clear that the Soviets were threatening a rout. They had in characteristic style deployed three vast armies – the Transbaikal Front and the 1st and 2nd Far Eastern Fronts, 1,577,725 troops backed by 5,556 tanks and self-propelled guns, as well as 27,000 artillery pieces. These formed two pincers which swung into Manchuria to swallow it up, and the Kwantung Army, supposedly Japan's best operating formation, was smashed apart. Prime Minister Suzuki knew then that the end was in sight – with the Emperor unconvinced about defensive preparations and without the stomach to rule over an Empire of the Dead. The army could stick its head in the sand about the atomic bombs all it liked but this battlefield reality was undeniable.

Discussions dragged on. The pro-peace faction, who believed they had the Emperor onside, spelled out the disaster that continuing the war offered. The pro-war or anti-peace faction became increasingly desperate, Army Minister Anami even introducing Flight Lieutenant McDilda's 'intelligence' that Tokyo would be the next atomic bomb target. Finally, Suzuki, to protests from Anami, asked the Emperor for his decision. Breaking the tense silence, he leaned forward and said: 'then I will express my opinion'. Addressing the Cabinet, he said that he couldn't bear to see his people suffer any more; moreover, the impression he had got since June was that preparations for the possibility of an invasion were falling short, and that the risk to Japanese life was too great. He sided with Suzuki's faction: Japan would accept the Potsdam Declaration but only if he remained in power: a 'sacred decision'. The Cabinet moved to ratify; Japan would surrender. The

Emperor continued, pointing out how unbearable it all was that his subjects should be suffering and that his loyal ministers should also be in the frame for what had befallen Japan, but he must 'swallow [his] tears' and recommended that they accept the Suzuki faction's proposal; the bitter truth known to all was that while he would remain in place, they might all hang. The privy council president then told Hirohito he would have to answer to his ancestors for his responsibility in the defeat Japan now faced, but the die was cast.

Immediately word began to seep out. The War Ministry, led by Anami, wanted to fight to the end. He had commanded troops in New Guinea and Halmahera, returning to Japan in late 1944. In April 1945 he was appointed War Minister by Suzuki. Ever the twentieth-century Samurai, Anami had issued orders that anyone speaking up in favour of peace be arrested. From the moment the Emperor cast his vote in favour of surrender, Anami became the focal point for discontent within the army. He had told the Emperor that the only honourable course of action was to carry on fighting, that if Japan was to surrender, then it could do so only after it had fought to defend itself. His argument, at its core, was that it was better to go down swinging:

> But even if the enemy repeats his thrusts and we cannot repel him, would it not be wondrous for this whole nation to be destroyed like a beautiful flower, leaving for the world's posterity only the great name of Japan and its brave, noble history? Would it not be glorious to be remembered as a people who refused to submit? Would it not be far better than surrendering ignominiously to our enemies? But if we are not to follow so stern a course, if we are to seek peace, let us insist that we seek it honourably.

Immediately, pro-war sentiment in the army surged. Outraged staff officers demanded of Anami what they should do once they had received the enemy's reply. He stated they should respond with discipline and obey their orders whatever they were. Discontent mutated further, leading to junior officers in the General Staff drawing up a message to be broadcast urging soldiers to fight on, and this message ran in the newspapers on 11 August, to the alarm of the pro-peace faction. The surrender was by no means a done deal within the Japanese government, despite the Emperor's divine approval. In the meantime, staff at Domei News took it upon themselves to transmit the news that the government had accepted the declaration on their shortwave radio. They had to smuggle the message past the military censors, resorting to sending it out in Morse code – stating plainly 'Japan Accepts Potsdam Proclamation' – until it was spotted and shut down. Fortunately, United Press registered the transmission and reported the news, and it was this rather than the message drawn up by the disgruntled General Staff which reached Truman in Washington at 7.33 a.m. on 11 August (20.33 p.m. Tokyo time on the 10th).

The response was twofold, strategic and diplomatic. Deliberation in Washington evolved quickly. Truman ordered a halt to any further atomic bombings, and the White House got to work deciding on a response. Consulting with their partners, the Americans accepted one British stipulation, that the Allies not insist Hirohito sign the surrender, while Chiang Kai-shek's disagreement was simply ignored. While it was contentious that the Japanese had attached a condition to their unconditional surrender, the overall feeling was that an end to the war with the Emperor still in place was a quick and cheap win, and one to cement before the Soviets gained too much ground. Secretary of State Jimmy Byrnes replied via the Swiss attaché with a masterpiece of doublethink. The Emperor would surrender authority to the Allied Powers, but would retain authority within Japan over the Japanese.

> With regard to the Japanese Government's message accepting the terms of the Potsdam proclamation but containing the statement, 'with the understanding that the said declaration does not comprise any demand which prejudices the prerogatives of His Majesty as a sovereign ruler,' our position is as follows:
>
> From the moment of surrender the authority of the Emperor and the Japanese Government to rule the state shall be subject to the Supreme Commander of the Allied Powers who will take such steps as he deems proper to effectuate the surrender terms . . .
>
> The armed forces of the Allied Powers will remain in Japan until the purposes set forth in the Potsdam Declaration are achieved.
>
> Accept, sir, et cetera

Byrnes's wire was received at 2 a.m. Tokyo time on 12 August and caused immediate consternation. While this conditional unconditional surrender had met the sole demand that Hirohito and his Cabinet had made, it was too much for the literal diehards. The Emperor, divine ruler, was subordinate to none – this notion was integral to the Japanese conception of sovereignty and the cornerstone of their polity – what the Japanese called the *kokutai.* Nationalism and militarism would not permit alteration to the *kokutai*, cemented in the Meiji revolution of 1889 and boiled down to its finest essence by years of war, even as a Japanese army was rounded up in Manchuko by the Soviets and two cities lay irradiated and devastated. Byrnes had given the Emperor, and his emerging not so reluctant opponents, what they wanted. The Ministry of Foreign Affairs interpreted Byrnes's wire as a restriction of sovereignty. The army – which was frantically demanding that someone, anyone build them an atomic bomb and as soon as possible – took it badly also, and again it was Anami they came to.

Time was running out for the anti-peace faction. In the afternoon of 13 August the Imperial Household Council accepted the surrender terms, and preparations began for the Emperor to announce domestically the government's new position. They reassured the Emperor that he was doing the right thing, and that saving the *kokutai*, even in this compromised form – and of course them with it – was the right thing to do. At the same time, grumbles coming from within the Big Six and without about how the peace settlement would overthrow the *kokutai* got louder. The unthinkable, disruption of the *kokutai*, was leading to the incredible: a coup against the surrender.

Army officers, led by Major Kenji Hatanaka – as in any self-respecting coup, colonels were well represented, among them Anami's brother-in-law, Lieutenant-Colonel Masahiko Takeshita – spoke to Anami, who refused to say whether he would stop them in their attempt to block the surrender. With Anami on the fence, the rebels pressed on, bringing other conspirators into the coup. They weren't short of volunteers. Time was running out too; at 7 p.m. on the 14th the national broadcaster, the NHK, alerted the population to an important announcement the following morning. Two and a half hours later, they put into action their plan to overturn Japan's chance to avoid any further bloodshed and surrender.

Hatanaka went to the palace and proceeded to bend the truth to get the numbers he felt he needed, lying to the Second Regiment of the Imperial Guards' commanding officer, Lieutenant-Colonel Jirō Shiizaki, that he had Anami's support as well as that of the commanding officers of Eastern District Army and the Imperial Guards Divisions; in his quest to maintain the army's honour and preserve the *kokutai*, clearly a lie or two didn't matter. He then went to the office of General Shizuichi Tanaka, commander of the Eastern District, to try to persuade him to join the coup. Tanaka not only refused, he ordered Hatanaka to go home. Meanwhile Anami, overcome by the contradictions he had been forced to face, opted out, committing suicide by *seppuku*, disembowelling himself rather than deal with the future. He made a mess of it. As the coup played out, he writhed in agony for three hours until a doctor was ordered to kill him by lethal injection. He left a note, but he bungled that too. It read: 'Believing in the eternity of our Divine Land, with my death I apologize to the Emperor for the great crime', yet another message open to misinterpretation, the crime unspecified. Anami not only didn't get to see the *kokutai* upended, nor Japan's ignoble surrender – he also avoided the likelihood of the Allied gallows.

Hatanaka encountered further opposition when the commanding officer of the 1st Imperial Guards Division, Lieutenant-General Takeshi Mori, refused to join the coup, not believing Hatakana's assertions that a wider revolt was afoot. Increasingly desperate and worried that the General would stop him, Hatanaka killed Mori. Collateral to this was Mori's brother-in-law, Lieutenant-Colonel Michinori Shiraishi, whom Hatanaka killed as well. Hatanaka then took Mori's place, literally, using the dead General's seal to authorize Imperial Guards Division Strategic Order No. 584, commanding the Guards to reinforce the Imperial Palace and Household, and do what praetorian guards have done since time immemorial: effectively hold the Emperor hostage for his own protection. The palace police were disarmed. Hatanaka and 1,000 insurrectionists frantically searched the complex, looking for the Emperor's recorded speech – if they could silence the Emperor, loyally of course, the *kokutai* would be preserved.

At the same time, technicians in the palace were preparing the phonograph recording equipment that would be used to record Hirohito's speech in the bunker underneath the Imperial Household Ministry. This in itself was a mark of the potentially revolutionary change to the *kokutai* the surrender had provoked: the Emperor until this point had been a god made flesh, but capturing his voice brought him down to earth. A pair of microphones was set up, the Emperor arriving at 23.25. His speech, which contained the extraordinary slice of understatement 'the war situation has developed not necessarily to Japan's advantage' – a phrase Anami had insisted upon during the wrangling around the text that afternoon, adamant that they were not losing the war – was yet another moment when clear communication was crucial.

This would be the first time the Emperor's subjects had heard his voice, and for many the first intimation that the war really hadn't developed to Japan's advantage. But a peculiar choice was made in which version of Japanese the Emperor would use. As if to obfuscate his meaning, or deflect somehow from the gravity of the situation, Hirohito's address was delivered in formal Japanese, *kanbun kundoku-tai*, not the entirely normal conversational language that he and his subjects used.

Only the most educated and upper-class Japanese would understand this *kanbun kundoku-tai*, and a translation would be needed for the ordinary listener. He fumbled some of the words, as he was unfamiliar with the pronunciation, and recorded a second take in the hope of improving his delivery. In a high-pitched and obviously nervous voice, the Emperor announced that his government would be accepting the Potsdam terms, that 'the security and well-being of our subjects is the solemn obligation which has been handed down by our Imperial Ancestors', not to mention saving his own skin. Four minutes and forty-five seconds long, the English translation was only 656 words, bringing to an end the war in the Far East, and finally speaking directly to the Allies. Though without mentioning the word 'surrender'.

But he made one thing clear, at least from where he sat, in the bunker recording this shattering message: the atomic bomb had changed everything. Echoing Truman's language about the power of the bomb, and anticipating the language that remains indelibly the mark of the nuclear age, he said: 'Moreover, the enemy has begun to employ a new and most cruel bomb, the power of which to do damage is indeed incalculable, taking the toll of many innocent lives. Should we continue to fight, it would not only result in an ultimate collapse and obliteration of the Japanese nation, but would also lead to the total extinction of human civilization.'

The plotters failed to find the recording, which was smuggled out of the Household Ministry, and despite another group of rebels in Yokohama unsuccessfully shooting up Suzuki's office, at 7.21 a.m. on 15 August 1945 the Japanese radio station Tateno interrupted its usual schedule to say that the Emperor would address the nation at noon, asking that subjects 'respectfully listen to the voice of the Emperor' and that public buildings ensure that the radios were ready. Hatanaka, with time running out, unsuccessfully tried to get himself ten minutes' airtime on NHK, was ordered to leave the Imperial Palace and, realizing that he had failed and that the plot was going nowhere, shot himself.

'To our good and loyal subjects,' the Emperor began, 'after pondering deeply the general trends of the world and the actual conditions obtaining to our empire today, we have decided to effect a settlement of the present situation by resorting to an extraordinary measure. We have ordered our government to communicate to the governments of the United States, Great Britain, China, and the Soviet Union that our empire accepts the provisions of their Joint Declaration.'

The Emperor had surrendered without surrendering, had attached conditions to the unconditional, had saved Japan and himself from annihilation. A war to conquer an empire of millions had resulted in a surrender to save one man, the Emperor.

Now it was a matter of putting pen to paper.

CHAPTER 12

THE FINAL ACT

The Japanese Signing of the Surrender, *2 September 1945*

It is now over, and we are at peace. But in the name of all my comrades who suffered with me, I pray that this nation will never again neglect the strength of its defenses; in all the joy I feel on returning to my land, there is the memory of the last days of Corregidor and the awful months that followed.

General Jonathan M. Wainwright, 9 September 1945

Sunday, 2 September 1945 was warm but the sky was covered with a high blanket of white cloud, giving Tokyo Bay a sullen, rather grey demeanour. It was, in many ways, a blessing; no one wanted to feel overheated or to be squinting in bright sunlight. In any case, overcast conditions were hardly going to dampen Allied spirits at the formal ceremony about to take place that would officially end the war. Stuart S. Murray, Captain of the mighty USS *Missouri*, had only been warned a few days earlier that the surrender ceremony would be taking place on the battleship's deck, which had prompted furious preparations, all undertaken at sea because there had been no time to make a call into a port first. Decks and bulkheads had been frantically repainted, brass fittings polished, uniforms had been cleaned and pressed, and, once it was known which dignitaries would be involved, sailors had been drafted to stand in so that the movements of the ceremony could be rehearsed and perfected to the tiniest detail.

It had been President Truman who had designated the *Missouri* for the ceremony, partly because it was one of the US Navy's most impressive warships – an *Iowa*-class battleship of nearly 58,000 tons – and appearances counted on occasions such as these; but also because it was named after his home state and he'd witnessed its launching. That had taken place at the Brooklyn Navy Yard in January 1944 and the ship had been christened by his daughter, Margaret. Truman had shouldered the responsibilities and burdens of the presidency stoically and now, at a moment of national and personal glory, no one could begrudge him this wish.

And the *Missouri* did look mightily fine to General Jonathan M. Wainwright, one of the US commanders being shipped out to the battleship that morning. He and a number of others had boarded a sleek – and much, much smaller – US Navy destroyer at Yokohama dock at 8 a.m. and had then sailed out to the *Missouri*, now anchored out at bay along with a further 250 Allied warships from the US, British, Australian and New Zealand Navies in an impressive display of immense military strength. It was on the *Missouri*, however, that Wainwright was transfixed. It was, quite simply, the most startling weapon of war he had ever seen. 'I simply could not believe', he wrote, 'that anything could be so huge, so studded with guns.' He thought the many barrels – which included nine 16-inch, ten 5-inch, ten quadruple 40mm cannons and forty-nine 20mm cannons – made the ship look rather like a giant hedgehog.

On board, Wainwright met up with Admiral Bill Halsey, commander of the US Third Fleet, whom he had not seen since the early 1930s when they'd both been far more junior in rank, as well as the Supreme Allied Commander, General MacArthur, but already the main deck was crammed. A table had been set up on the starboard side between a 40mm gun turret and turret no. 2 of three 16-inch guns, overlooked by the ship's superstructure, which included a magazine and supply room, as well as the Captain's and Admiral's cabins. Wainwright had never seen so many generals, admirals and air marshals in one place in his life, while every spare space on the mighty battleship, save the area cleared for the ceremony, was covered with sailors, pressmen and dignitaries: every turret, every deck, every vantage point.

At 8.56 a.m. the eleven Japanese representatives were brought to the ship on a small launch, headed by the Japanese Foreign Minister, Mamoru Shigemitsu, dressed in formal morning coat, stiff collar and top hat. As they stepped aboard they passed through a corridor of 'sideboys', enlisted sailors standing to attention who had all been chosen because they were at least six foot tall. Everything about this ceremony was meant to demonstrate the vastly superior might of the Allies, and especially the United States. As if to further underline this physical discrepancy, Shigemitsu had a wooden leg – he'd lost the one he'd been born with when a Korean rebel threw a grenade at him in Shanghai. It meant he now limped across the deck to stand in front of the surrender table.

Then, at 9.02, MacArthur and Fleet Admiral Chester Nimitz emerged. MacArthur stood at the microphone to the side of the table and began the proceedings, but before he sat down he said, 'Will General Wainwright and General Percival step forward while I sign?'

Wainwright and the British General then emerged from the dignitaries lined up behind the table and stood either side of MacArthur as he sat down and signed the surrender documents. The Supreme Commander had also brought with him five fountain pens with which to sign the documents, and after writing his first signature turned to Wainwright. 'He gave me the pen,' noted Wainwright, who saluted awkwardly and took it, 'a wholly unexpected and very great gift.'

MacArthur gave the second pen used to Percival, and the two generals returned to their places after the Allied signatures had been completed and it was the turn of the Japanese. First Shigemitsu hobbled forward and, bending over the table, signed. Then General Yoshijirō Umezu, the Chief of the Army

General Staff. 'We were, I felt,' noted one of the Japanese delegates, the diplomat Toshikazu Kase, 'being subject to the torture of the pillory. A million eyes seemed to beat on us with the million shafts of a rattling storm of arrows barbed with fire. I felt them sink into my body with a sharp physical pain.'

They were experiencing the humiliation of defeat. Of surrender. It was a terrible thing to endure, and yet General Wainwright, watching this, was unique among American senior commanders there that day in having signed an instrument of surrender of his forces – to the very regime that stood before him now. So too had General Percival, who stood alongside him; it had been Percival who had surrendered the British colonies of Malaya and Singapore – Britain's largest ever defeat – in February 1942. And Wainwright had surrendered the whole of the Philippines three months later, in May; that also ranked as one of the worst military defeats in American history. The difference was that Percival had been the British C-in-C in Singapore from the outset, whereas Wainwright had not. Rather, the American was handed the poisoned chalice of command of the Philippines when MacArthur was ordered out by the President. And the defeat and surrender that had followed had been in part down to MacArthur himself and to the lack of preparation by the United States. It was certainly not Wainwright who was to blame, although in the long years since that day of infamy he had suffered plenty for it.

General MacArthur already had a long and distinguished military career behind him well before the war had begun. He'd been wounded and much decorated in the First World War, had been made a Brigadier-General aged thirty-eight in 1918, and soon after became the youngest Major-General in the US

Army. He'd first taken over command of the Philippines, an American possession, in 1922, but had returned home in 1930 to become the Chief of Staff of the Army, the most senior military post in the United States. Officially, he had then retired in 1937 and returned to live in Manila in his beloved Philippines as a Filipino Field Marshal and as President Manuel Quezon's military advisor. With the onset of war in 1939, with the sabre-rattling of the Japanese and with America's direct involvement looking increasingly likely, MacArthur had been recalled on 26 July 1941 as Commander of US Army Forces in the Far East.

The Philippines had been ceded to the United States by Spain in 1898 following the Spanish–American War, but in 1935 the archipelago gained commonwealth status and it was agreed by the USA that after a ten-year transition period the islands would become fully independent. In 1941 American influence was still very strong, with a firm military base there, but the Filipino government also had its own burgeoning military. None the less, on matters of defence the Americans were still in the driving seat, and MacArthur very much the Commander-in-Chief. In other words, defending the Philippines was his responsibility.

Whether he could ever have successfully saved the islands was a moot point, but there is no question that the lack of preparation and the disagreements over the best strategy sealed the fate of the Philippines for certain. In terms of air power, the USAAF there had been outnumbered by more than three to one by the Japanese, but indecision had led to most of the 100-plus fighters and thirty-five B-17 Flying Fortresses being destroyed on the ground before they had engaged with the Japanese at all. The slaughter had ensured that when General

Masaharu Homma's Fourteenth Army invaded the island of Luzon – which included the capital city of Manila – they would be untroubled by American air power. To make matters worse, at the time Homma's men landed in Lingayen Gulf to the north of Manila, the US warships were sailing towards the Dutch East Indies as part of a pre-war agreement to create an Allied Fleet. So MacArthur could expect almost no naval support either.

On the other hand, there had been contingency plans to prepare the Bataan Peninsula, a large jungle-clad and hilly land mass of two extinct volcanoes that extended southwards and almost closed off Manila Bay and the Philippines' capital city. Orange 3, as it had been code-named, planned for Bataan to be built up with ammunition dumps, food and fuel supplies, medical stocks and, of course, prepared defensive positions. This could then become a defended redoubt until reinforcements might arrive. MacArthur, however, had cancelled Orange 3 as he considered it defeatist. Even after the Japanese attack on Pearl Harbor on 7 December, MacArthur had still refused to make any provision for the defence of Bataan. While the Japanese might have taken Manila, preparing Bataan for a long defence really could have bought the Americans considerable time. And with time, a counter-attack plan could have been worked out and the Philippines gradually strengthened. Rather as they had in China, the Japanese would have then found themselves holding part of the country but, crucially, not all.

Nor was Homma's Fourteenth Army especially strong; it contained just two reinforced divisions, which amounted to only around 46,000 troops. MacArthur, by contrast, had nine divisions and a significant manpower advantage. What's more, defending was always more straightforward and generally less costly, in terms of lives, than attacking. However, he'd also divided his forces, so that in the north Wainwright had command of just two Philippines divisions, which was not enough to resist the full force of the invasion, supported as it was by overwhelming Japanese air and naval power. Then, on 26 December 1941, four days after the invasion, MacArthur decided to invoke Orange 3 after all and ordered all his forces to pull back to Bataan under the command of Wainwright. This amounted to some 80,000 troops of the Filipino-American Army and 26,000 civilians from the Manila area. Yet by abandoning the rest of Luzon at this moment MacArthur had effectively sealed the fate of the Philippines. Certainly, the Japanese had considered the American situation so hopeless they'd withdrawn Homma's veteran 48th Division and sent it off to tackle the Dutch East Indies instead, replacing it with a mere brigade of army reservists. This switchover bought MacArthur time to get his troops to Bataan, but because no preparations had been made for such a defence there his forces found themselves numerically double in size to the Japanese but without enough food, medical supplies, fuel or ammunition. From the outset, he ordered all his men to go on to half-rations. Nor was existing in Bataan for the faint-hearted. This was a place of mountainous jungle, of malaria-infested mosquitoes, of millions of insects and an array of potential diseases. Defending Bataan required careful preparation. But almost no preparation had been made.

At the same time, MacArthur had retreated to his bunker complex on the small island of Corregidor, lying just off the southern end of the Bataan Peninsula in the mouth of Manila Bay. From Christmas Eve 1941 MacArthur remained in the

Malinta Tunnel bastion, spending most of his time firing off communiqués to Washington demanding urgent and substantial reinforcements and also to the press, underlining his heroic single-handed defence of the Philippines against an over-mighty enemy but saying nothing of his lack of foresight or the ill-prepared and ill-judged nature of the defence of the country. He also diverted considerably more supplies to his 12,000-man garrison on Corregidor than they needed while Wainwright's forces wasted away on Bataan.

It was clear, however, that what reinforcements could be sent would be too little, too late, and in March 1942 President Roosevelt ordered MacArthur to leave the Philippines; he did not want him to become a martyr there as MacArthur had already declared he would rather die on Corregidor than surrender to Homma. A direct order from the President was a different kettle of fish, however, and so on the night of 11–12 March MacArthur was whisked off Corregidor in a US Navy PT boat – a small, fast torpedo boat – and later flown to Australia, vowing to the press, 'I shall return!' Somehow, MacArthur had turned defeat into an heroic last stand to rival Thermopylae and given the Filipinos a shard of hope that would, in part, sustain them in resistance to the brutal rule of the Japanese in the long years ahead.

Wainwright could expect no such last-minute escape, however. He had been rung by Major-General Richard Sutherland, MacArthur's Chief of Staff, on the night of 9 March and told to come and see the Chief immediately. By that point his troops on Bataan were already woefully short of food, ammunition and supplies, and suffering catastrophically from malaria and a host of other diseases. Wainwright himself was exhausted. Tall, at six foot one, tough, lean and hard-drinking, he was an extremely able field commander. The military ran through his family. His grandfather had been a naval officer for the Union in the Civil War, while his father had fought in Cuba and the Philippines and had died of disease there. This had not deterred his son, however, who had passed out of West Point in 1906, joined the 1st Cavalry Regiment when it was still very much on horseback and, like his father, served in the Philippines, seeing action during the Moro Rebellion. He later saw service in France with the 82nd Infantry Division before slowly but surely rising through the ranks in the inter-war army; by 1938 he was a Brigadier-General and commanding 3rd Cavalry Regiment. Then, in September 1940, he was posted back to the Philippines as commander of the Philippine Department. By the time of the Japanese invasion he was MacArthur's senior field general and commanded both US and Filipino troops, men still equipped with the British-style Brodie helmets, Springfield rifles and not half the modern weaponry – and uniforms – that were on the cusp of entering US service. Wainwright's force was very much representative of the inter-war army, albeit in no way lacking in courage and determination. The problem was that while guts and fortitude might be inexhaustible, supplies were not. And a force with no supplies was no force at all.

Homma's troops were not in great shape, having suffered significantly since the invasion, but their lines of supply were shorter and, crucially, they had ports, now including Manila, and control of the skies above and seas all around. Wainwright had around 70,000 men, of whom 22,000 were American, which included around 10,000 on Corregidor and the rest on Bataan; there were also some resistance groups to the north that were still in radio contact. His air force comprised just one P-40 fighter plane and his naval power amounted to four PT boats, a handful of minesweepers and a few other launches. This meant that Wainwright's new command would, inevitably, face defeat and surrender.

Now back on Bataan, he lined up all his officers and told them about MacArthur's departure. Unsurprisingly, they were all quite depressed at the news. 'But I soon saw that they understood, just as I understood,' he noted. 'They realized as well as I what the score was.'

In the days and weeks that followed, Wainwright did what he could. Unlike MacArthur, who did not like interacting with front-line troops, Wainwright made himself a very visible commander. He was constantly at the front in Bataan, talking to the men, urging them on, ensuring that hit-and-run patrols on the Japanese wore down the enemy and that remaining stocks of artillery shells, especially, were used to best advantage. He was also promoted to Lieutenant-General and given command of all the newly created United States Forces in the Philippines, much to the chagrin of MacArthur, now in Australia, who had not been told of this first by Washington. Wainwright also began parcelling out many of the supplies MacArthur had stockpiled on Corregidor to the beleaguered men on Bataan.

None the less, all these moves could only delay the inevitable. For the troops on Bataan, this came in early April. They were being bombed daily, supplies were almost out, and renewed Japanese attacks were denting the front line. While Wainwright was now on Corregidor, the defence of Bataan was in the hands of Major-General Edward P. King. On the afternoon of the 7th King's Chief of Staff, Brigadier-General Arnold

J. Funk, arrived to warn Wainwright that King might have to soon surrender. Sitting on Wainwright's desk, however, were MacArthur's written orders: *When the supply situation becomes impossible there must be no thought of surrender. You must attack.* Wainwright repeated those orders to Funk then warned Washington that the outlook was rapidly worsening. But two days later, on 9 April, Wainwright learned that King had offered to surrender regardless of his orders to the contrary. He tried to stop him but it was too late. Distraught though he was, Wainwright received a message of support from Roosevelt at this critical hour. The President still hoped that he might hold out on Corregidor and that naval supply ships might break the Japanese blockade. 'However,' FDR signalled, 'you are assured of complete freedom of action and my full confidence in your wisdom in whatever decisions you may make.' This released him from MacArthur's orders, but the American grip on the Philippines had now shrunk to this one small island a little over two square miles in size, shaped rather like a wriggling tadpole, and lying thirty miles west of Manila at the mouth of Tokyo Bay. The defences on the island were not insignificant, but as with Bataan there could be only one outcome, as Wainwright well knew. Daily, the island was hammered by Japanese air forces for what was clearly a prelude to invasion. On 28 April he managed to evacuate thirty female nurses and twenty men on to two seaplanes, but for those who remained, all they could do was wait.

The Japanese duly landed at 11.15 p.m. on 5 May and were soon swarming west along the island. At 4 a.m. the following day another message arrived from the President. 'The American people', he told Wainwright, 'ask no finer example of tenacity, resourcefulness and steadfast courage. The calm determination of your personal leadership in a desperate situation sets a standard of duty for our soldiers throughout the world.'

Yet Wainwright had barely read this when it became clear that he would soon have to make the worst possible decision for any commanding general. 'I had to make up my mind,' he noted, 'a mind then reeling with the task of trying to find ways of averting the inevitable.' He thought about their situation: beach defences pulverized, forty-six out of forty-eight coastal guns knocked out, machine gun nests obliterated and communications down. At 10.15 a.m. he came to his conclusion. Farewell messages were sent, communications with the Japanese were made, and then that was it. Their stoic defence was over. 'Promptly at noon this terrible day, May 6, 1942, I ordered the white flag run up and our firing ceased,' he wrote. 'It was with the sickest of feelings that I gave the white-flag raising order.'

After the surrender, Wainwright was taken to Fort McKinley in Manila and repeatedly grilled: about his own troops, about his thoughts on the Japanese, about what had happened to their cash reserves, about why irregulars were still resisting elsewhere on the Philippines. They'd burnt all banknotes, he told them over and over, the bullion had been earlier sent to the States, and from his prison Wainwright could not tell Filipinos in the jungle what to do. Meanwhile, his troops on Bataan had been treated appallingly. Before the invasion the Japanese had not expected to have to deal with tens of thousands of prisoners of war, and certainly not stuck in the jungle of Bataan. They could have lifted them by boat or by motor transport, but Homma was preparing for his attack on Corregidor and did not want to spare the vehicles. Instead the 60,000 or so still standing were marched sixty-five miles to the nearest train station at San Fernando, north-west of Bataan, and then again from the station at Capas to various prison camps.

Many of those marching were already in a weakened state but they soon became weaker because their captors gave them little water and even less food. Many died of exhaustion or disease, but a significant number were also summarily executed along the way: shot, stabbed, beheaded and beaten. As many as 650 Americans died and 10,000 Filipinos. It became known as the 'Bataan Death March'.

By comparison Wainwright had been treated well so far, but on 9 June he and other officers were transferred to Tarlac, to the north of Manila, which had once been one of his own bases. The town was wrecked when he got there. He and other officers were placed in a barracks that had previously housed eighty Philippine Army trainees, but where there were now 180 prisoners of war. Wainwright was given a cot but no bedding, although he'd brought two blankets with him, one of which he gave to Brigadier-General Lewis Beebe, MacArthur's former Assistant Chief of Staff, who had been left behind by the Chief. They were also told not to consider themselves the equals of any of their captors. If hatless, they were to bow to any passing Japanese soldier, regardless of rank. If wearing a hat, they were to salute. 'I got my first lesson in bowing from a Jap sergeant,' noted Wainwright. 'I can still feel the wish to retch that I felt when I first was forced to do it.' The food was terrible and mainly rice-based, which they were not really used to; all struggled with stomach upsets and diarrhoea.

They were moved from Tarlac on 11 August 1942 and taken first by train back to Manila, then by truck to Pier 7; it was where Wainwright had said farewell to his beloved wife, Adele, before she'd headed back to the States fifteen months earlier. Now he had no way of telling her where he was, that he was still alive and not dead; and he had no idea at all whether he'd ever get back home or see Adele again. His anguish was considerable.

The ship taking them away from Manila was a stinking tub on which there were far too many prisoners for its size. Wainwright and General King, who had surrendered in Bataan, were given a small cabin. They were treated better than all the other prisoners but were ordered not to leave this cabin, so suffered a claustrophobic existence. The humiliations also continued, including a distressing physical check. 'Much of the examination,' noted Wainwright, 'centred about the rectum.'

They landed at Karenko on the former Chinese island of Formosa, now Taiwan. It was a steaming-hot, barren and dirty little port and they were made to wait in the heat before being marched through the streets and watched by thousands of Chinese and Japanese, who stared at them as though they were freaks. At mid-afternoon they arrived at their new camp: a square compound of around 150 yards each side, with a dozen buildings and toilet block and a small, grassy parade ground. On arrival they were formed up, bawled at and told to surrender all personal luggage. Wainwright tried to keep his toiletries but they were snatched away. Even toilet roll was confiscated. He felt a sense of despair. Clearly, Karenko was going to be worse than anything they'd experienced so far.

And so it proved. They were told to strip and were searched again. Their clothes were eventually handed back but not their boots, which were replaced by ill-fitting wooden clogs. In the days that followed they were systematically starved. After a few weeks many of them began to dramatically deteriorate physically. Malnutrition, aggravated by the clogs, led to the swelling of feet and ankles. One of the greatest challenges was keeping spirits going when they had no idea how long their incarceration would last or what the future held in store for them in the camps. Maintaining self-respect was also vital, but difficult when faced by repeated and ritual humiliation.

A morale boost of sorts came with the arrival of a number of British and Commonwealth prisoners on 28 September, including General Percival and Major-General William F. Sharp, who had been commanding US-Filipino forces on Mindanao, one of the other major islands of the Philippines. Also among the new arrivals was Major-General Merton Beckwith-Smith. He had commanded the British 1st Guards Brigade in France and the Low Countries in 1940 and had taken over 1st Division from General Alexander when the latter had taken command of the Dunkirk evacuation. 'We have been given the supreme honour of being the rearguard at Dunkirk,' he had told his officers. 'Go and tell your platoons the good news!' Given command of 18th Division after his return to England, they were later posted to Singapore. They had barely arrived before the island was overrun and the entire British force surrendered. Beckwith-Smith had an indomitable spirit which inspired them all; always cheerful, always looking to find the best, he did, however, finally crack one particular Sunday. He was the only one among them who had a prayer book so volunteered to conduct a brief service each week. In the middle of reading one prayer, in which he asked God for His blessings on their families and loved ones, his voice suddenly broke and he began to weep. 'He could not stop it,' noted Wainwright, 'and nor could we. He turned his back to us for a long time and when he could control himself he turned again and continued.'

Soon after this incident, Beckwith-Smith gave a salute to a passing Japanese but for some reason the guard did not like it and turned on him, punching him in the face twice. Beckwith-Smith reeled but did not fall. All who saw this were outraged and Wainwright and Percival wrote a joint letter to Captain Imamura, the commandant. It achieved nothing.

Meanwhile, the privations were worsening. On 3 October Wainwright weighed just 132 pounds; he should have been at least 170. They were also told they needed to carry out manual work and when they refused their rations were cut further. Then, on 11 November, Beckwith-Smith tragically died of a combination of diphtheria and malnutrition. 'The American officers had become very fond of this plucky Englishman,' noted Wainwright, 'but while we were grieved to see him go some of us felt in our hearts that he was better off than the rest of us.' Certainly, life grew progressively worse for them all, and not least Wainwright, who was now fifty-nine years old. By 12 December his weight had dropped to 125 pounds – just nine stone. This was the day he was first allowed to write to his wife, albeit only a few anodyne lines that told her little except that he was alive. That same night he grew sick and lay cramped on his bunk with shivers and a fever. Malnutrition and a dose of beriberi had got to him. He was also suffering from 'foot slap', a numbness to the feet caused by the illness.

He recovered, but all of them were soon forced to work – it was that or literally starve to death. As they began labouring they were given extra rice, but at the same time the beatings increased. Everyone was struck at some point. Wainwright was first hit one evening after returning from the latrine. Seeing a guard, he bowed with the usual feeling of nausea, but the guard just yelled at him.

Wainwright paused, only for the guard to slap him across the face. 'It was a stinging blow,' he noted, 'and in my throat I felt a rising gorge of hate and despair.' The guard slapped him again – and again, four times in all. Determined not to fall, Wainwright took it until the guard swung his fist and punched him full on the left jaw and at this he fell. When he eventually got back to his bunk, he found that sleep eluded him. Maybe it was fatigue, but the very next morning, during their hut inspection, he accidentally dropped a mess bowl, which shattered on the floor. The Japanese guard bellowed at him and, with his bayoneted rifle in one hand and his other fist drawn back, charged at him. His bayonet pierced Wainwright's left wrist while he was then beaten about the face. Screaming at him some more, the guard told him to pick up the broken pieces before marching him to the guardhouse. He felt faint; his wrist was bleeding and he'd taken quite a pummelling over the last twelve hours or so. Fortunately he was then sent to the camp hospital, where Colonel Harold Glattley of the US Army Medical Corps bandaged his wrist. The stinging sense of humiliation, however, had been worse than the physical pain.

The cruelty never ended. Beatings continued. Humiliations continued. A large consignment of Red Cross parcels reached the camp but all were kept by the Japanese, something that Wainwright found harder to take than any of the beatings. Then suddenly, and with no warning, on 2 April 1943 he and five other generals, thirteen brigadier-generals, a naval captain and eleven enlisted men as well as the British and Dutch officers were all rounded up and told they would be leaving Karenko.

*

Over the next few months Wainwright was moved several times, first to Tamazato camp and then to Moksak, both on Formosa. Conditions did improve dramatically. Red Cross parcels were allowed, they were permitted books to read and no longer expected to work. He and his fellows put on a little weight and in March he was able to write a second letter to his wife and a third that June; moments that normally would have been of little consequence came to take on enormous significance in this timeless incarceration in which the future was so unknowable. While Japanese prison camps had become bywords for brutality, there was no standard way of treating prisoners. Camp commandants were not instructed to be barbaric, nor their guards; however, the same warped version of *bushidō* that prevented the Japanese from surrendering was also turned into supreme contempt for any enemy willing to fly a white flag rather than die.

While this led to some camps being more cruelly run than others, those running the camps could not afford to give prisoners much food because they did not have much themselves. Medical supplies were also insufficient, so it was not surprising that prisoner welfare was a low priority. The rapidly industrialized Japan of the 1930s, with a burgeoning urban population, had invaded China in 1937 because it was short of food and other vital natural resources. Four years of war had not solved Japan's shortcomings and so, with the cost of the conflict in China rising horrifically, they began to look further afield. Thus began their war of conquest and a series of stunning, sweeping victories. These, however, were not enough. They simply did not have the shipping to transfer the plunder they needed nor the resources to maintain and grow their new empire. What's more, while the United States might have abandoned the Philippines, it had none the less taken the fight to the Japanese sooner and more effectively than had been expected. In April 1942 the Americans had bombed Tokyo. In May they had given the Japanese Navy a bloody nose at the Battle of the Coral Sea. At the beginning of June the US Navy had won a truly decisive naval victory at Midway and in August had invaded the Solomon Islands in the South Pacific, only recently captured by the Japanese. By February 1943 the Japanese had been beaten on the ground, in the air and at sea on and around Guadalcanal and MacArthur had begun his stepping-stone approach back towards the Philippines with an army that looked different and was far better equipped than it had been a year earlier. And all the while Japanese shipping was being sunk: troopships, supply ships, oil tankers and warships. The war with Japan was, above all, a war at sea, because no matter where the fighting took place, it could only happen by keeping the sea lanes open.

Wainwright knew nothing of these developments, however; he had had almost no news at all. At Moksak camp the Japanese Propaganda Department tried to recruit him to write to Roosevelt to urge him to stop the war; Wainwright accepted the lavish picnic at a nearby Shinto shrine but flatly refused to speak out against the American war effort.

Despite this stance, conditions did continue to improve. He and his fellow prisoners were allowed to keep and tend pigs, chickens and goats, which, although they were forced to share them with their captors, did substantially increase their diets and improve their health. The winter was bitterly cold and they did not have enough clothes, but they got through it; at any rate, Christmas 1943 was better than the previous year. The spring of 1944 brought warmer weather but with it the largest mosquitoes they had ever seen. All were persecuted relentlessly by these vicious insects. Then, in May 1944, Wainwright received his first letter from his wife. 'I read it so often', he wrote, 'that I nearly wore it out.' Life continued. It was monotonous, their incarceration seemingly without end.

It was in October 1944 that they were suddenly told they were being moved once again, this time to Manchuria, the area of northern China that the Japanese had invaded in 1931. 'All we knew when told that we would be sent north', noted Wainwright, 'was the sinking feeling a man gets when he learns his prison sentence has been prolonged.'

They were flown to Korea, then passed through a series of camps that were every bit as awful as Karenko, until they were taken by train to a further camp in a remote part of northern Manchuria called Sian. It was bleak, freezing cold and conditions were once again brutal, with a sadistic commandant and terrible food. Red Cross packages reached them, and although distributed were then taken away again before they had had a chance to eat much of the contents. Physically they all began to decline badly again; Wainwright's teeth were in a terrible state. He was not alone. And it was still bitterly cold up there in northern Manchuria when, on 21 March, they were ordered to hand over their winter clothes and were given summer wear instead; nearly all of them consequently came down with colds and influenza.

Rumours did reach them, however; guards would occasionally let slip that the Allies were winning and their movement north, to Manchuria, also suggested Japan had been losing ground. After all, why else send them there? Wainwright had learned not to read too much into such rumours, but in the summer of 1945 he began to work on a hypothetical estimation of the war's progress. Drawing on his training in military planning and on suppositions of the Allies' build-up of supplies, he conjectured that the war would only end with the invasion of Japan and that this would be unlikely to occur until the end of 1946. As it happened, American planners had been concluding much the same. But then had come the atomic bomb and the attacks on Hiroshima and Nagasaki – of which Wainwright and his fellow prisoners had known nothing.

Wainwright finished his deliberations in the middle of August and was mentally preparing himself for another year at least of imprisonment when, on the 18th, news reached them that the war was over. This was confirmed the following morning during roll call. By the order of the Emperor, the Japanese interpreter told them, the war had been amicably terminated. At this the prisoners all began laughing, then laughing some more. 'There was no stopping the laughter,' wrote Wainwright. 'It came up in me, and in the others, with an irresistible force: something born of the combination of our relief, the look on the Jap's face, the blind preposterousness of his beginning, the release from years of tension, the utter, utter relief over having survived to see this blessed day.'

It took a while to get them out. First they were visited by a medical doctor from the Airborne arm and then connected with the Office of Strategic Services. When Wainwright had been taken prisoner, neither airborne troops nor the OSS had existed. Not until 24 August did they finally leave Sian, when they were taken by Soviet Red Army troops in American jeeps to Mukden and then flown to Chungking. There they were given fresh uniforms, Wainwright was presented with the Distinguished Service Cross he'd been awarded back in 1942 – MacArthur had rejected his nomination for a Medal of Honor – and were put up in a decent hotel. He made a radio broadcast to the United States before finally being flown back to Manila on 30 August. Seeing it for the first time in over three years, which before the war had been one of the most beautiful cities in the Far East, he was shocked by the scale of destruction. The fighting there in the early months of the year, part of MacArthur's reconquest of the Philippines, had been as brutal as any and had seen as many as 200,000 civilians killed, mainly by the Japanese, although it had been mostly American shells that had wrecked the city.

Here, though, back in Manila, Wainwright was sent a tailor to adjust his uniform to fit his emaciated frame and also issued with a pistol, an item above any other that signified to him that he really was free and back as a Three-Star General in the US Army. The next day, 31 August, he, General Percival and others were up early and flown to Yokohama on a C-54; Wainwright could scarcely believe the speed, size and luxury of the aircraft. It was also strange to be driven from the airfield to the Grand Hotel, Japanese officers snapping to attention and saluting them after years of humiliating servility before enemy guards. 'I thought of all the beatings we had taken for failing to bow and scrape before illiterate latrine sentries,' he wrote, 'and great waves of thankfulness passed over me.'

That evening he was reunited with MacArthur for dinner. Seeing Wainwright, MacArthur stood up, reached out his arms, took hold of him and looked him up and down. Wainwright had always been slim – his nickname had been 'Skinny' – but he remained woefully underweight after his long ordeal.

'Well,' MacArthur said at last, 'I'm glad to see you.'

'I'm glad to see *you*,' was all Wainwright could think to say in return.

After dinner, Wainwright addressed a number of war correspondents who were waiting for him. 'Tonight in Yokohama, again a free American officer with a weapon in my hand,' he told them, 'my gratitude goes out to the American people for their generous and sympathetic understanding of the misfortune which befell me in the Philippines in May 1942. Through the generosity of my great commander, General MacArthur, I am here to witness the greater misfortune of my enemy.'

Wainwright must have been utterly exhausted after his ordeal and from the immense amount of travelling he had done over the past few days. Such feelings, however, were cast aside as he stood tall and unflinchingly behind MacArthur on the deck of the *Missouri* as the surrender ceremony got under way. What a moment that must have been. For three and a half years he'd been in captivity, kept in a time trap. When he emerged, the world had changed utterly. An era-defining weapon had been launched, the atomic bomb; they had entered a new age. Yet it wasn't just that; Wainwright had suddenly been confronted by an American military that had developed almost out of all recognition during those years of incarceration: the luxury of the C-54, the enormity of the battleship and now, the ceremony over, the thunderous roar of hundreds of American aircraft flying over in salute. Wainwright had suffered the ignominy of surrender, and yet here on board the USS *Missouri*, on 2 September 1945, he was witness to a far, far greater defeat for the Japanese. The Second World War, the most cataclysmic in the history of the world, was over.

POSTSCRIPT

General Wainwright's official duties were not quite over with the signing of the surrender document on the *Missouri*. The Imperial Japanese forces were still spread far and wide and subsequent surrender ceremonies were held in China and Manchuria, in Burma and the Pacific Islands, and also in the Philippines. Despite their still-weakened state, Wainwright and Percival were immediately flown back to Manila via the tiny volcanic outcrop of Iwo Jima, where the US Marine Corps had fought yet another terrible battle in February and March that year. It was 1.45 a.m. on 3 September, the sixth anniversary of the start of Britain's war. Allowed a brief rest, they then took a C-47 Dakota to Laguna and, once landed, clambered into a car heading to Baguio, 150 miles north of Manila. Like most towns and cities in Luzon, Baguio had been a pretty, modern town of broad boulevards before the war, but now looked to Wainwright as though it had been hit by a giant hammer. Their journey finished at the still-intact High Commissioner's residence. A table had been prepared in the main reception room, and once all the dignitaries were assembled General Tomoyuki Yamashita was brought in. The 'Tiger of Malaya' had routed the British back in 1942 and it had been to him that Percival had surrendered Singapore. More recently, Yamashita had been the defender of the Philippines, an assignment he had guessed, when appointed, would lead to his death. Now here was Wainwright, the man who had surrendered the Philippines back in May 1942, and Percival, who had lost Singapore, to witness this moment of revenge.

Yamashita, a big man, wept as he was taken away. Seeing this, Wainwright could not help feeling a wave of compassion. 'This might seem a little strange, coming from me,' he said to one of his fellow American officers, 'but I hope Yamashita is shown the courtesy due his rank, in the matter of personal accommodations, housing and food.' He was assured he would be.

With this final act over, Wainwright then began the long journey home, reunited first with his son, a naval officer, in California and then, in Washington, with his wife, Adele. It was 12.30 p.m. on 10 September, and also waiting for him was General Marshall and Secretary of War Henry Stimson. From the airport in Washington they drove to the Pentagon, where, to his immense surprise, a crowd of over 100,000 was waiting on the Monument Grounds. As he stepped on to a prepared rostrum he was cheered, a moment that brought tears to his eyes. 'My comrades and I have been profoundly touched by all these evidences of your great regard,' he told them. 'I thank you in their name and in my own. This is truly such a welcome as a man dreams of, locked away behind barbed wire and the bayonets of cruel jailers. It is the surest evidence I could have that you will keep before you the words which I know fired you to great effort after our sorrowful defeat: "Remember Bataan! Remember Corregidor!"'

His homecoming was still not over, however, because he'd been summoned to see the President – a different man, of course, to the one who had been sending missives to him on

Corregidor. Truman invited Wainwright to step out with him into the White House garden where some photographers were waiting. And there Truman bestowed upon him the Medal of Honor that MacArthur had denied him three years earlier.

Wainwright had kept a tiny secret diary during his time in captivity and later used it to write his wartime memoirs. He concluded his book by urging magnanimity on the Allies' former enemies but also greater preparedness in years to come. 'The expense of making ourselves big enough and tough enough to have prevented that war would have been but a brief fraction of its eventual cost,' he noted. 'Such preparedness would be a microscopically briefer fraction of the cost of a World War III.' His words remain as pertinent now as they were eighty years ago. The dawn of the nuclear age that ended the Second World War helped prevent a global conflict, but the world remains a fragile place and the future deeply uncertain. We face many challenges, and patterns of human behaviour that led to conflict in the 1930s are being repeated. It is incredible to think that in Ukraine and the Middle East the scale of destruction and numbers of casualties are once again comparable to certain parts of the Second World War.

And while the threat of another global conflict remains, and that of nuclear Armageddon, it is vital to remember that nuclear capability is now shared by many nations, not just the United States. It might be the ultimate deterrent but it is also one that, if used, would surely bring about the end of the known world. Anyone poised with their finger over the red button will already have lost. What recent conflicts have illustrated, which has been largely forgotten by the West since the end of the Cold War, is that a conventional deterrent is the best way to ensure lasting peace. The Second World War also showed, beyond any doubt, that when the Western democracies pull together towards a common, single goal they can beat autocracies, riven as they always are by paranoia, corruption and mistrust. Just consider the enormity of what was accomplished by the Allies: the harnessing of technology, industry and immense global reach. Whether it be the B-29 Superfortresses and hordes of technologically advanced fighter planes flying over the USS *Missouri* on 2 September 1945, or the enormous armada assembled for D-Day on 6 June 1944, this was an astonishing achievement. Nor was it just down to the industrial muscle and technological vision of the United States. Some 31 per cent of all US supplies in the European Theatre of Operations were provided by Britain. On D-Day itself, two-thirds of the troops delivered to those shores were British Commonwealth. Two-thirds of the 12,500 aircraft were British; 792 of the 1,213 warships were British and 3,261 landing craft of the 4,127 were British. This is not to gloat about British contributions but rather to point out that the Allied victory in the west and in the war against Japan was a collective effort. Even the atomic bomb was only possible with the contributions of British scientists. Moreover, many other nations – peoples who wanted a freer, democratic future – also played a notable part in the victory that took place in 1945.

The unity of purpose that brought victory has been lost in the West. The great leaders, whose vision and geopolitical understanding proved decisive, are absent. Truman, when he took on the mantle of the presidency in April 1945, did so through a deep belief in the importance of his mission and the values the democracies stood for. No one could possibly deny that the

Western Allies were guilty of extreme ruthlessness or even war crimes by today's standards. Britain was also a colonial power with very different post-war aims; both nations were imperfect then, and remain so, but their leaders sincerely wanted a better, peaceful world to follow. We in the West have enjoyed that vision for eighty years, yet now it suddenly feels more vulnerable again. Britain, for example, enjoys none of the wealth, global reach and industrial capacity that enabled it to prepare its navy and air force for war in the late 1930s and dramatically increase its output during the conflict. Today, the United Kingdom and her European neighbours have allowed their armed forces to become woefully depleted and overly dependent on the United States. Europe's leaders should heed the warning of General Wainwright.

The global conflict cost a staggering 75.5 million lives, dislocation on an unprecedented scale and created a new global order which continues to influence our lives to this day. It is, without question, the most cataclysmic conflict the world has ever witnessed. What is remarkable is how quickly the monstrous regimes that ignited the war developed. In the first decades of the twentieth century, Imperial Japan had shown little sign of the sadistic militarism that emerged in the early 1930s. Germany, too, was well on the way to being a successful manufacturing-based economy before the Wall Street Crash of October 1929 brought economic disaster. The lessons from history are that competition for resources and economic catastrophe very often bring about political unrest and upheaval as people search for an alternative to a norm that appears to have failed. Peace is always fragile, even when it does not appear to be. The past is endlessly fascinating and the human drama of the Second World War remains captivating, but we should never forget that history provides a compass that leads us to the present and helps us prepare for the future.

At the core of the Second World War, what started it, and what dragged it way beyond the point at which its outcome was decided, was endless unworldly delusion – delusion that drove the German and Japanese regimes. That both governments, in their last gasps, sought some kind of military honour in defeat demonstrates clearly how far detached from reality they were. Their war aims, after all, were explicitly genocidal, and they pursued those aims enthusiastically. The wicked fallacy that expunging Germany and then the expanded Reich of Jews would somehow solve Germany's problems – whatever they might be – persisted to the very end of the war. Japanese disregard for civilian lives in the territories they had conquered was as brutal and murderous as in Europe – 16 million Chinese civilians died as a result of Japan's war in Asia. The Japanese government quibbling over words and the precise meaning of *kokutai* in the jaws of atomic annihilation speaks only of their grotesque detachment from reality, but one consistent with Imperial Japan's war of conquest and expansion. The rump of the Reich that Dönitz's administration claimed to command tried to make demands of the Allies that were of a piece with the rest of Germany's conduct of the war. The recurring insistence in May 1945 that millions of German soldiers should make their way to the Western Allied lines to surrender when no such thing was possible was no less hare-brained than the notion that the vast expanses of the Soviet Union could be conquered in a swift knockout blow. What Dönitz had failed to understand, however, was that the spell had been shattered with Hitler's death and the oath men had made to him broken. The Nazi Age of Delusion was over. No one believed it any more. That it had taken so much bloodshed to snap the followers of Nazism out of this bewitchment is the world's tragedy.

And spells, which can endure for generations, can be broken still. At the end of 2024, in Syria, where the brutal Ba'ath Party and subsequent Assad regime had endured for sixty-three years – only eight years fewer than the Soviet Union – the world watched in astonishment as the seemingly permanent edifice collapsed. It happened in a giddy rush comparable to the fall of the regime in Afghanistan in August 2021, when its Western backers, principally the USA, withdrew; in contrast, in Syria the Assad regime crumbled before the Russians could pull out. While there are, of course, countless differences, Assad's power, receding like the tide, revealed for all to see the shipwrecks it had concealed. This was not unlike the end of the Second World War: the discovery of atrocities; a population having to come to terms with the end of what had seemed permanent; new factions seeking expression in the ruins; the feeling that while one disaster may have ended, the future remains uncertain, and in the shadow of what has gone before. Doubtless future historians will make sense of what has happened in Syria, find the underlying causes, point to the contingencies and personalities that have brought about the end of the Assad regime, but, like a currency, once no one believed in it any more, literally stopped giving it credit, it had no value, it was worth nothing.

And the delusions continue, not least in President Putin's mind about what constitutes the real Russia. These have plunged Europe into a bitter war of conquest and unremitting bloodshed in Ukraine; how that spell can be broken, how that belief can also lose its currency, is a question that needs to be answered.

*

Ever since the Soviets first questioned Hitler's death, conspiracy theories have surrounded what became of him. Really, though, there is no need now for any mystery over his fate. A fragment of his skull was later found close to where his body had first been discovered with a neat bullet hole piercing the bone; this along with both Hitler's and his wife's teeth remain in the state archives in Moscow. The SMERSH report on the autopsy had still not been given to Stalin by 26 May 1945, when the Russian premier met Harry Hopkins, Truman's representative, in Moscow. None the less, Stalin did know that Hitler's body had very likely been located but chose to cast doubt and continued to do so over the years following, primarily to test the response of American and British intelligence services. But Hitler was indisputably dead, at his own hand, and the Russians had enough of him to prove it.

In fact, the fate of all those who had shared Hitler's final days in the Führerbunker is known. Martin Bormann's body was discovered in 1972 during some roadworks; he'd been missing since the early hours of 2 May, fuelling yet more wild theories about an escape to South America. When his remains were unearthed they were exactly where a witness to his death had reported seeing him killed and his teeth matched surviving dental records. Later, in 1998, his body was DNA-checked beyond any doubt. There were some claims about his skull having traces of clay that could only have come from South America, but that was ludicrous nonsense. Heinz Linge and Erich Kempka survived, however, as did various others including one of Hitler's secretaries, Traudl Junge. Like Linge, she later published a memoir of her time in the service of the Führer. Linge had been captured by the Russians on 2 May and in captivity was grilled over and over about those final days.

He spent ten years as a prisoner of war before finally being released.

The rest of the remains of Hitler, his wife of one day, of Josef and Magda Goebbels and of General Krebs, who had also taken his own life, were originally buried in a wood near the small town of Rathenow, west of Berlin. In February 1946 they had been disinterred and taken even further west to SMERSH headquarters in Magdeburg. This was purely so that SMERSH could safely store the bodies and prevent any other part of the Soviet apparatus getting hold of them; it also allowed Stalin to keep the fate of Hitler a mystery to the outside world. In Magdeburg the boxes of remains were buried once more, and there they remained until 1970, when Yuri Andropov, later leader of the Soviet Union but then Chairman of the KGB, ordered the bodies to be disinterred yet again and this time incinerated. The ashes were flung into a tributary of the River Elbe. Forensic work on the piece of skull and teeth in 2017 proved a further match for Hitler and Eva Braun, first through analysing tartar remaining on the Führer's teeth and then by matching with dental X-rays that had been first examined on 9 May 1945. No one outside Russia will be getting to see these macabre remains any time soon, and probably very few inside Russia either. That does not matter, though, as the forensic pathologists who carried out the work were French and their findings were fully written up and reported. The issue had never been over whether Hitler had died by his own hand on 30 April 1945, but what had happened to his corpse. Petrol does not burn at a particularly high temperature, and no matter how carbonized the flesh had become, there was always likely to be part of the skeleton. What happened to these bones was the only mystery. That has since been solved.

Of the senior Nazis, Dönitz and Kesselring were extremely lucky to get off lightly and served comparatively short prison terms; Kesselring had his death sentence commuted after lobbying from senior Allied commanders who had failed to understand the depth of his war crimes in Italy. By 1952 he was suffering from cancer of the throat and released from prison on compassionate grounds; he lived for another eight years, dying in 1960 of a heart attack, rather than cancer, aged seventy. Dönitz was tried at Nuremberg but given only a ten-year sentence, which he spent at Spandau until being released in October 1956. He retired to a village in Schleswig-Holstein, wrote his memoirs, which, like those of Kesselring, neatly edited out his rampant anti-Semitism and war crimes, and died peacefully at the ripe old age of eighty-nine in 1980.

Keitel was put on trial alongside Kaltenbrunner, Göring, Hans Frank, Albert Speer and other leading Nazis. Some, like Speer, were spared execution, but Kaltenbrunner, Göring and Keitel all received the death sentence. Göring managed to take cyanide before he could be hanged, but Keitel and Kaltenbrunner went to the gallows on 16 October 1946. Keitel appealed to God to save him, then hit his head as he dropped and this prevented a clean snap of the neck. He had a terrible end, convulsing for twenty-four minutes before finally breathing his last.

That most reluctant of presidents, Harry S. Truman, performed well at the Potsdam Conference in the summer of 1945, proved largely uncompromising with regard to the Soviet Union in the years that followed, presided over the Berlin airlift in 1948, which really marked the start of the Cold War, backed the Marshall Plan that helped rehabilitate West Germany, Japan, Italy and other parts of Europe and successfully stood for a second term in 1948. He was replaced in 1952 by Eisenhower, who similarly served two terms before another war veteran, John F. Kennedy, won in 1960. Truman died in 1972, aged eighty-eight, Eisenhower in 1969, aged seventy-eight. General Wainwright, meanwhile, sadly died in September 1953, aged just seventy, following a stroke, and was buried among other American military heroes in Arlington National Cemetery, Virginia. He did, however, outlive both General Homma and General Yamashita. Homma was tried and executed for the atrocities of the Bataan Death March, Yamashita primarily for the massacres of civilians in Manila. Yamashita's conviction has remained highly controversial as he had issued orders to his troops not to contest the city; the local commander on the ground, Admiral Sanji Iwabushi, chose to ignore those orders. Several American lawyers questioned the legitimacy of the Yamashita trial. But it seems that MacArthur wanted vengeance and was determined to make him pay the ultimate price for what had happened to his beloved city. He was hanged on 23 February 1946.

Field Marshal Montgomery was as unsuited to peace as he had been made for war. Administering the stricken Germany was a task the army was poorly adjusted to do. Men wanted to go home – and not to the Far East. Fraternization, which had been banned, was rampant, and Montgomery felt the task not to be beneath him as such, but a tremendous anti-climax. He had enjoyed the war, and he had proved himself as one of Britain's great captains – an assessment he immodestly agreed with; the peace that followed, however, would see him do plenty to ensure he would not be held in the regard in which he held himself. On return from Germany he settled into his next role as Chief of the Imperial General Staff, succeeding Brooke. It was not one he relished, and as he did what he could to bend the British Army to the Monty way of doing things he made enemies and earned grudges. And he had made mistakes, of course. Perhaps his greatest reputational error was the publication in 1958 of his memoirs. These constitute the worst character reference a man could ever give himself: he was right about everything, surrounded by amateurs and ditherers. He doled out judgement of Ike, and his predecessor in the desert, Field Marshal Auchinleck, among others. The Auk sued, retractions were issued, apologies and qualifications made, but it was now open season on him as a commander, as a person, as a father, and it has been ever since. His staff, at least those to whom he had remained loyal, were steadfastly loyal to him. He died on 24 March 1976 aged eighty-eight.

Yelena Kagan returned to Moscow after being demobilized and became a celebrated and prize-winning writer, adopting the pen name Yelena Rzhevskaya in honour of those who fell at Rzhev during the Great Patriotic War. She died in 2017. Helmut Altner also became a writer and a journalist of some repute, as the Paris correspondent for several German publications. After recovering from his ordeal, Hugo Gryn emigrated to Britain in 1946, won a place at Cambridge to study mathematics and then volunteered to serve in the Israeli Army during the Palestinian War. After this, he went to the United States with the intention of becoming a Reform rabbi but returned to Britain in 1964 and was Senior Rabbi at the West London Synagogue. He also became a regular contributor on BBC Radio 4. In 1989 he returned to Berehovo to make a documentary film with his daughter, Naomi, called *Chasing Shadows*. He died in 1996. Alan Moskin went back to the States after the war and lived a long life. In his later years he worked tirelessly to campaign against prejudice and injustice and became a member of the Speakers Bureau of the Museum of Jewish Heritage. He died in 2023.

What is so striking in writing about these different surrenders and about some of the men and women who were directly involved is the astonishing delusion and arrogance of the vanquished and the incredible determination, dedication and bravery of the victors. It is impossible not to feel inspired by men like Truman, who remains to this day somewhat in the shadows of his predecessor. Similarly, the stoicism of General Jonathan Wainwright or the incredible courage of young boys such as Hugo Gryn and, frankly, even Helmut Altner really are remarkable. The war took a long time to play out, was fought all around the globe, and at the end there were a lot of very exhausted men, whether Eisenhower, Wainwright, Churchill or even Roosevelt, whose life was almost certainly cut short by the immense strain of leading the United States into becoming a war-winning nation. Even Hitler, for all his hubris and the fantasy world in which he existed, was a shattered wreck by the time he blew out his brains on 30 April.

The surrenders of 1945 are also a reminder of the terrible cost and sacrifices that were made to reach that point. The freedoms and the peace we enjoy here in the West should not be taken for granted; they were hard won. We must never, ever forget it.

TIMELINE

1938

NOVEMBER
Carpathian Ruthenia annexed from Czechoslovakia into Hungary

1941

SUNDAY, 7 DECEMBER
Japanese attack on the US Pacific Fleet at Pearl Harbor, Hawaii

MONDAY, 22 DECEMBER
Japanese Fourteenth Army under General Masaharu Homma invades the Philippines at Lingayen Bay, Luzon

FRIDAY, 26 DECEMBER
General Douglas MacArthur invokes Orange 3 – the retreat to the Bataan Peninsula

1942

MONDAY, 9 MARCH
General Jonathan M. Wainwright told to report to MacArthur on Corregidor

WEDNESDAY, 11 MARCH
Night MacArthur evacuated from Corregidor – Wainwright takes over

THURSDAY, 9 APRIL

Wainwright learns that Major-General Edward P. King has offered to surrender in Bataan

TUESDAY, 28 APRIL

Wainwright evacuates fifty personnel including thirty women from Corregidor

TUESDAY, 5 MAY

11.15 p.m. Japanese invasion of Corregidor

WEDNESDAY, 6 MAY

12 p.m. Wainwright surrenders Corregidor

TUESDAY, 9 JUNE

Wainwright and other senior American commanders transferred to Tarlac camp on Luzon

TUESDAY, 11 AUGUST

Wainwright leaves the Philippines to go to Karenko camp on Formosa

MONDAY, 28 SEPTEMBER

British generals and officials arrive at Karenko, including General Arthur Percival

SATURDAY, 3 OCTOBER

Wainwright weighs 132 pounds

WEDNESDAY, 11 NOVEMBER

Major-General Merton Beckwith-Smith dies at Karenko

SATURDAY, 12 DECEMBER

Wainwright weighs 125 pounds

1943

Wainwright repeatedly moving camps

1944

MARCH

Germany invades Hungary

MAY

Wainwright receives first letter from wife

JUNE

Jews of Berehovo sent to Auschwitz

Hugo Gryn's younger brother, Gabi, murdered on arrival

JULY

Hugo Gryn and father moved to Lieberose forced labour camp

Democratic Convention in USA – Harry S. Truman chosen to be Franklin D. Roosevelt's running mate for November 1944 presidential election

OCTOBER

Wainwright and other prisoners moved to Manchuria

1945

SATURDAY, 20 JANUARY

Roosevelt and Truman sworn in as President and Vice-President

FRIDAY, 2 FEBRUARY

Hugo Gryn and father start forced march to Sachsenhausen

TUESDAY, 6 FEBRUARY
US 71st 'Red Circle' Infantry Division lands in France

MONDAY, 19 FEBRUARY
US invasion of Iwo Jima

WEDNESDAY, 28 FEBRUARY
Heavy Allied bombing of Bolzano

Obergruppenführer Karl Wolff meets with senior commanders to discuss peace feelers via Allen Dulles and the OSS in Switzerland

Hugo Gryn and father reach Mauthausen

SATURDAY, 3 MARCH
Eugen Dollmann and Luigi Parilli head to Switzerland and meet Dr Gero von Schulze-Gaevernitz

TUESDAY, 6 MARCH
Wolff agrees to free Ferruccio Parri and Antonio Usmiani from prison

THURSDAY, 8 MARCH
Wolff travels to Switzerland

FRIDAY, 9 MARCH
Overnight: Operation MEETINGHOUSE – the fire bombing of Tokyo by 334 B-29 Superfortresses

SUNDAY, 11 MARCH
US 71st Infantry Division in action for first time near Ratzwiller

MONDAY, 19 MARCH
Wolff travels to Ascona in Switzerland to meet with Dulles

THURSDAY, 22 MARCH
US Third Army starts crossing the Rhine

FRIDAY, 23 MARCH

Wolff in Bad Nauheim meeting with Feldmarschall Albert Kesselring

Operation PLUNDER – 21st Army Group's crossing of the Rhine begins

SATURDAY, 24 MARCH

Midday: Wolff flies into Tempelhof

Afternoon: Wolff meets with Heinrich Himmler and Ernst Kaltenbrunner in Berlin

Operation VARSITY – Allied airborne landings on eastern side of the River Rhine

SUNDAY, 25 MARCH

Wolff and Kaltenbrunner in Burg Rudolfstein

MONDAY, 26 MARCH

Wolff and Kaltenbrunner in car crash

End of Battle of Iwo Jima – American victory

THURSDAY, 29 MARCH

Wolff back in Italy

Helmut Altner, aged seventeen, conscripted into German Army

FRIDAY, 30 MARCH

Himmler warns Wolff not to move his family to Italy

SUNDAY, 1 APRIL

Allied invasion of Okinawa led by the Americans

MONDAY, 2 APRIL

Wolff due to meet Dulles but cancels

MONDAY, 9 APRIL

General Mark W. Clark launches final Allied offensive in Italy

WEDNESDAY, 11 APRIL
Nordhausen liberated

THURSDAY, 12 APRIL
Roosevelt writes to Stalin about the Italian surrender negotiations

Afternoon: Roosevelt has a cerebral haemorrhage and dies

5.25 p.m. Truman reaches White House

7.09 p.m. Truman sworn in as President of the United States

FRIDAY, 13 APRIL
Wolff asked to visit Himmler in Germany

Hugo Gryn and father leave Mauthausen

SUNDAY, 15 APRIL
Wolff ordered to Germany by Himmler

Bergen-Belsen liberated

Roosevelt's funeral

MONDAY, 16 APRIL
Wolff flies into Berlin then drives to Hohenlychen for meeting with Himmler. Kaltenbrunner also present.

Truman addresses Congress

Red Army assault on the Oder starts with attack by Zhukov's 1st Belorussian Front. The Battle for Berlin has begun.

Helmut Altner in firing line of Red Army attack

TUESDAY, 17 APRIL
Kaltenbrunner and Wolff drive to Berlin to see Hitler

WEDNESDAY, 18 APRIL
3 a.m. Kaltenbrunner and Wolff reach Führerbunker

THURSDAY, 19 APRIL

German collapse along the Oder Front

Hitler decides to take personal command of the Battle for Berlin and to remain in the city to the end

5 p.m. Hitler walks with Wolff and Kaltenbrunner in Reichskanzlei garden and instructs Wolff to continue talking to Dulles

FRIDAY, 20 APRIL

Hitler's fifty-sixth birthday

Evacuation of personnel and papers to Berchtesgaden begins on Martin Bormann's orders

Hitler orders 9. Armee to restore the Oder Front and instructs Obergruppenführer Flex Steiner to attack from the north with his Germanische SS-Panzerkorps – but it no longer really exists

SATURDAY, 21 APRIL

Last raid on Berlin by RAF Bomber Command

1 p.m. German Army headquarters at Zossen abandoned

6 p.m. Major John Poston killed and Captain Peter Earle wounded during German ambush

SUNDAY, 22 APRIL

Afternoon: Hitler bawls at his generals and accuses them of treachery

Göring is instructed to take over command of German forces from Berchtesgaden

Wolff at conference with Ambassador Rudolf Rahn, General Heinrich von Vietinghoff and others near Verona

Truman meets with Averell Harriman, US ambassador to the Soviet Union

MONDAY, 23 APRIL

Evening: General Helmuth Weidling, commander LVI Panzerkorps, appears at the Führerbunker to protest against accusations of treachery. Hitler appoints him commander of the defence of Berlin.

Wolff, Oberst Victor von Schweinitz and Obersturmbannführer Eugen Werner reach Lucerne, Switzerland

Second of two meetings between Truman and Vyacheslav Molotov

TUESDAY, 24 APRIL

Albert Speer arrives at the Führerbunker to say farewell to Hitler

The Goebbels family move into the Führerbunker

WEDNESDAY, 25 APRIL

Albert Speer leaves the Führerbunker for the last time

Wolff leaves Switzerland

Obersalzberg heavily bombed by RAF Bomber Command. Hitler's house, the Berghof, largely destroyed.

Henry Stimson briefs Truman about the atomic bomb

THURSDAY, 26 APRIL

Hanna Reitsch and Generaloberst Robert von Greim reach the Führerbunker

Partisans surrounding Wolff's villa at Cernobbio

FRIDAY, 27 APRIL

Obergruppenführer Hermann Fegelein arrested

News that Himmler has been trying to make contact with the Allies

139 *Prominenten* hostages reach Niederdorf

Wolff learns that Allies have authorized Operation SUNRISE, the surrender of German forces in Italy

Benito Mussolini captured by partisans

SATURDAY, 28 APRIL

Fegelein executed in the Reichskanzlei garden

Discussion in Führerbunker over best way to commit suicide

Siege of Niederdorf over and *Prominenten* saved

Mussolini executed

SUNDAY, 29 APRIL

Early hours: Hitler and Eva Braun marry

Hanna Reitsch and von Greim escape by flying an Arado 96 down the Charlottenburger Chausee

2 p.m. Unconditional surrender of all German forces in Italy signed in Caserta

Hitler dictates his last will and testament

Yelena Kagan reaches Berlin

MONDAY, 30 APRIL

3.15 p.m. (approx.) Hitler shoots himself in the Führerbunker and Eva Hitler takes cyanide

4 p.m. (approx.) Both bodies burnt in the Reichskanzlei garden

10 p.m. Soviet flag raised above the Reichstag

TUESDAY, 1 MAY

1 a.m. Last resistance at the Reichskanzlei

Early: Helmut Altner learns that Hitler is dead

General Hans Krebs visits General Chuikov and tells him Hitler is dead

Grossadmiral Karl Dönitz appointed head of state, Hitler's successor

Ruth Andreas-Friedrich and companions head back to their home in Steglitz, Berlin

British 6th Airborne Division captures Wismar on Baltic coast

Hamburg surrenders to the British

10.15 a.m. Massive Soviet artillery barrage directed on to the centre of Berlin

6 p.m. (approx.) Murder of six Goebbels children

11 p.m. Breakout from the Führerbunker begins

WEDNESDAY, 2 MAY

2 a.m. Wolff argument with Kesselring

Helmut Altner and 2,000 others break out of Spandau barracks

8 a.m. Keitel has meeting with Dönitz in Plön

8.30 a.m. General Weidling surrenders Berlin unconditionally

Ruth Andreas-Friedrich and companions learn of Hitler's death

12 p.m. Helmut Altner reaches Döberitz

2 p.m. Surrender in Italy comes into force

Kesselring orders General Friedrich Schulz to make contact with the Allies

US 7th Infantry Regiment captures Salzburg

5 p.m. Bodies of Josef and Magda Goebbels discovered

THURSDAY, 3 MAY

Generaladmiral Hans-Georg von Friedeburg visits Lieutenant-General Sir Miles Dempsey's British Second Army Headquarters

Surrender negotiations at Field Marshal Sir Bernard Montgomery's HQ

Goebbels children found in the Führerbunker

The war is over for Helmut Altner

Small Japanese force surrenders to Australians on New Guinea

FRIDAY, 4 MAY

Morning: Alan Moskin and men of 71st Infantry Division liberate Gunskirchen – Hugo Gryn and father liberated

Afternoon: Hitler's body discovered in the Reichskanzlei garden

Lieutenant Sherman W. Pratt and men of 3rd Battalion, 7th Infantry, US 3rd Infantry Division, capture Berchtesgaden and the Obersalzberg

Yelena Kagan interrogating staff from the Führerbunker

5 p.m. German surrender delegation arrive at Montgomery's HQ

5 p.m. French troops at edge of Berchtesgaden

6.30 p.m. Germans surrender all troops in northern Germany to Montgomery

SATURDAY, 5 MAY

8 a.m. Surrender of German troops in northern Germany takes effect

2.30 p.m. Surrender of all German troops in Bavaria and Austria to US 6th Army Group

Hitler and Eva Hitler's bodies recovered

SUNDAY, 6 MAY

Early: Yelena Kagan party to SMERSH abduction of Hitler's body

Dönitz fires Himmler

Evening: General Alfred Jodl reaches Eisenhower's Supreme Allied HQ in Reims

9 p.m. Eisenhower warns Dönitz he will close American lines to surrendering German troops unless they immediately sign unconditional surrender

MONDAY, 7 MAY

2.41 a.m. German unconditional surrender signed in the Collège Moderne et Technique in Reims

3 a.m. General Sir Hastings Ismay in London learns of surrender in Reims

Kaltenbrunner leaves Altaussee for the Totes Gebirge

2.27 p.m. Count Schwerin von Krosigk announces German surrender on national radio

3.30 p.m. Ed Kennedy sends report to Associated Press in London about the surrender

4.10 p.m. Prime Minister Winston Churchill talks to Admiral William Leahy in Washington DC

Géza Gryn dies in son Hugo's arms

TUESDAY, 8 MAY – VE DAY IN THE WEST

8.15 a.m. (Eastern War Time) Truman addresses the press at the White House

2 p.m. (approx.) Feldmarschall Wilhelm Keitel flies into Tempelhof then is driven to Karlshorst

3 p.m. Churchill victory speech

Autopsy on Hitler's remains – Yelena Kagan given his teeth in a jewellery box

11.01 p.m. Reims surrender due to take effect

WEDNESDAY, 9 MAY

12.43 a.m. Surrender ceremony in Karlshorst finished

7 a.m. War against Nazi Germany officially over

Yelena Kagan and SMERSH officers secure X-rays of Hitler's dental records

Wolff invites von Schulze-Gaevernitz to Bolzano

SATURDAY, 12 MAY

Kaltenbrunner captured

SUNDAY, 13 MAY

Wolff's forty-fifth birthday – and arrest at party

FRIDAY, 22 JUNE

End of Battle of Okinawa with Allied victory

THURSDAY, 5 JULY
General election in Britain

MONDAY, 16 JULY
Trinity Test of atomic bomb at Los Alamos in New Mexico – a success

TUESDAY, 17 JULY
Start of Potsdam Conference

WEDNESDAY, 25 JULY
Truman authorizes dropping of atomic bomb on Japan

THURSDAY, 26 JULY
Results of British general election: Churchill loses and Clement Attlee becomes Prime Minister

Potsdam Declaration by USA, Britain and China demanding unconditional surrender by Japanese

THURSDAY, 2 AUGUST
End of Potsdam Conference

MONDAY, 6 AUGUST
8.15 a.m. First atomic bomb dropped on Hiroshima

TUESDAY, 7 AUGUST
Truman reiterates the Potsdam Declaration

WEDNESDAY, 8 AUGUST
Lieutenant Marcus McDilda shot down in his P-51 over Osaka

THURSDAY, 9 AUGUST
11.01 a.m. Second atomic bomb dropped, on Nagasaki

Soviet Union invades Manchuria

Fevered discussions among Japan's war leaders

FRIDAY, 10 AUGUST

Emperor Hirohito expresses desire to surrender

8.33 p.m. (Tokyo time) Japan sends Morse code signal accepting unconditional surrender (7.33 a.m. on 11 August in Washington)

SATURDAY, 11 AUGUST

Pro-war faction in Japan make announcement in Japanese newspapers

SUNDAY, 12 AUGUST

2 a.m. (Tokyo time) US Secretary of State Jimmy Byrnes accepts Japanese surrender offer and agrees Hirohito can stay in power

TUESDAY, 14 AUGUST

7 p.m. (Tokyo time) National Japanese broadcaster tells people to expect an important announcement the following morning

11.25 p.m. (Tokyo time) Emperor Hirohito records radio broadcast to Japanese people for first time and announces unconditional surrender

WEDNESDAY, 15 AUGUST

7.21 a.m. (Tokyo time) Japanese radio announces the Emperor will speak at noon

SATURDAY, 18 AUGUST

Wainwright learns that war is over

12 p.m. (Tokyo time) Hirohito addresses the nation and announces surrender

FRIDAY, 24 AUGUST

Wainwright finally leaves Sian camp

THURSDAY, 30 AUGUST

Wainwright flown back to Manila

FRIDAY, 31 AUGUST

Wainwright and Percival flown to Yokohama

Wainwright meets MacArthur for first time since March 1942

SUNDAY, 2 SEPTEMBER

9 a.m. Formal surrender by Japanese aboard the USS *Missouri*

MONDAY, 3 SEPTEMBER

Wainwright oversees surrender of all Japanese forces on the Philippines

MONDAY, 10 SEPTEMBER

Wainwright awarded Congressional Medal of Honor by Truman

1946

WEDNESDAY, 16 OCTOBER

Kaltenbrunner and Keitel hanged at Nuremberg

NOTES

Abbreviations used in the Notes

IWM Imperial War Museum, London

NARA National Archives and Records Administration, College Park, Maryland

TNA The National Archives, Kew

Prologue

1 **'Then we suddenly . . .'**: Robert E. Sherwood (ed.), *The White House Papers of Harry L. Hopkins*, Vol. 2, Eyre & Spottiswoode, 1949, p. 670

2 **'Much good talk . . .'**: ibid., p. 671

4 **'win through to absolute victory'**: cited in speech by Franklin D. Roosevelt, Library of Congress, www.loc.gov

11 **'The elimination . . .'**: cited in Frank Freidel, *Franklin D. Roosevelt: A Rendezvous With Destiny*, Little, Brown, 1991, p. 463

11 **'popped into my mind'**: cited in Robert Sherwood, *Roosevelt and Hopkins*, Harper & Brothers, 1948, p. 696

11 **'unconditional surrender'**: cited in Winston Churchill, *The Second World War*, Vol. 4, Cassell, 1951, p. 614

Chapter 1: A Bullet to the Head

15 **'Decrepit, scruffy, often . . .'**: cited in Kempowski, *Swansong 1945*, p. 261

18 **'Pity we couldn't take him . . .'**: conversation recited in Zhukov, *The Memoirs of Marshal Zhukov*, p. 468

19 **'Tell him that if Goebbels . . .'**: ibid., p. 468

19 **'As world capital . . .'**: cited in Heim, Picker and Bormann (eds), *Hitler's Table Talk*, p. 466

21 **'Berlin is to be given . . .'**: cited in Albert Speer (trans. Richard and Clara Winston), *Inside the Third Reich*, Macmillan, 1970, p. 249

21 **'Sadly, not exactly . . .'**: both quotes cited in Kempowski, *Swansong 1945*, p. 1

27 **'You will see . . .'**: cited in Christian Shakespeare, *Bunker 1945: The Last Ten Days of Adolf Hitler*, p. 37

29 **'Even the SS . . .'**: cited in Linge, *With Hitler to the End*, p. 189

31 **'Believe me, Speer . . .'**: cited in Speer, *Inside the Third Reich*, p. 690

32 **'You're going then . . .'**: ibid., p. 697

32 **'By staying . . .'**: cited in Brisard and Parshina, *The Death of Hitler*, p. 85

33 **'Jawohl, mein Führer . . .'**: Linge, *With Hitler to the End*, p. 192

34 **'Her eyes lit up . . .'**: ibid., p. 195

35 **'"Linge," Hitler told him . . .'**: ibid., p. 199

Chapter 2: The Duel Part 1

48 **'It was only at . . .'**: TNA WO 208/4517

50 **'If Wolff was trying . . .'**: ibid.

50 **'I control the SS forces . . .'**: ibid.

51 **'Gentlemen, if you can be . . .'**: ibid.

56 **'Based on the Führer's . . .'**: NARA RG239/M194

57 **'If there is no . . .'**: cited in von Lang, *Top Nazi*, p. 276

58 **'I have laid the ground work . . .'**: cited in Dulles, *The Secret Surrender*, p. 118

59 **'Everything possible . . .'**: ibid.

59 **'He seemed quite . . .'**: TNA WO 208/4517

Chapter 3: The Duel Part 2

65 **'That was a grave . . .'**: cited in von Lang, *Top Nazi*, p. 280

65 **'I thank you . . .'**: cited in Dulles, *The Secret Surrender*, p. 151

67 **'out of the conviction . . .'**: ibid., p. 158

70 **'If they hang me . . .'**: von Lang, *Top Nazi*, p. 288

70 **'I am happy . . .'**: ibid.

70 **'Actually, what I had done . . .'**: TNA WO 208/4517

72 **'Here we have . . .'**: cited in von Lang, *Top Nazi*, p. 293

73 **'I will never forget . . .'**: ibid., p. 295

75 **'I shall put in . . .'**: TNA WO 208/4517

78 **'I understand that . . .'**: recounted by von Schulze-Gaevernitz in Dulles, *The Secret Surrender*, pp. 208–9

79 **'poisoned his mind'**: TNA WO 208/4517

79 **'Without ringing me . . .'**: ibid.

80 **'There were tears . . .'**: ibid.

80 **'You are tearing . . .'**: ibid.

81 **'Three times in . . .'**: ibid.

81 **'That is what . . .'**: ibid.

84 **'For ten minutes . . .'**: Robert E. Matteson, Oral History Interview, Accession Number 1993.A. 0097.5, US Holocaust Memorial Museum

Chapter 4: Monty's Men

87 ***'daily express from . . .'***: Tom Pocock, *Alan Moorehead*, Kindle edn, Pimlico, 1991, pp. 272–3

93 **'No. of prisoners taken . . .'**: 5th Battalion, King's Own Scottish Borderers, War Diary, https://www.royalscotskosbwardiaries.co.uk/_files/ugd/29af12_7e44e0eda08947f7918852f1b0ca3679.pdf

93 **'come far in advance . . .'**: 1st Canadian Parachute Battalion War Diary, https://www.pegasusarchive.org/varsity/war_1stCdn.htm

93 **'innumerable policemen . . .'**: 5th Battalion, King's Own Scottish Borderers, War Diary

94 **'probably the last in 7th . . .'**: 1st Battalion Royal Tank Regiment Diary, 27 April, http://desertrats.org.uk/WarDiaries/1st_RTR/1stRTR1945.htm

94 **'conducted blindfold . . .'**: ibid.

94 **'Staff cars with negotiators . . .'**: ibid., 1 May

97 **'I now have . . .'**: Horne and Montgomery, *The Lonely Leader*, Kindle edn, Picador, 2012, p. 211

98 **'Well, my man . . .'**: Henderson, *Watching Monty*, Kindle edn, The History Press, 2005, p. 206

99 **'one was right at the heart . . .'**: Carol Mather, *When the Grass Stops Growing*, p. 407

100 **'all I knew is . . .'**: ibid.

100 **'left forearm is badly shattered . . .'**: letter from Monty to Frank 'Simbo' Simpson quoted in Horne and Montgomery, *The Lonely Leader*, Kindle edn, p. 382

100 **'he would have sailed . . .'**: Peter Earle, Henderson Papers, Eton College Archives

102 **'Regret to report . . .'**: ibid.

102 **'I am going to give you . . .'**: Horne and Montgomery, *The Lonely Leader*, Kindle edn, p. 402

102 **'I was completely devoted . . .'**: Richard Mead, *The Men Behind Monty*, Kindle edn, Pen & Sword Books, 2015, p. 429

104 **'a magnificent looking officer . . .'**: personal account of Trumbull Warren communicated to Nigel Hamilton in *Monty: The Field Marshal*, p. 502

105 **'The Chief is putting . . .'**: ibid.

106 **'Certainly not . . .'**: Moorehead, *Eclipse*, Kindle edn, Transworld Digital, 2022, p. 324

106 **'You should have thought . . .'**: Hamilton, *Monty: The Field Marshal*, p. 504

108 **'the implications of your . . .'**: *New York Times*, Bill Downs, 'Montgomery Scorns Nazis, Exults, "This Is the Moment"; the surrender of Hamburg to the British Germans get scorn from Montgomery anxious about civilians' map shocks enemy', https://www.nytimes.com/1945/05/05/archives/montgomery-scorns-nazis-exults-this-is-the-moment-the-surrender-of.html

108 **'And my third point . . .'**: ibid.

109 **'I really do think . . .'**: Hamilton, *Monty: The Field Marshal*, p. 507

110 **'My generation . . .'**: Moorehead, *Eclipse*, Kindle edn, pp. 326–7

112 **'No doubt that if . . .'**: dispatch by R. W. Thompson quoted in Hamilton, *Monty: The Field Marshal*, p. 513

112 **'He was very dejected . . .'**: Montgomery, *The Memoirs of Field Marshal Montgomery*, Kindle edn, Pen & Sword, 2006, loc. 5823

113 **'INSTRUMENT OF SURRENDER'**: the text is from an image at the Imperial War Museum, London, IWM (Documents.5000), https://www.iwm.org.uk/collections/item/object/1030005005

113 **'This to include all naval ships in these areas.'**: this Montgomery added by hand; it had been left out of the original typed-up document and Henderson had to point it out to his boss

114 **'von Friedeburg down to Major Friedl . . .'**: von Friedeburg killed himself later in the month, on the 23rd, using poison, the same day as Kinzel. Friedl, who was promoted to Oberst – Colonel – immediately, also died in May, in a car accident.

115 **'4 May ALL GERMAN . . .'**: 5th Battalion, King's Own Scottish Borderers War Diary, 4 May 1944, https://www.royalscotskosbwardiaries.co.uk/_files/ugd/29af12_b54493cd0a674d20bb4b53065a79c17f.pdf

115 **'Russian-British liaison . . .'**: 1st Canadian Parachute Battalion War Diary, 4 May, 1st Canadian Parachute Battalion

115 **'That concludes the surrender . . .'**: dispatch by R. W. Thompson quoted in Hamilton, *Monty: The Field Marshal*, p. 513

Chapter 5: The Camp

117 **'Of all the horrors . . .'**: Gunskirchen Lager Liberation Pamphlet, published by 71st Infantry Division

122 **'You are nineteen . . .'**: Gryn, *Chasing Shadows*, p. 175

122 **'Well, perhaps . . .'**: ibid.

122 **'I'm afraid they may . . .'**: ibid., p.176

122 **'All right, you will go to work'**: ibid.

122 **'Come on . . .'** ibid., p. 177

123 **'Under the present . . .'**: ibid., p. 194

124 **'This is a good omen . . .'**: ibid., p. 215

127 **'We were marched . . .'**: IWM 9280

128 **'It was an extraordinarily . . .'**: ibid.

132 **'Do you think . . .'**: cited in John C. McManus, 'The Race to Seize Berchtesgaden', *World War II Magazine*, May 2005

133 **'We rounded a bend . . .'**: Pratt, *Autobahn to Berchtesgaden*, p. 607

138 **'I had nightmares . . .'**: Alan Moskin Oral History, National World War II Museum, New Orleans

138 **'Guys were peeing . . .'**: ibid.

139 **'We just looked . . .'**: ibid.

139 **'I saw, all down his back . . .'**: ibid.

140 **'And that was . . .'**: Gryn, *Chasing Shadows*, p. 240

140 **'And he died . . .'**: ibid., p. 241

141 **'He was there . . .'**: ibid.

Chapter 6: The Supreme Commander Will See You Now

147 **'The great leader . . .'**: The American Presidency Project website, 'Address at Meeting Sponsored by the Republican National Committee', 17 April 1956

149 **'Berlin was no longer . . .'**: Bedell Smith, *Eisenhower's Six Great Decisions*, Kindle edn, Lucknow Books, 2014, p. 182

153 **'Well, I have never before . . .'**: Carlo D'Este, *Eisenhower: A Soldier's Life*, Henry Holt, 2002, p. 737

155 **'Still having trouble . . .'**: John Toland, *The Last 100 Days: The Tumultuous and Controversial Story of the Final Days of World War II in Europe,* Kindle edn, Random House, 2003, p. 552

155 **'The Boss's face . . .'**: McKeogh and Lockridge, *Sgt. Mickey and General Ike*, Kindle edn, Lucknow Books, 2016, p. 179

155 **'immediate, simultaneous . . .'**: quoted in Ullrich, *Eight Days in May*, Kindle edn, Penguin, 2021, p. 123

156 **'another of the iniquitous crew . . .'**: Bedell Smith, *Eisenhower's Six Great Decisions*, p. 197

156 **'I wonder . . .'**: ibid., p. 199

157 **'Obviously, you do not entirely realize . . .'**: ibid., p. 205

157 **'Try to explain . . .'**: Ullrich, *Eight Days in May*, Kindle edn, p. 183

158 **'looked pretty much . . .'**: McKeogh and Lockridge, *Sgt. Mickey and General Ike*, Kindle edn, p. 186

159 **'General Eisenhower insists . . .'**: Ullrich, *Eight Days in May*, Kindle edn, p. 184

159 '[**who**] **earlier had been . . .'**: Ludde-Neurath, *Unconditional Surrender*, Kindle edn, Frontline Books, 2010, p. 87

162 **'thought it rather lonely . . .'**: Summersby quoted in Whiting, *Finale at Flensburg*, Kindle edn, p. 152

162 **'I want to say a word . . .'**: German surrender scene described by Boyd Lewis, United Press war correspondent, https://www.upi.com/Archives/1945/05/07/German-surrender-scene-described/1123163084011/

163 **'You will get details . . .'**: Kay Summersby quoted in Charles Whiting, *Finale at Flensburg: The Story of Field Marshal Montgomery's Battle for the Baltic* (Forgotten Aspects of World War Two), Kindle edn, Sapere Books, 2024, p. 154

163 **'"This isn't much . . ."'**: McKeogh and Lockridge, *Sgt. Mickey and General Ike*, p. 187

164 **'In January 1943 . . .'**: transcribed from YouTube, https://youtu.be/iLBRAi_ZNVo

Chapter 7: VE Day

167 **'The unconditional surrender . . .'**: Winston Churchill, *The Second World War*, Vol. 6, Cassell, 1954, p. 477

170 **'may well be . . .'**: ibid., p. 574

170 **'the PM does not seem . . .'**: Lord Moran, *Winston Churchill: The Struggle for Survival, 1940–1965*, Sphere, 1968, p. 269

170 **'very tired . . .'**: Churchill, *The Second World War*, Vol. 6, p. 616

173 **'We walked all over . . .'**: 'Who Were The Women In The Trafalgar Square Fountains On VE Day?', https://www.iwm.org.uk/history/who-were-the-women-in-the-trafalgar-square-fountains-on-ve-day

173 **'this supreme day . . .'**: Telegram 'From Moscow to Foreign Office', the Churchill Archive CSCT 1/29/62, Churchill College, University of Cambridge

174 **'With warm affection . . .'**: Truman Library, Messages to Allied Leaders and to General Eisenhower on the Surrender of Germany | Harry S. Truman

174 **'Your message is cherished . . .'**: Churchill, *The Second World War*, Vol. 6, p. 571

175 **'Moved towards Trafalgar Sq . . .'**: Mass Observation Archive, The Keep, https://www.thekeep.info/mass-observation-records-the-victory-celebrations-marking-the-75th-anniversary-of-ve-day/

177 **'Yesterday morning, at 2.41 a.m . . .'**: full text accompanied by an audio recording, The Churchill Project, Hillsdale College, https://winstonchurchill.hillsdale.edu/victory-in-europe/

181 **'the best of both . . .'**: Harold Nicolson, *The Harold Nicolson Diaries: 1907–1964*, Kindle edn, Weidenfeld & Nicolson, 2024, p. 257

181 **'The peer next to me . . .'**: Lord Moran, *Winston Churchill: The Struggle for Survival, 1940–1965*, p. 269

182 **'strongest foundation . . .'**: Hansard, 8 May 1945, House of Commons Column 1869 https://hansard.parliament.uk/Commons/1945-05-08/debates/860a9828-1c45-4dd3-8ca7-8798a88f0ed9/CommonsChamber

183 **'He [Winston] then proposes . . .'**: Nicolson, *The Harold Nicolson Diaries: 1907–1964*, p. 352

185 **'it's a victory of the . . .'**: ibid.

186 **'Almighty God for . . .'**: King George VI's VE Day broadcast https://www.royal.uk/king-george-vis-ve-day-broadcast with audio

188 **'crowd was stupendous . . .'**: Sheridan Morley and Graham Payn, *The Noel Coward Diaries*, with a Foreword by Stephen Fry, Kindle edn, Weidenfeld & Nicolson, 2022, p. 29

188 **'I wish I had not gone . . .'**: Nicolson, *The Harold Nicolson Diaries: 1907–1964*, Kindle edn, p. 353

188 **'I suppose this . . .'**: Morley and Payn, *The Noel Coward Diaries*, p. 29

188 **'A Grenadier officer . . .'**: 'The Queen remembers D-Day 1945', interview with Godfrey Talbot, first broadcast on BBC Radio 4 on 8 May 1985

189 **'There were places . . .'**: 'A Royal Night Out: What really happened the night the Princesses left the palace for VE Day', https://www.tatler.com/article/the-queens-night-out-ve-day

189 **'We are utterly indifferent . . .'**: Gilbert, *The Day the War Ended*, p. 209, telegram no. 2505 to Moscow, 8 May 1945, FO papers 371/50581

Chapter 8: Happy Birthday, Mr President

193 **'Is that you, Pug?'**: Ismay, *The Memoirs of General Lord Ismay*, p. 394

193 **'It was impossible . . .'**: ibid., p. 395

194 **'I will address you . . .'**: TNA FO 371/50581

195 **'This is Ed Kennedy . . .'**: cited in Kennedy Cochran (ed.), *Ed Kennedy's War*, loc. 51

196 **'There is nothing official . . .'**: cited in Gilbert, *The Day the War Ended*, p. 94

196 **'As the whole world . . .'**: TNA FO 371/50581

201 **'I was floored . . .'**: cited in McCullough, *Truman*, p. 314

202 **'Never before have . . .'**: The American Presidency Project website, 'Address to Congress on the Yalta Conference', 1 March 1945

202 **'I saw the President . . .'**: Truman, *Memoirs, Volume One*, p. 3

203 **'Harry, the President is dead'**: ibid., p. 5

204 **'I made it clear . . .'**: ibid., p. 9

205 **'Their experience . . .'**: ibid., p. 10

205 **'Boys, if you ever pray . . .'**: ibid., p. 19

206 **'Today, the entire world . . .'**: The American Presidency Project website, 'Address Before a Joint Session of the Congress', 16 April 1945

208 **'Since the Yalta . . .'**: cited in Truman, *Memoirs, Volume One*, p. 15

208 **'Russia will emerge . . .'**: cited in McCullough, *Truman*, p. 373

209 **'We must clearly . . .'**: ibid., p. 372

210 **'I have never . . .'**: Truman, *Memoirs, Volume One*, p. 82

210 **'Within four months . . .'**: cited in McCullough, *Truman*, p. 377

213 **'You have plenty of time'**: The American Presidency Project website, 'The President's News Conference on V-E Day', 8 May 1945

213 **'This is a solemn . . .'**: ibid.

Chapter 9: Amid the Ruins Part 1

220 **'When we were riding . . .'**: cited in Zhukov, *The Memoirs of Marshal Zhukov*, p. 629

222 **'It was very difficult . . .'**: Rzhevskaya, *Memoirs of a Wartime Interpreter*, p. 129

222 **'We were interested . . .'**: ibid., p. 131

223 **'We clamber over . . .'**: Andreas-Friedrich, *Battleground Berlin*, p. 11

224 **'Buffaloes must have . . .'**: ibid., p. 13

224 **'Only chaos . . .'**: ibid.

224 **'Suddenly, we become aware . . .'**: ibid., p. 14

225 **'"But then," he wrote . . .'**: Altner, *Berlin Soldier*, p. 196

226 **'All the dams of discipline . . .'**: ibid., p. 199

226 **'The oath of loyalty . . .'**: ibid., p. 200

226 **'Whoever wants to . . .'**: ibid.

228 **'ruthlessly'**: Gorlitz, *The Memoirs of Field Marshal Wilhelm Keitel*, p. 224

231 **'I jump up again . . .'**: Altner, *Berlin Soldier*, p. 209

231 **'Death plays his dance . . .'**: ibid.

233 **'I look at it in horror . . .'**: ibid., p. 214

234 **'But I hurry on . . .'**: ibid., p. 215

Chapter 10: Amid the Ruins Part 2

237 **'All of a sudden . . .'**: cited in Kempowski, *Swan Song 1945*, pp. 413–14

239 **'The children seemed alive . . .'**: Rzhevskaya, *Memoirs of a Wartime Interpreter*, p. 158

240 **'I saw them only . . .'**: ibid., p. 157

240 **'It had seemed . . .'**: ibid., p. 161

241 **'Strength returns to my body . . .'**: Altner, *Berlin Soldier*, p. 231

242 **'Somewhere a lark . . .'**: ibid., p. 240

242 **'War over!'**: ibid.

242 **'It was obvious to us . . .'**: Gorlitz, *The Memoirs of Field Marshal Wilhelm Keitel*, p. 228

243 **'Hauling water . . .'**: Andreas-Friedrich, *Battleground Berlin*, 4 May 1945

243 **'They look right . . .'**: ibid.

244 **'Alles kaputt!'**: Rzhevskaya, *Memoirs of a Wartime Interpreter*, p. 173

245 **'Dismay and terror . . .'**: Andreas-Friedrich, *Battleground Berlin*, 6 May 1945

246 **'She is eighteen . . .'**: ibid.

246 **'"Commissars," he hissed . . .'**: ibid., p. 18

247 **'Hitler kaputt!'**: Rzhevskaya, *Memoirs of a Wartime Interpreter*, p. 221

248 **'It was decidedly . . .'**: ibid., p. 227

249 **'Liberated from bombs! . . .'**: Andreas-Friedrich, *Battleground Berlin*, 8 May 1945, p. 20

249 **'Our patience . . .'**: Gorlitz, *The Memoirs of Field Marshal Wilhelm Keitel*, p. 231

250 **'Every corner . . .'**: ibid.

250 **'We flew straight back . . .'**: ibid., p. 232

251 **'God almighty . . .'**: Rzhevskaya, *Memoirs of a Wartime Interpreter*, p. 228

253 **'The world goes wild . . .'**: Andreas-Friedrich, *Battleground Berlin*, 9 May 1945

254 **'at the afflictions . . .'**: Rzhevskaya, *Memoirs of a Wartime Interpreter*, p. 228

Chapter 11: Lost in Translation

259 **'We will not deviate . . .'**: Potsdam Declaration | Birth of the Constitution of Japan

260 **'including those who have . . .'**: ibid.

261 **'the Japanese government . . .'**: Kumiko Torikai, *Voices of the Invisible Presence: Diplomatic Interpreters in Post-World War II Japan*, John Benjamin's, 2009, p. 33

269 **'If one is first to issue . . .'**: Herbert P. Bix, 'Japan's Delayed Surrender: A Reinterpretation', *Diplomatic History*, Vol. 19, No. 2 (Spring 1995), pp. 197–225

270 **'Its duration was . . .'**: ibid., p. 131

270 **'Witnesses say that . . .'**: ibid., pp. 131–2

270 **'were killed as it were . . .'**: ibid., p. 141

271 **'4 square miles . . .'**: USAAF Bomber Survey film

272 **'The target will be . . .'**: Diary entry of Harry S. Truman, 25 July 1945, in which he reflects on the atomic bomb tests and the destructiveness of it,

and the plan for using the bomb on military targets only. Papers of Harry S. Truman: President's Secretary's File.

272 **'Today 3 B-29s . . .'**: quoted in Sadao Asada, 'The Shock of the Atomic Bomb and Japan's Decision to Surrender: A Reconsideration', *Pacific Historical Review* (1998) 67 (4), pp. 477–512, https://doi.org/10.2307/3641184

273 **'Sixteen hours ago . . .'**: Truman Statement on Hiroshima, Atomic Heritage Foundation

274 **'We are now prepared . . .'**: https://ahf.nuclearmuseum.org/ahf/key-documents/truman-statement-hiroshima/#:~:text=We%20are%20now%20prepared%20to,Japan's%20power%20to%20make%20war.

275 **'great victory over us'**: Tristan Grunow, 'A Reexamination of the "Shock of Hiroshima": The Japanese Bomb Projects and the Surrender Decision', *The Journal of American-East Asian Relations*, Vol. 12, No. 3/4 (Fall/Winter 2003), p. 168

275 **'If we could defeat . . .'**: ibid., p. 183

276 **'If Truman's broadcast . . .'**: ibid.

277 **'As you know . . .'**: FEPoW under the Japanese: Marcus McDilda

278 **'About four minutes . . .'**: https://discovery.nationalarchives.gov.uk/details/r/C4123058

279 **'He is a typical . . .'**: William L. Laurence, Eyewitness Account of Atomic Bomb Over Nagasaki | The Bombing of Hiroshima and Nagasaki | Historical Documents

281 **'then I will express . . .'**: quoted in Tsuyoshi Hasegawa, *Racing the Enemy: Stalin, Truman, and the Surrender of Japan*, Harvard University Press, 2006, p. 315

282 **'But even if the enemy . . .'**: Coffey, *Imperial Tragedy*, p. 332

284 **'With regard to the Japanese . . .'**: Foreign Relations of the United States: Diplomatic Papers, 1945, The Far East, China, Vol. 7, Nanking Embassy Files, Lot F–73: telegram, *The Secretary of State to the Ambassador in China (Hurley)*, Washington, 11 August 1945, Historical Documents – Office of the Historian

286 **'Believing in the eternity . . .'**: John Toland, *The Rising Sun: The Decline and Fall of the Japanese Empire 1936–1945*, Random House, 1970, p. 1280

288 **'the security and well-being . . .'**: https://ahf.nuclearmuseum.org/ahf/key-documents/jewel-voice-broadcast/

288 **'Moreover, the enemy has . . .'**: ibid.

289 **'respectfully listen to the voice . . .'**: Toland, *The Rising Sun*, p. 1284

289 **'To our good and loyal . . .'**: https://ahf.nuclearmuseum.org/ahf/key-documents/jewel-voice-broadcast/

Chapter 12: The Final Act

291 **'It is now over . . .'**: cited in Wainwright, *General Wainwright's Story*, p. 293

294 **'I simply could not believe . . .'**: ibid., p. 279

295 **'Will General Wainwright . . .'**: https://www.youtube.com/watch?v=mxUkoSTBRIU

295 **'He gave me the pen . . .'**: ibid., p. 280

296 **'We were, I felt . . .'**: Kase, *Journey to the Missouri*, p. 4

300 **'I shall return!'**: cited in MacArthur, *Reminiscences*, p. 145

302 **'But I soon saw . . .'**: Wainwright, *General Wainwright's Story*, p. 67

303 **'"However," FDR signalled . . .'**: ibid., p. 84

303 **'The American people . . .'**: ibid., p. 118

304 **'I had to make up my mind . . .'**: ibid., p. 123

304 **'Promptly at noon . . .'**: ibid., p. 123

305 **'I got my first . . .'**: ibid., pp. 158–9

306 **'Much of the examination . . .'**: ibid., p. 173

307 **'We have been given . . .'**: Christ Church College, Oxford, Archives

307 **'He could not stop it . . .'**: Wainwright, *General Wainwright's Story*, p. 183

308 **'The American officers . . .'**: ibid., p. 188

309 **'It was a stinging blow . . .'**: ibid., p. 189

312 **'I read it so often . . .'**: ibid., p. 226

312 **'All we knew . . .'**: ibid., p. 233

313 **'There was no stopping . . .'**: ibid., p. 259

314 **'I thought of all . . .'**: ibid., p. 277

314 **'"Well," MacArthur said' . . .'**: ibid., p. 278

315 **'Tonight in Yokohama . . .'**: ibid.

Postscript

318 **'This might seem . . .'**: Wainwright, *General Wainwright's Story*, p. 286

318 **'My comrades and I . . .'**: ibid., p. 298

319 **'The expense of making . . .'**: ibid., p. 303

SELECTED SOURCES

General Histories

Baron, Scott, *USS Missouri: The Mighty Mo and the Men Who Sailed Her*, self-published, 2021

Bass, Gary J., *Judgement at Tokyo: World War II On Trial and the Making of Modern Asia*, Picador, 2024

Beevor, Antony, *Berlin: The Downfall 1945*, Penguin, 2007

Brisard, Jean-Christophe and Parshina, Lana, *The Death of Hitler: The Final Word on the Ultimate Cold Case: The Search for Hitler's Body*, Hodder, 2019

Caddick-Adams, Peter, *1945: Victory in the West*, Hutchinson Heinemann, 2022

Citino, Robert M., *The Wehrmacht's Last Stand: The German Campaigns of 1944–1945*, University Press of Kansas, 2017

Clinger, Fred, Johnston, Arthur and Masel, Vincent, *The History of the 71st Infantry Division*, Arcole Publishing, 2017

Coffey, Thomas, *Imperial Tragedy: Japan in World War II, the First Days and the Last*, World Publishing Co., 1970

Daly-Groves, Luke, *Hitler's Death: The Case Against Conspiracy*, Osprey, 2019

Eberle, Henrik and Uhl, Matthias (eds), *The Hitler Book: The Secret Dossier Prepared for Stalin*, John Murray, 2005

Edsel, Robert M., *Saving Italy: The Race to Rescue a Nation's Treasures from the Nazis*, W. W. Norton, 2013

Gilbert, Martin, *The Day the War Ended*, HarperCollins, 1995

Holland, James, *Italy's Sorrow*, HarperCollins, 2007

Jähner, Harald, *Aftermath: Life in the Fallout of the Third Reich, 1945–1955*, W. H. Allen, 2019

Kempowski, Walter, *Swansong 1945: A Collective Diary of the Last Days of the Third Reich*, W. W. Norton, 2015

Kershaw, Ian, *The End: Hitler's Germany 1944–45*, Allen Lane, 2011

Le Tissier, Tony, *The Battle of Berlin 1945*, The History Press, 2007

– *Death Was Our Companion: The Final Days of the Third Reich*, Sutton, 2003

Mayo, Jonathan and Craigie, Emma, *Hitler's Last Day: Minute by Minute*, Short Books, 2015

McManus, John, *American Courage, American Carnage*, Forge, 2009

– *Island Infernos: The US Army's Pacific War Odyssey, 1944*, Caliber, 2021

– *To the End of the Earth: The US Army and the Downfall of Japan, 1945*, Caliber, 2023

Middlebrook, Martin and Everitt, Chris, *The Bomber Command War Diaries*, Penguin, 1990

Murray, Williamson and Millett, Allan R., *A War To Be Won: Fighting the Second World War*, Belknap Press, 2000

Rees, Laurence, *The Nazi Mind: 12 Warnings From History*, Viking, 2025

Scott, James M., *Rampage: MacArthur, Yamashita and the Battle of Manila*, W. W. Norton, 2018

Steinacher, Gerald, *Nazis on the Run: How Hitler's Henchmen Fled Justice*, Oxford University Press, 2012

Steinbacher, Sybille, *Auschwitz: A History*, Penguin, 2004

Ullrich, Volker, *Eight Days in May: How Germany's War Ended*, Allen Lane, 2021

Weale, Adrian, *Eyewitness Hiroshima: A Detailed Account of One of the Most Destructive Attacks in Human History*, Robinson, 1995

Whiting, Charles, *Finale at Flensburg: The Story of Field Marshal Montgomery's Battle for the Baltic (Forgotten Aspects of World War Two)*, Leo Cooper, 1973

Williams, Dayna Spear (ed.), *71st Infantry Division: The Red Circle Division*, Turner Publishing Company, 2001

Memoirs, Biographies

Altner, Helmut, *Berlin Soldier*: *The Explosive Memoir of a 17 Year-old German Boy Called Up to Fight in the Last Weeks of the Second World War*, The History Press, 2008

Andreas-Friedrich, Ruth, *Battleground Berlin: Diaries 1945–1948*, Paragon House, 1990

Bedell Smith, General Walter, *Eisenhower's Six Great Decisions: Europe, 1944–1945*, Longmans, 1956

Daniels, Jonathan, *The Man of Independence*, Victor Gollancz, 1951

Dulles, Allen, *The Secret Surrender*, Weidenfeld & Nicolson, 1967

Gorlitz, Walter (ed.), *The Memoirs of Field Marshal Wilhelm Keitel*, Cooper Square Press, 2000

Gryn, Hugo with Gryn, Naomi, *Chasing Shadows*, Penguin, 2001

Hamilton, Nigel, *Monty: The Field Marshal 1944–1976*, Hamish Hamilton, 1986

Heim, Heinrich, Picker, Henry and Bormann, Martin (eds), *Hitler's Table Talk: The Complete Edition 1941–1944*, Scrawny Goat Books, 2024

Henderson, Johnny, *Watching Monty: The Everyday Life of General Bernard Montgomery*, The History Press, 2024

Horne, Alistair and Montgomery, David, *The Lonely Leader: Monty 1944–45* (Pan Military Classic Series), Macmillan, 1994

Ismay, General Lord Hastings, *Memoirs of General the Lord Ismay*, Viking, 1960

Kase, Toshikazu, *Journey to the Missouri*, Yale University Press, 1950

Kennedy Cochran, Julia (ed.), *Ed Kennedy's War: VE Day, Censorship & The Associated Press*, Louisiana State University Press, 2012

Kershaw, Ian, *Hitler*, Penguin, 2013

Lang, Jochen von, *Top Nazi: The Man Between Hitler and Himmler*, Enigma Books, 2005

Linge, Heinz, *With Hitler to the End: The Memoirs of Adolf Hitler's Valet*, Frontline, 2013

Ludde-Neurath, Walter, *Unconditional Surrender: The Memoir of the Last Days of the Third Reich and the Dönitz Administration*, US Naval Institute Press, 2010

MacArthur, Douglas, *Reminiscences*, Bluejacket, 2001

Manchester, William, *American Caesar: Douglas MacArthur 1880–1964*, Back Bay Books, 1978

Mather, Carol, *When the Grass Stops Growing: A War Memoir*, Leo Cooper, 1998

McCullough, David, *Truman*, Simon & Schuster, 1992

McKeogh, Michael James and Lockridge, Richard, *Sgt. Mickey and General Ike*, G. P. Putnam's Sons, 1946

Montgomery of Alamein, Viscount, *The Memoirs of Field Marshal Montgomery*, Collins, 1958

Moorehead, Alan, *Eclipse (Second World War Voices 3)*, Hamish Hamilton, 1967

O'Brien, Phillips Payson, *The Second Most Powerful Man in the World: The Life of Admiral William D. Leahy, Roosevelt's Chief of Staff*, Caliber, 2020

Pocock, Tom, *Alan Moorehead*, The Bodley Head, 1990

Poen, Monte M. (ed.), *Strictly Personal and Confidential: The Letters Harry Truman Never Mailed*, Little, Brown, 1992

Pratt, Sherman W., *Autobahn to Berchtesgaden*, Gateway, 1992

Rzhevskaya, Yelena, *Memoirs of a Wartime Interpreter: From the Battle of Rzhev to the Discovery of Hitler's Berlin Bunker*, Greenhill Books, 2018

Tedder, Marshal of the Royal Air Force Lord, *With Prejudice*, Cassell, 1996

Truman, Harry S., *Memoirs, Volume One: Year of Decisions*, Doubleday, 1955

– *Where the Buck Stops: The Personal and Private Writings of Harry S. Truman*, Warner Books, 1989

Ullrich, Volker, *Hitler: Downfall 1939–1945*, Vintage, 2020

Wainwright, General Jonathan M., *General Wainwright's Story*, Greenwood Press, 1946

Warlimont, Walter, *Inside Hitler's Headquarters 1939–45*, Presidio, 1964

Wendel, Else, *Hausfrau at War: A German Woman's Account of Life in Hitler's Reich*, Odhams, 1957

Zhukov, Marshal, *The Memoirs of Marshal Zhukov*, Jonathan Cape, 1971

ACKNOWLEDGEMENTS

Huge thanks from Al to the following:
Merryn Walters, Andy Aitcheson, Scarlett Murray, Ingram Murray: 'The Colonel', Mary Grace Brunker, Richard Allen-Turner, and, of course, Eleanor and Daisy.

And from James:
Peter Caddick-Adams, Martin Davidson, Matt Doncaster, Freya Eden-Ellis, Cassandra Han, Cora MacGregor, John McManus, Roger Moorhouse, Steve Prince, Dorothee Schneider, Gerard Steinacher, Lorenzo Viti, Patrick Walsh, Merryn Walters, Aaron Young, and, of course, Rachel, Ned and Daisy.

And from both of us:
Bill Scott-Kerr, Linden Lawson, Phil Lord, Lucy Upton, Katrina Whone, Nicole Witmer, Sally Wray and all at Bantam Press; Morgan Entrekin, George Gibson, Jenny Choi and all at Grove Atlantic.

PICTURE ACKNOWLEDGEMENTS

Photographs not credited here are in the public domain

CHAPTER OPENERS

Chapter 1: *A BULLET TO THE HEAD*
German soldiers and officers laying down arms: Courtesy of the author

Chapter 2: *THE DUEL PART 1*
Ernst Kaltenbrunner, Heinrich Himmler and August Eigruber at Mauthausen concentration camp: Bundesarchiv, Bild 192-029 / CC-BY-SA 3.0

Chapter 3: *THE DUEL PART 2*
Lieutenant Williams S. Leinberger inspects the painting *Adam and Eve* by Frans Floris: United States Army Signal Corps Photograph Collection

Chapter 4: MONTY'S MEN
Field Marshal Montgomery receives Generaladmiral von Friedeburg and other members of the German surrender delegation: Imperial War Museum BU 5145

Chapter 5: *THE CAMP*
Captured German soldiers remove bodies from inside a barracks in Gunskirchen: CBW/Alamy Stock Photo

Chapter 6: *THE SUPREME COMMANDER WILL SEE YOU NOW*
General Eisenhower: Courtesy of the John Henderson Collection, Eton College Archives

Chapter 7: *VE DAY*
American soldiers and British girls celebrate VE Day in Piccadilly Circus, London: Pictorial Press Ltd/Alamy Stock Photo

Chapter 8: *HAPPY BIRTHDAY, MR PRESIDENT*
President Truman, VE Day in America: Associated Press/Alamy Stock Photo

Chapter 9: *AMID THE RUINS PART 1*
VW car with bullet holes, ruins of Berlin: Courtesy of the author

Chapter 10: *AMID THE RUINS PART 2*
Soldier sitting among ruins: Courtesy of the author

Chapter 11: *LOST IN TRANSLATION*
Nuclear bomb mushroom cloud: United States Army Signal Corps Photograph Collection

Chapter 12: *THE FINAL ACT*
US Fleet Admiral Chester Nimitz signs surrender documents: Hulton Archive/Stringer/Getty Images

PLATE SECTION

Page 1, top left
Hitler shortly before his death

Page 1, top right
The sofa where Hitler committed suicide

Page 1, centre
Crater where Hitler's corpse was found

Page 1, bottom
The Goebbels family: Bundesarchiv, Bild 146-1978-086-03/CC-BY-SA 3.0

Page 2, top left
Wolff with Himmler: Courtesy of the author

Page 2, top right
Signing the surrender in Caserta: Courtesy of the author

Page 2, centre
Wolff with von Schulze-Gaevernitz and von Vietinghoff: Supplied by the author courtesy of the Imperial War Museum

Page 2, bottom
Recovering stolen Italian art: Supplied by the author courtesy of the Imperial War Museum

Page 3, top
Montgomery signing the surrender on the Lüneburg Heath: Imperial War Museum BU 5208

Page 3, centre
The link-up of British and Soviet forces near Wismar: Imperial War Museum BU 5239

Page 3, bottom left
John Poston with Carol Mather: Courtesy of the John Henderson Collection, Eton College Archives

Page 3, bottom right
Montgomery with Sir Alan Brooke: Courtesy of the author

Page 4, top
US troops in Nuremberg: Courtesy of the author

Page 4, centre
The liberation of Gunskirchen concentration camp

Page 4, bottom left
US 3rd Division troops in Berchtesgaden: United States Army Signal Corps Photograph Collection

Page 4, bottom right
The end in Germany: United States Army Signal Corps Photograph Collection

Page 5, top
Jodl signs the surrender at Reims: Popperfoto via Getty Images

Page 5, centre left
Kay Summersby: Bettmann/Getty Images

Page 5, centre right
Celebrations in Trafalgar Square: Imperial War Museum EA 65799

Page 5, bottom
Crowds at Piccadilly Circus: Imperial War Museum EA 65879

Page 6, top left
Truman being sworn in as President: Courtesy of the author

Page 6, top right
Truman's address on VE Day: Associated Press/Alamy Stock Photo

Page 6, centre
Berliners with Red Army troops: Courtesy of the author

Page 6, bottom left
Soviet flag being raised over the Reichstag

Page 6, bottom right
Keitel and the German surrender in Karlshorst: Courtesy of the author

Page 7, top
The crew of the *Enola Gay*

Page 7, centre
The remains of Hiroshima

Page 7, bottom left
Kenji Hatanaka

Page 7, bottom right
Korechika Anami

Page 8, top left
MacArthur with Hirohito

Page 8, top right
MacArthur meeting Wainwright

Page 8, centre
Japanese representatives on USS *Missouri*

Page 8, bottom
Fly-past over Tokyo Bay: Courtesy of the author

PRINCIPAL CHARACTERS

All courtesy of the author with the exception of:

Grossadmiral Karl Dönitz: *Süddeutsche Zeitung* Photo/Alamy Stock Photo

General Dwight D. Eisenhower: American Photo Archive/Alamy Stock Photo

Generaladmiral Hans-Georg von Friedeburg: Keystone-France/Gamma-Rapho via Getty Images

Obergruppenführer Ernst Kaltenbrunner, Feldmarschall Wilhelm Keitel: *Süddeutsche Zeitung* Photo/Alamy Stock Photo

General Douglas MacArthur: Granger Historical Picture Archive/Alamy Stock Photo

Field Marshal Sir Bernard Montgomery: Associated Press/Alamy Stock Photo

Major John Poston: piemags/archive/military/Alamy Stock Photo

President Harry S. Truman: NB/USC/Alamy Stock Photo

INDEX

Abwehr, the 53
Adachi, General Hatazō 267
Addison, Christopher Addison, 1st Viscount 183
Aid to Russia Fund 173
Airey, General Terence 58, 77
Alamein, Battle of El (1942) 153
Alexander, Sir Frank, Lord Mayor of London 172
Alexander, Field Marshal Sir Harold 46, 58, 72, 77, 80, 148, 178, 307
Alexander, Sidney, Canon of St Paul's 172–3
Allied Airborne Army, First 146
Altaussee, Austria 83–4; salt mines 56–7; Villa Kerry 83
Altner, Helmut 224–6, 230–34, 240–42, 243, 253, 328
Alvensleben, Hauptmann Wichard von 76, 77
Anami, General Korechika 267–8, 275, 280, 281, 282–3, 285, 286, 287
Andreas-Friedrich, Ruth *ix*, 222–4, 243, 245–6, 249, 253–4
Andropov, Yuri 325
Appomattox Court House, Battle of (1865) 11
Apsley, Lieutenant-Colonel Allen 184
Ardennes offensive *see* 'Battle of the Bulge'
Arisue, General Seizō 275, 276
Armin, General Hans-Jürgen von 147
Arnold, Lieutenant-Colonel Dick 152
al-Assad, Bashar 323
Associated Press news agency (AP) 195
Atlantic Charter, the 2, 9, 10
atomic bomb, the 183, 211–12, 271–2, 273, 274, 280 281, 283, 288, 315, 320; *see also* Hiroshima; Nagasaki
Attlee, Clement 259
Auchinleck, Field Marshal Claude 92, 328
Augsburg, Germany 131
Auschwitz-Birkenau concentration camp, Poland 48, 121, 122–4, 125, 128
Australia/Australians 109, 266, 267; Navy 294
Austria/Austrians 20, 43, 45, 47, 51, 55, 56–7, 83, 84, 136, 156
Avondale Park, SS 169

Bader, Obersturmbannführer Friedrich 74, 75, 76, 77
Baguio, Philippines 317–18

Baldham, Germany 135
Bataan, Philippines 298, 299, 300, 301, 302, 303, 304; 'Bataan Death March' (1942) 305, 327
Batchelor, Lieutenant-Colonel Hugh 93
'Battle of the Bulge' (Ardennes offensive) 99, 148
Bauer, Hauptmann Hans 24
BBC, the 169, 172, 177, 188–9
Beckwith-Smith, Major-General Merton *ix*, 307–8
Bedell Smith, Lieutenant-General Walter ('the Beetle') *ix*, 155–7, 158–9, 160, 162, 177
Beebe, Brigadier-General Lewis 305
Berchtesgaden, Germany 22, 23, 25, 28, 29, 30, 31, 131–5, 252
Berehovo, Czechoslovakia 120, 121
Bergen-Belsen concentration camp, Germany 95, 106, 135–6
Berghof, Germany 23–4, 131, 133, 135
Bergonzoli, Generale Annibale 92
Berlin 10, 19–21; Führerbunker 22–3; battle for 26–8, 33, 91, 224, 228–9; surrender of 15, 17–19, 37, 206, 227; destruction of 127, 217, 219–22, 223; airlift (1948) 326
Bernays, Robert 184
'Berne Incident', the 65
BERNHARD, Operation 52–4, 128
Bernstorff, Countess Ingeborg Maria von 44
Best, Sigismund Payne 74–7
Bevin, Ernest 186
Birkenau concentration camp *see* Auschwitz-Birkenau concentration camp
Blaczeck (German soldier) 232–3
Blaschke, Dr Hugo 252, 253
Blondi (dog) 35, 245
Blum, Léon 67
Bockscar (B-29) 279
Bohr, Niels 273
Bols, Major-General Eric 93
Bolzano, Italy 43, 48, 73, 77, 80, 81, 82, 85; Palazzo Ducale 42–3, 79, 82
Bonin, General Bogislaw 76
Bonnier de La Chapelle, Fernand 8
Borchard, Leo (Andrik Krassnow) *xi*, 222–4, 243
Bormann, Martin: oversees building of the Eagle's Nest (1939) 24; his house at Berchtesgaden 131, 133; and Italian art treasures 56; with Hitler in the Führerbunker 23, 24, 25, 28, 31, 230; and Speer 31; as witness at Hitler's marriage ceremony 34; and Hitler's suicide 35, 36; death 37, 103, 324
Bradley, General Omar 90, 130, 145, 154
Braun, Eva 23, 31–4, 35, 36, 245, 324, 325
Braun, Dr Wernher von 119
Bremen, Germany 93
Brenner Pass, Italy 43, 50, 53, 59, 73, 80
Brief Encounter (film) 173
British Army 20, 89, 91, 95–6, 327
  6th Airborne Division 92, 93
  Armies: First 4; Second 103, 146; Eighth 4, 92, 100
  21st Army Group 115, 145
  1st Guards Brigade 307

11th Hussars 100, 102
1st Infantry Division 307
Irish Guards 174
King's Own Scottish Borderers (5th Battalion) (KOSB) 93, 115
Royal Tank Regiment 94, 115
Royal Welch Fusiliers 102
Westminster Garrison Battalion 173–4
British Mechanised Transport Corps (MTC) 152
Brooke, General Sir Alan 109, 111, 115, 148–9, 327
Buch, Berlin: SMERSH HQ 245, 247, 253
Buchenwald concentration camp, Germany 135, 155
Buckingham Palace, London 173, 188, 189, 194
Bunker Hill, USS 262
Burgdorf, General Wilhelm 27, 29, 33, 35
Burma 261, 263, 317
Busch, Generalfeldmarschall Ernst 104, 105
Byrnes, James F. ('Jimmy') *ix*, 200–201, 205, 284, 285
Bystrov, Major 229–30, 240, 251

Campbell, John 184
Camrose, William Berry, 1st Viscount 187
Canadian forces: First Army 146; paratroopers 115; 1st Canadian Parachute Battalion 92–3
Canterbury Cathedral, Kent 173
Capone, Al 199
Caravaggio, Michelangelo Merisi da: *Bacchus* 82
Carnock, Arthur Nicolson, 1st Baron 181
Casablanca Conference (1943) 1–3, 4–7, 10–11, 164, 206
Caserta, Italy 77; Reggia 78
Cernobbio, Italy: Villa Locatelli 73
Chandos pub, St Martin's Lane, London: VE Day 174
Channel Islands, the 115, 178
Channon, Henry 'Chips' 188
Charité Clinic, Berlin 251–2
Chasing Shadows (film) 328
Chiang Kai-shek 259, 260, 283
Chicago Tribune 153
China/Chinese 259, 260, 263, 276, 283, 289, 298, 310, 312, 317, 322; *see also* Formosa
Chourakov, Ivan 244–5
Chuikov, General Vasily 17–18, 19, 229
Churchill, Clementine 173, 181, 187
Churchill, Colonel 'Mad Jack' 67
Churchill, Sarah (Lady Audley) 187
Churchill, Winston *ix*; first meeting with Roosevelt 2; makes a toast to 'unconditional surrender' 11; with Roosevelt at Casablanca Conference 2, 10, 11, 164; and Montgomery 102, 113; told of Germany's surrender 169, 170–71, 193, 194; and Stalin's insistence on postponing announcement 194–5, 196–7, 212–13; on VE Day 167, 171, 173, 174–5, 177–88, 189; at Yalta Conference 202; loses election 259
CIA, the 8, 84, 85
Ciano, Count Galeazzo 47

Clark, General Mark W. 7, 8, 59, 66
COMPASS, Operation 92
Coral Sea, Battle of the (1942) 311
Corregidor Island, Philippines 299–300, 301, 302, 303
Covello, Cynthia 172–3, 174, 176–7
Coward, Noël 174, 188
Cranach, Lucas, the Elder: *Adam and Eve* 82
Curry, Sergeant Ralph D. 279
Czechoslovakia/Czechs 20, 66, 67, 120, 136, 146

Daily Express 107
Daily Mail 171
Daily Mirror 171
Daily Telegraph 171
Daniels, Jonathan 196
Darlan, Amiral François 8
Dawnay, Colonel Kit 103, 105
D-Day (6 June 1944) 130, 150, 151, 152, 320
de Guingand, Freddie 97
de Labilliere, Paul, Dean of Westminster 183, 184
Demmin, Germany: suicides 96
Dempsey, Lieutenant-General Miles 103, 104
Deryabin, Captain 245
Devers, General Jacob L. 130, 132, 145
Digney, Joyce 172–3, 174, 176–7
Dollmann, Eugen 48, 49
Domei News 268, 274, 283
Donelson, Tennessee: battle (1862) 3, 10
Dönitz, Grossadmiral Karl *ix*; and Hitler's birthday 24; returns to Flensburg 24; joined by Keitel and Jodl 31; and Karl Wolff 61; succeeds Hitler as head of state 19, 225–6, 228, 242–3, 322; and Kesselring 80; sends delegation to Montgomery to negotiate surrender terms 103, 104, 107–9, 110–11, 156; refuses Himmler's services 111, 228, 246–7; incensed by Allied demand for total surrender 157; orders Jodl to delay surrendering to Eisenhower 157–9; finally authorizes him to sign surrender terms 159; sends Keitel to sign unconditional surrender with Soviets 249; after the war 326
Donovan, William 'Wild Bill' 46
Dornberger, General Walter 119
Downs, Bill 108
DRAGOON, Operation 130
Dufving, Oberst Theodor von 18
DUKEX contingent (Canadian First Army, British Second Army) 145–6, 149
Dulles, Allen 46–51, 57–8, 59, 64–7, 69, 70, 72–3, 79–80, 82
Dunkirk 115, 307

Earle, Captain Peter 101–2
Early, Steve 203
Eden, Anthony 8
Edinburgh: VE Day 189
Eichmann, Adolf 47, 83–4, 85
Eicken, Carl von 251–2
Eisenhower, General Dwight D. *x*; and the French 7, 8; appointed Supreme Commander (1943) 149; diverts

Allied armies from Berlin 90–91, 131; and Montgomery 90, 97, 98, 106, 113, 148, 149; responsibilities 145–7; relations with fellow generals 130, 150; under strain 150–51; rumoured to be having an affair with his driver 151–3; his successes 153–4; horrified by Ohrdruf concentration camp 154–5; and German surrender 111, 114, 115, 147–8, 150, 155–6, 157–64, 178, 179, 193, 194, 213, 219, 247; becomes President 326–7; death 327
Eisenhower, John 151
Eisenhower, Mamie 151
Elizabeth, Princess 184, 188–9
Elizabeth, Queen Consort 184, 188, 189
Enola Gay (B-29 Superfortress) 269–70
Evening Standard 195
Ewart, Colonel 107, 112, 114
Exeter, HMS 278

Falkenhausen, General Alexander von 75
Fasano, Lake Garda, Italy 66
Fegelein, Gretl (*née* Braun) 33
Fegelein, Gruppenführer Hermann 32–3, 63
Fisher, Geoffrey, Archbishop of Canterbury 173, 183
Flensburg, Germany: German government 104, 108, 109, 111, 148, 157, 159, 169, 195, 242, 247, 249, 250
Florence, Italy: Uffizzi Gallery 55, 83
Foggia, Italy 43
Formosa 306–9, 310
France/the French 2, 7, 8, 9, 12, 20–21, 54, 149, 182; Communists 8; 2ème Division Blindée 132; First Army 130, 132, 145; Free French 8; Navy 7; *see also* Reims
Frank, Anne 48
Frank, Hans 326
Friedeburg, Generaladmiral Hans-Georg von *x*; leads delegation to surrender to Montgomery 104–5, 107–9, 110–11, 112, 114, 147; tries delaying strategy with Eisenhower 155–9; finally signs surrender document 161–2; surrenders to the Soviets 249–50
Friedl, Major Hans Jochen 104, 105, 108, 109, 111, 114
Funk, Brigadier-General Arnold J. 302–3

Garda, Lake, Italy 48, 51, 52, 56, 66
Gaulle, General Charles de 8
Gavin, Brigadier James M. 152–3
George VI 174, 176, 177, 184, 186–7, 188, 189
German armed forces
  Armeen: 6. 4, 30; 9. 26–7, 28, 31; 10. 80; 12. 30, 224, 226, 232, 241; 14. 80
  Heeresgruppen: C 134; G 129, 134, 135; Mitte 26; Weichsel 26, 106
  'Berlin' Infanterie-Division 224–6
  Luftwaffe 6, 32
  I.SS Panzer-Division 48

German armed forces – *cont.*
II. SS Freiwilligen Panzergrenadier-Division Nordland 27
LVI Panzerkorps 27, 31
III (Germanische) SS-Panzerkorps 27
U-boats 4, 104; U-2336 169
Volkssturm 18, 94, 225, 241, 264
Waffen-SS 31, 41, 63, 79, 225, 231, 233, 241
Glattley, Colonel Harold 309
Goebbels, Josef 19, 26, 28, 32, 33, 34, 37, 103, 230, 239, 325
Goebbels, Magda 32, 33, 37; children 32, 37, 239, 240
Gorbushin, Colonel Vassily 248, 252
Göring, Reichsmarschall Hermann 24–5, 29, 30, 31, 103, 131, 133, 134, 227, 326
Gott, Lieutenant-General William 100
Gotthard Pass, Switzerland 49
Grant, Ulysses S. 3, 10
Greenwood, Arthur 183
Greim, Generaloberst Robert von 32. 34
Groves, General Leslie R. 211, 212
Gryn, Bella *x*, 120, 122, 123–4
Gryn, Gabi 120, 122, 123
Gryn, Géza *x*, 120, 121–5, 126–9, 140–41
Gryn, Hugo *x*, 119–29, 140–41, 328, 329
Gryn, Naomi: *Chasing Shadows* 328
Guadalcanal, Solomon Islands 311
Gunji Sangiin *see* Big Six, the
Günsche, Otto 23, 36
Gunskirchen concentration camp, Austria 117, 136, 139–41
Häcklingen, Germany 89
Halder, General Franz 67–8
Halmahera, Indonesia 282
Halsey, Admiral Hill 294
Hamburg, Germany 89, 94, 109, 225
Hanley, Major 77
Hansell, Brigadier-General Haywood 263
Harden, Major Richard 100
Harriman, Ambassador W. Averell 208–9
Harris, Air Chief Marshal Sir Arthur 'Bomber' 6
Harrisson, Tom 175
Harster, Gruppenführer Wilhelm 48, 59, 64
Hatanaka, Major Kenji 285–7, 289
Hawkins, Lewis 195
Hay, Kathleen 176
Heinrici, General Gotthard 26, 27
Heintges, Colonel John A. 132, 134, 135
Henderson, Johnny 89, 98
Herr, General Traugott 80
Herriot, Édouard 181–2
Herten, Jack van 54
Heusermann, Käthe 252--3
Heydrich, Reinhard 39, 45, 52
Himmler, Reichsführer Heinrich: and Wolff 44, 56–7, 59, 63, 64–5, 67, 68–70, 81; on Hitler's fifty-sixth birthday 24; offers to surrender to the Allies 33; and Florentine artworks 56–7; busted for negotiating with Swedes 103; his services refused by Dönitz 111, 228, 246–7
Hirohito, Emperor 267, 269, 280, 281–2, 283, 284–5, 287–9, 313
Hiroshima, bombing of 269–77

Hitler, Adolf: his home city 136; in the 1930s 222, 225; meets Dulles 46; his love of art 55, 56, 57; his Alpine retreat 131–2; his pre-war vision of Berlin 19–20, 21; his policy of divide and rule 45; and 1940 celebrations 20–21; his fiftieth birthday 23–4; and Dönitz 103, 104, 111, 226, 322; and Kesselring 51, 79; and Stauffenberg's assassination attempt 68; and Roosevelt's call for unconditional surrender 9–10; refuses to accept defeat 22, 25–9; in the Führerbunker 22–3; and Wolff 69–70, 80, 81; his fifty-sixth birthday 22, 23, 24–5; his last week 29–34; and Keitel 227–8, 249; marries Eva Braun 34; his last will and testament 35, 161–2; death 18, 34–6, 37, 41, 80, 91, 96, 224, 225, 229, 322, 329; identification of his body 239, 240, 244–5, 247–8, 251–3, 323–4, 325
Hitler Youth 138–9, 231
HMV 172
Hobart, Lieutenant-Colonel O. R. C. 94
Hodges, General Courtney 99
Hofer, Gauleiter Franz 43, 71, 72, 79, 85
Hohenlychen , Germany 68–9
Homma, General Masaharu x, 297–8, 299, 300, 301, 304–5, 327
Hopkins, Harry 1, 2, 324
Horthy, Admiral Miklós 67
Höttl, Sturmbannführer Wilhelm 47, 51, 53, 84
Hradecký, Václav 66, 79
Hull Daily Mail 171
Hungary/Hungarians 47, 67, 120–21; Jews 47, 121
Hunger Plan 75
HUSKY, Operation 153–4
Husmann, Dr Max 48, 50

Ilyin, Lieutenant Leonid 239
Imamura, Captain Hitoshi 308
Insole, Lieutenant P. G. 93
International Committee of the Red Cross 54
Ismay, General Sir Hastings 193–4
Italy/Italians 5, 11, 12, 41, 43–4, 47, 48–51, 57–9, 247, 326; Jews 50, 52, 85; theft of artworks 54–7, 82–3; surrender of German troops 41, 61*ff.*; and Stalin 204, 209, *see also* Bolzano
Iwabushi, Admiral Sanji 327
Iwo Jima 212, 317

Japan/Japanese 2, 3, 5, 7, 11, 12, 90, 186, 193, 206, 208, 212, 214, 257, 321, 322; the Big Six 267–9, 280, 285; Kempeitai (Japanese secret police) 276–7; surrender 259*ff.*, 291*ff.*, 317–18; post-war 326, 327; *see also* Hiroshima; Nagasaki
Japanese forces
  Armies: Fourteenth 298, 304; Eighteenth 267; Kwantung 280–81, 285

Japanese forces – *cont.*
329th Infantry (Takenaga Unit) 266–7
Ketsu-Go strategy 280
Navy 266, 311
Jennings, Humphrey 175
Jews 42, 52–3, 83, 119; Berlin 222–3; Dutch 48, 54; Hungarian 47, 121, *see also* Gryn, Hugo; Italian 50, 52, 85
Jodl, General Oberst Alfred *x*; with Hitler in the Führerbunker 29; asks Göring to take over decision-making 30; joins Dönitz 31; and Keitel 227, 228; and Montgomery's insistence on unconditional surrender 110; signs surrender at Reims 147, 148, 157–63, 169, 177, 195, 247
Johnson, President Andrew 206
Johnson, Hewlett, Dean of Canterbury 173
Junge, Traudl 324

Kagan, Yelena *x*, 217, 220–22, 229–30, 239–40, 243–5, 247–8, 251, 254, 328
Kaltenbrunner, Obergruppenführer Ernst *x*, 39, 45; and Operation BERNHARD 52–4, 128; rivalry with Wolff 42, 45, 48, 51–2, 54, 58–9, 63–4; and Dulles 46, 47, 58; survives car accident 64; plans to use VIP prisoners (*Prominenten*) as hostages 67–8, 73–4, 77, 79; accuses Wolff of treason 69; goes with him to see Hitler 69–70, 71; plans his escape 79, 81; reaches his house in Austria 83; arrested by American Counter Intelligence Corps 84; death 85, 326
Kansas City Star 198
Karenko, Formosa 306–9
Kase, Toshikazu 296
Kasserine, Battle of, Tunisia 153
Kehlsteinhaus (Eagle's Nest) 24, 131–2, 133, 135
Keitel, Feldmarschall Wilhelm: appearance *xi*; 227; career 227; loyalty to Hitler 227; in the Führerbunker 24, 29, 227; hears of Hitler's death 228; holds discussions with Dönitz 31, 228, 242; realizes importance of surrendering to the Allies rather than the Soviets 105–6, 242–3; concerned with Germany's military honour 110; orders Himmler to no longer visit Dönitz's HQ 247; at Wismar 226–7; forced to accept Eisenhower's conditions 159, 178; appalled by the destruction of Berlin 219–20; signs unconditional surrender 249–50; flown back to Flensburg 250–51; faces months of interrogation 254; trial and execution 254, 326
Kempka, Erich 33, 36, 37, 229, 324
Kennedy, Ed *xi*, 195, 196, 213
Kennedy, President John F. 327

Kesselring, Feldmarschall Albert 50, 51, 57, 58, 59, 61, 66, 79, 80–81, 134, 326
King, Major-General Edward P. 302–3, 306
King, Admiral Ernest J. 7, 205, 207
Kinzel, General Eberhard 104, 105, 108, 109
Kislenko, Major-General A. P. 77–8
Klimenko, Colonel 229–30, 244–5, 248
Knee, Captain Derek 104, 109
Kokura, Japan 278
Konev, Marshal Ivan 26, 28
Krassnow, Andrik *see* Borchard, Leo
Krebs, General Hans *xi*, 17–18, 19, 23, 28 29, 35, 229, 325
Krichevsky, Ilya 237
Krosigk, Count Schwerin von 195
Kunstschutz (organization) 55
Kyoto, Japan 272, 277

Lange, Wilhelm 229–30
Langsdorff, SS Standartenführer Professor Alexander 55–6, 57, 82
Lattre de Tassigny, Général Jean de 132, 178, 219
Laurence, William L. 279
League of Nations 3, 46
Leahy, Admiral William 196, 205, 207, 211, 212
Leclerc, Général Philippe 132, 134, 135
LeMay, General Curtis 263
Lemelsen, General Joachim 80
Lemnitzer, General Lyman 58, 77
Lieberose concentration camp, Germany 124–7, 128
Lincoln, Abraham 206
Linge, Sturmbannführer Heinz 23, 29, 33, 34, 35–6, 37, 324
Linz, Austria 55, 136
London: the Blitz 2, 6, 152, 172; VE Day 171–7, 180–81, 182–5, 187–9
London Can Take It (film) 175
Lüneburg Heath 87, 89, 91, 92, 147, 157

MacArthur, General Douglas *xi*; military career 207, 296–300, 305, 311, 314; and Wainwright 300, 301, 302, 303, 313–15; signs Japanese surrender documents 294, 295, 315; and General Yamashita's conviction 327
MacCarthy-Morrogh, James 152
McDilda, Flight Lieutenant Marcus 276–7, 281
McKeogh, Sergeant Michael 155, 163
McQueen, Flight Lieutenant Alastair 99
Madge, Charles 175
Magdeburg, Germany: SMERSH HQ 325
Malaya 296
Manchuria/Manchuko 280–81, 285, 312, 317; Sian camp 312–13
Manhattan Project 210–11, 273; Trinity Test 259–60, 273
Manila, Philippines 298, 299, 305, 312, 317, 327; Fort McKinley 304
Marants, Major Anna 248
Margaret, Princess 184, 188, 189
Marshall, General George 150, 153, 205, 207, 211, 318; Marshall Plan 326

Mass Observation (MO) 175–6
Mather, Bill 99
Mather, Carol 99–100
Matteson, Captain Robert E. 83–4
Matthews, Walter, Dean of St Paul's Cathedral 172
Mauthausen concentration camp, Austria 128–9
MEETING-HOUSE, Operation 263
Merano, Italy 52, 54; Schloss Labers 54
Mers-el-Kébir, Algeria 7
Midway, Battle of (1942) 311
Ministry of Food 169–70
Ministry of Information 169
Missouri, USS 293–6, 315, 317, 320
Moksak camp, Formosa 310, 311
Molotov, Vyacheslav 208, 209–10, 212
Montgomery, Field Marshal Bernard *xi*; character and personality 89, 90, 95, 97–8, 99, 147, 327–8; and Eisenhower 90, 145, 146, 148, 149, 159–60, 162; and Carol Mather 99–100; and John Poston 100, 101–3; at TAC HQ on Lüneburg Heath 89–90, 91–2, 96–7; accepts German surrender 87, 103–15, 147, 155, 157, 162; death 328
Montgomery, David 97, 109
Moorehead, Alan 107
Moran, Charles Wilson, 1st Baron 170, 181
Morell, Dr Theodor 23, 28
Morgan, Lieutenant-General Sir William 78
Mori, Lieutenant-General Takeshi 286–7
Moskin, Staff Sergeant Alan 136–40, 141, 328
Munich, Germany 131, 223
Murphy, Robert 8
Murray, Captain Stuart S. 293
Murrow, Ed 8
Mussolini, Benito 5, 42, 46, 47, 55, 67, 73, 77

Nagasaki, bombing of 270, 278–80, 313
New Guinea 263, 266, 282
Nicolson, Harold 181, 183, 184, 188
Niederdorf, Italy 74–7
Niizuma, Lieutenant-Colonel Seiichi 275–6
Nimitz, Admiral Chester 207, 295
Nishina, Yoshio 273, 275–6
Nordhausen concentration camp, Germany 135
Norway/Norwegians 8, 20, 27, 109, 169, 182
Novello, Ivor 188
Nuremberg, Germany 131; Trials 85, 326

Oberammergau, Germany 119
Obersalzberg, Germany 131, 133–4, 135, 136
O'Daniel, Major-General John 'Iron Mike' 131, 132, 134
Oder, River 21, 23, 26, 27, 28
Office of Strategic Services (OSS) 8, 46, 48, 49, 51, 57, 66, 67, 73, 208, 313
Ohrdruf concentration camp, Germany 154
Okinawa, Battle of (1945) 208, 212, 261–2, 264, 266, 267

OKW (Oberkommando der Wehrmacht) 24, 29, 68, 75, 104, 110, 157, 227, 247
OSS *see* Office of Strategic Services
OVERLORD, Operation 146, 149, 154
Oxenius, Major Wilhelm 161, 162

Pacific Islands 317
Parilli, Baron Luigi 48–9, 57, 65, 66, 67, 72
Paris Peace Conference (1919–20) 46
Parri, Ferruccio 49, 50
Patch, General Alexander 130, 132, 136
Patton, General George S. 97–8, 130, 132, 136, 137, 154, 198
Pavolini, Alessandro 73
Pearl Harbor (1941) 2, 261, 273–4, 298
Peenemünde, Germany 119
Peleliu, Battle of (1944) 212
Pendergast, Thomas J. 199
Percival, General Arthur 295, 296, 307, 308, 314, 317, 318
Petacci, Clara 73
Philippines, the 263, 296, 297–9, 300, 301–3, 304, 305, 311, 314, 317–18
Piccadilly Circus, London: VE Day 176
Pichko, Major 251
Pim, Captain Richard 169
Pletcher, Captain J. D. 117
Pohl, General Max von 71, 80
POINTBLANK, Operation 6
Poland 20, 24, 120, 179–80, 209–10
Poleck, Generalmajor Fritz 111–12
Poston, Major John *xi*, 100–101, 102–3, 112
Potsdam Conference (1945) 259, 326; Declaration 257, 259, 260, 268, 274, 280, 281, 283, 284, 288
Pragser Wildsee, Italy 73–4, 76, 77
Pratt, Lieutenant Sherman W. *xi*, 133, 136
Pravda 229
Prominenten 67–8, 73–7, 79
Putin, Vladimir 323

Quezon, President Manuel 297
Quisling, Vidkun 8

RAF *see* Royal Air Force
Rahn, Ambassador Rudolf 71
Ramsay, Admiral Bertram 97
Rathbone, Flight Lieutenant John 184
Rathenow, Germany 325
Rauff, Standartenführer Walter 48, 73
Rayburn, Samuel 203
Red Army: and Battle of Stalingrad (1942–3) 4, 9, 30, 121; advance on Germany 43–4; surrounds German 6. Armee 30; attempts to reach Denmark 92–3; final offensive 21–2, 23, 26–7, 28, 31, 33, 71, 74, 111, 194, 206; and surrender of Berlin 15, 17–19, 21, 91, 106, 219, 220, 237, 243, 244; Third Shock Army 217, 220, 228, 229, 243–5; Fifth Shock Army 245; German fear of 92, 96, 104, 106, 109, 148, 156, 157, 242; and rape of German women 245–6; aircraft 234; and the Japanese 264–5, 280–81, 285, 313; *see also* Zhukov, Marshal Georgy

Red Cross parcels 309, 310, 312
Reichssicherheitshauptamt (RSHA) 45, 47, 53; *see also* Kaltenbrunner, Obergruppenführer Ernst
Reims, France 143, 149, 155, 157, 169, 179, 194, 195, 247
Reitsch, Hanna 32, 34
Repubblica Sociale Italiana (RSI) 55
Reynolds, Phyllis and Tom 97, 110
Rhine, River 44, 59, 89, 92, 93, 95, 130, 137, 149
Rhineland, Germany 20
Ribbentrop, Joachim von 24
Roberts, Major-General Pip 101
Romania 209
Rommel, General Erwin 4, 92
Roosevelt, Eleanor 203–4
Roosevelt, Elliott 1, 11
Roosevelt, President Franklin D.: prepares for massive rearmament 149–50, 200; wins a third term 200; charges his friend, Donovan, with creating the Office of Strategic Services 46; enters the war and calls for Hitler's unconditional surrender 7, 9–12; orders MacArthur to leave the Philippines 296, 300; sends Wainwright messages of support 303–4; at Casablanca Conference (1943) 1–5, 10–11, 164, 206; determined to remain in office until war is won 199–200; ill-health 200; chooses Truman as his Vice-President 200–201; wins a fourth term 201; comparisons with Truman 197–8, 204, 207; at Yalta Conference 202, 259; backs the Manhattan Project 211; death 65, 145, 174, 203–4, 205, 329; funeral 206
Roosevelt, President Theodore 205
Rose, Alfred, Bishop of Dover 173
Röttiger, Generalmajor Hans 66, 71, 76–7, 79, 80
Royal Air Force 95, 320
  Bomber Command 6, 22, 26, 133, 134
  Second Tactical Air Force 146
  Volunteer Reserve 184
Royal Navy 145, 320, 321
RHSA *see* Reichssicherheitshauptamt
Rubens, Peter Paul: paintings 82
Ruhr, the 6
Russia 323; *see* Soviet Union/Soviets
Rutherford, Ernest 273
Rzhevskya, Yelena *see* Kagan, Yelena

Sachsenhausen concentration camp, Germany 53, 125, 128
Sackville-West, Vita 181
St Alban's Cathedral 173
St Paul's Cathedral 172–3
Samuel, Herbert Samuel, 1st Viscount 183
Sandys, Diana (*née* Churchill) 187
Sandys, Duncan 187–8
Satō, Ambassador Naotake 268
Savoy Hotel, London: VE Day 174
Scarborough Evening News 171
Schellenberg, Brigadeführer Walter 63–4, 75
Schneider, Karl 229
Schörner, Feldmarschall Ferdinand 26

Schulz, General Friedrich 79, 80, 134
Schulze-Gaevernitz, Dr Gero von 49, 50, 73, 77, 78, 82
Schweinitz, Oberst Victor von 72, 73, 77, 78, 80
Schwend, Friedrich 53–4, 85
SD *see* Sicherheitsdienst
Sevez, Général François 162, 177
Seyss-Inquart, Reichskommisar Arthur 156–7
SHAEF *see* Supreme Headquarters Allied Expeditionary Force
Sharp, Major-General William F. 307
Shigemitsu, Foreign Minister Mamoru 295
Shiizaki, Lieutenant-Colonel Jirō 286
SHINGLE, Operation 130
Shiraishi, Lieutenant-Colonel Michinori 286
Shkaravsky, Conlonel Faust 248
Sicherheitsdienst (SD) 45, 47, 48, 52, 64,66
Singapore 182, 296, 307, 317, 318
Skorzeny, Colonel Otto 79
Slovik, Eddie 146
SMERSH 229, 239, 245, 248, 324, 325
Sneland I (ship) 169
Sokolovsky, General Vasily 18, 19
Solomon Islands 311
Soltau, Germany: British hospital 102
Southampton Docks 171
Soviet Union/Soviets: invasion of Poland and Hungary 24, 120–21; and Hitler's death 229, 240, 244–5, 247–8, 323–4, 325; and peace negotiations 50, 57–8, 77–8; and German surrender 160–62, 171, 177–8, 189, 212–13; and Japan 264–5, 268, 283–4, 289; relations with the West 197, 214, 326; *see also* Red Army; Stalin, Joseph
SMERSH 229, 239, 245, 247, 248, 324, 325
Spaatz, General Carl 'Tooey' 219, 250
Spandau, Berlin 225, 230, 241, 326
Special Air Service (SAS) 99, 146
Speer, Albert 19, 21, 22, 31–2, 103, 131, 135, 326
SS (Schutzstaffel) 24, 33, 36, 41, 42, 44, 47, 48, 49, 50, 54, 63, 68–9, 74, 76, 77
SS-Totenkopfverbände 74, 75
Stalin, Joseph: absent from Casablanca Conference (1943) 5; at Tehran Conference (1943) 264–5; correspondence with Roosevelt 65, 204; and Hitler's death 18, 324, 325; wants unconditional capitulation from Germans 18; pressures Truman to quash peace treaty with Italy 72; given symbolic victory over Nazis by Eisenhower 90, 164; George VI unconcerned about 187; and VE Day (9 May) 189, 194–7, 249, 250; at Yalta Conference 202, 210; and Truman 208, 209, 210; and the Manhattan Project 259–60
Stalingrad, Battle of (1942–3) 4, 9, 30, 121

STARVATION, Operation 263
Stauffenberg, Claus von 68, 75
Steimle, Standartenführer Eugen 64
Steiner, Obergruppenführer Felix 27–8, 33
Stettinius, Edward 202, 204, 208
Stichler, Leutnant 225, 232–3
Stiller, Obersturmbannführer Edgar 74, 76, 77
Stimson, Henry 205, 210, 272, 318
Stone, Chief Justice Harlan 204
Straight Flush (aeroplane) 270
Strong, Major-General Kenneth 155, 157, 158, 163
Stumpfegger, Dr Ludwig 37
Stumpff, Generaloberst Hans-Jürgen 219, 249, 250
Summersby, Gordon 152
Summersby, Captain Kay (*née* Kathleen MacCarthy-Morrogh) *xii*, 151–3, 158; *Past Forgetting* 143, 152, 162, 163
SUNRISE, Operation 58, 65, 72
Supreme Headquarters Allied Expeditionary Force (SHAEF) 90, 145, 155, 156, 157, 159
Susloparov, General Ivan 162, 163, 178
Sutherland, Major-General Richard 300
Suzuki, Admiral Kantarō 267–9, 274, 280, 281, 282, 288
Syria: Ba'ath Party 323

TAC HQ 89–90, 91–2, 96–7, 98, 103, 104, 112; staff 89, 96, 107, 108, 109
Takenaga, Lieutenant-Colonel Masaharu 267
Takeshita, Lieutenant-Colonel Masahiko 285
Tanaka, General Shizuichi 286
Tarlac, Philippines 305
Taylor, General Maxwell 132
Tedder, Air Chief Marshal Sir Arthur 163–4, 178, 219, 250
Tehran Conference (1943) 264–5
Thiele, Hannelore 246
Thomas, General Georg 68, 75, 76
Thompson, John 'Beaver' 153
Tibbets, Colonel Paul W. 269, 270
Time magazine 199
Timeloberg, Germany 89, 103
Times, The 102
Titian: paintings 82
Tōgō, Shigenori 267–8, 280, 285????
Tokyo 263, 272, 277, 281, 284, 311
Tokyo Bay 293, 303
TORCH, Operation 7, 8, 130, 153
Townsend, Group Captain Peter 188
Toyoda, Admiral Soemu 267–8, 277, 280
Trafalgar Square, London: VE Day 175–7
Truman, Bess (*née* Elizabeth Wallace) 198, 204
Truman, President Harry S. *xii*, personality 199, 207, 329; background 197–9; becomes Vice-President 201–3, then President 203–7, 320; meets Averell Harriman 208–9, and Molotov 209–10; is told about Manhattan Project 210–12; communications with Churchill 174, 194, 212–13; on VE Day 191, 212–15; and Stalin 72, 194–5, 196–7; at Potsdam

Conference (1945) 259, 272, 326; and bombing of Hiroshima 271–2, 273–4, 275; orders a halt to further atomic bombings 283; designates USS *Missouri* for surrender ceremony 293–4; awards General Wainwright the Medal of Honor 318–19; death 327
Truman, Margaret 293

Ukraine 75, 319, 323
Umezu, General Yoshijirō 267–8, 280, 295–6
'Uncle Emil' resistance movement 222–3, 249–50
'unconditional surrender' 11–12
United Press 283
United States Army Air Forces (USAAF) 6, 8, 28, 90, 150, 208, 271, 274–5
  Airborne Divisions: 82nd 152; 101st ('Screaming Eagles') 132–3, 134, 135
  Air Forces: Ninth 146; Fifteenth 43
    B-29 bombers (Superfortresses) 262–3, 264, 269–70, 272, 279, 320
  American Expeditionary Force 198
  Armies: First 145; Third 132, 136, 137, 145; Seventh 81, 130, 132, 136, 145; Ninth 145; Fifteenth 145
  4th Armored Division 154
  Army Groups: 6th 130, 136, 140, 145; 12th 90, 130, 145; 21st 91, 92, 94, 95, 96, 98, 109, 157
  II Corps 4
  80th Counter Intelligence Corps (CIC) 83, 85
  Infantry Divisions: 3rd 129, 130–31, 135, 136; 7th 'Cottonbalers' 129, 131, 132, 133, 135; 38th 82; 71st 'Red Circle' 117, 136–41; 82nd 301; 85th 'Custer' 81, 82
  66th Infantry Regiment 137
  506th Parachute Infantry Regiment 135
United States Navy 7, 200, 205, 208, 300, 311
  casualties 262
  Marine Corps 7
  Third Fleet 294
  see also Missouri, USS
Uraevsky, Lieutenant 78
Usmiani, Antonio 49, 50

V-2s 119, 135
Vatican, the 47, 48
Venlo incident, Holland 74–5
Verona, Italy 48, 49, 52
Versailles, Treaty of (1919) 3, 10, 20
Vietinghoff, General Heinrich von 58, 65, 66–7, 71–2, 73, 76, 77, 78, 79, 80
Voss, Vizeadmiral Hans-Erich 239–40

Wagner, Konteradmiral Gerhard 104, 108
Wagner, Dr Herbert 119
Waibel, Max 72, 73
Wainwright, Adele 306, 308, 310, 312, 318
Wainwright, General Jonathan M.: appearance *xii*, 300; background 301; and Japanese invasion of Philippines 299,

Wainwright – *cont.* 300, 301, 302–4; surrenders 304; as prisoner of war 304–7, 308–10, 311–13, 319, 329; awarded DSC 313–14; in Manila with MacArthur 314–15; witnesses Japanese surrender aboard USS *Missouri* 291, 294, 295, 296, 315; and Yamashita's surrender ceremony 317–18; reunited with family 318; awarded Medal of Honor 318–19; death 327
Wallace, Henry A. 200, 201, 204
Warren, Lieutenant-Colonel Trumbull 104, 105, 109, 111
weather forecasting 172
Wegner (German soldier) 225
Weidling, General Helmuth *xii*, 27, 31, 35, 37
Wenck, General Walther: 12. Armee 30, 224, 226, 232, 241
Wentzell, Generalmajor Fritz 79, 80
Werner, Obersturmbannführer Eugen 72, 73, 77, 78, 80
Westarp, Countess Gisela von 83, 84
White Rose resistance group 223
Wilmot, Chester 109
Wilson, Arnold 184
Wilson, President Woodrow 3; Fourteen Points 12
Windhorst, Hermann 225
Wismar, Germany 92–3, 115, 227
Wolff, Obergruppenführer Karl: appearance *xii*, 44; background 44; on Kaltenbrunner and Heydrich 39; his plans to end the war and for self-preservation 41–2, 47; lives in style in Bolzano 42–3; rivalry with Kaltenbrunner 42, 45, 51; contacts Allen Dulles 46, 48–50; and Kesselring 50–51; survives strafing 51; and Florence's art treasures 54–7, 82–3; further negotiations with Dulles 57–8; talks with Kesselring 59, 61, 80–81, 134; his plans thwarted by Himmler 58–9, 63–5; further contact with Dulles 65–7; bluffs his way out of danger 68–71; finalizes negotiations with the Allies 71–3, 76–80; escapes death 81–3; after the war 85
Woodroffe, Jean 189
Wünsche, Obersturmbannführer Max 63

Yalta Conference (1945) 202, 205, 210, 259
Yamashita, General Tomoyuki *xii*, 317–18, 327
Yokohama, Japan 314–15
Yonai, Admiral Mitsumasa 267–8, 269, 270

Zaun, Inge 246
Zevelyov, Piotr: letter home 15
Zhukov, Marshal Georgy: launches offensive against Berlin 21, 27, 28, 30, 224, 228; told of Hitler's death 18; demands unconditional surrender from Germans 19; and German capitulation 178, 194, 219
Zimmer, Guido 66

ABOUT THE AUTHORS

James Holland and Al Murray are the hosts of the acclaimed Second World War podcast *We Have Ways of Making You Talk*. This is their first book together.

James Holland is an internationally acclaimed and award-winning historian, writer and broadcaster. The author of many books, including the bestsellers *Normandy '44* and *Cassino '44*, he has also presented and written a large number of television programmes and series. He is a fellow at St Andrews University and the Co-Founder and Creative Director of the Chalke Valley History Festival.

Al Murray has written many successful books including *Watching War Films with My Dad*, *Command* and, most recently, the bestselling *Arnhem: Black Tuesday*. He is also the award-winning creator of The Pub Landlord, one of the most recognizable and successful comic creations of recent times, who, for over twenty years, has been filling arenas and theatres around the world.